ROYAL SAILORS

ROYAL SAILORS

A. Cecil Hampshire

WILLIAM KIMBER: LONDON

First Published by
WILLIAM KIMBER AND CO. LIMITED
Godolphin House, 22a Queen Anne's Gate
London, S.W.1

TYPESET BY
SPECIALISED OFFSET SERVICES LTD., LIVERPOOL,
AND PRINTED IN GREAT BRITAIN BY
W. & J. MACKAY & CO. LTD., CHATHAM

CONTENTS

LIST OF ILLUSTRATIONS

AUTHOR'S NOTE

With the entry of the Prince of Wales into Dartmouth the long and historic tradition by which members of Britain's Royal Families have served in the Royal Navy is being carried on. Not without reason, the truth of the dictum of William IV that, 'There is no place in the world for making an English gentleman like the quarterdeck of an English man of war,' is thus still recognised. Of his forthcoming naval service Prince Charles himself has said, 'It is to me a worthwhile occupation and one which I am convinced will stand me in stead for the rest of my life.'

Despite the difficulty of maintaining a clear line of demarcation between the exalted status of a royal personage and his Service identity as a naval officer, and the necessity on occasion of 'wearing two hats', few of the royal sailors of the past were merely royal dummies. Some had to endure hardships, if not actual privations, and were forced to suffer special indignities because of their royal birth. 'It never did me any good to be a prince, and many was the time I wished I hadn't been,' commented the late King George V of his early life in the Navy. Most sought to be true professional sailors, and several triumphantly succeeded. For some, fate brought their naval careers to a premature end.

In this book the naval service of eleven royal sailors has been traced over a period of two hundred years, which span the transition of the Royal Navy from the days of sailing warships to the modern nuclear age and from muzzle-loading guns to guided missiles. For certain biographical details I have drawn on the works of other authors, some dead, some still living, and to these I am very grateful. In particular, I owe special thanks to the following for their kind permission to quote from the copyright material indicated: John Murray (Publishers) Ltd., from John

Gore, *King George V – A Personal Memoir;* St. Martin's Press, Inc., New York, and Macmillan, London & Basingstoke, from Sir Henry F. Stephenson, *A Royal Correspondence,* and Sir John Wheeler-Bennett, *George VI;* Evans Bros., Ltd., from Roger Fulford (Ed), *Dearest Child;* Constable & Co Ltd., and Nigel Nicolson, Esq., Literary Executor to Sir Harold Nicolson, from *King George V;* Longman Group Ltd., from H. Bolitho, *A Century of British Monarchy;* Cassell & Co., Ltd., from H.R.H. The Duke of Windsor, *A King's Story;* Hodder & Stoughton from Carola Oman, *Nelson;* and the Hamlyn Publishing Group Ltd., from Winston S. Churchill, *World Crisis, 1911-1918.*

I should also like to thank the staffs of the Naval Library, Public Record Office, National Maritime Museum, and Imperial War Museum, for their help and patience.

A.C.H.

'Aboard ship you learn to live with people'

Prince Philip

CHAPTER I

THE SOVEREIGN AND THE NAVY

Throughout the centuries, from the time of Alfred the Great to the present day, close links have existed between the Sovereign and the Navy. Indeed, although the affairs of the Fleet are today administered by a Board of Admiralty within the Ministry of Defence, the Queen is still titular Lord High Admiral.

When King Alfred built his own fleet of galleys and trained the crews to man them in order to repel the marauding Danes at sea before they could reach our shores, he not only 'fathered' the Navy, he was the first English monarch to recognise the importance of sea power to an island race. Successive rulers played a considerable part in the furtherance of this doctrine as a basis of the English state. Specifically, Richard I, for the proper conduct of the fleet which conveyed him and his Crusaders to Palestine, drew up the first written ordinances, or laws of the sea, upon which the disciplinary code of the Royal Navy is based today.

King John of Magna Carta fame appointed the first civilian official to look after the welfare of his warships, thus foreshadowing the present Board of Admiralty. Edward I adopted the Arabic title of 'admiral' for the commander of a fleet at sea, and founded the 'Court of Admiralty of England' for the administration of all maritime law – the functions of which are today carried out by the Ministry of Defence and the High Courts of Justice. Henry VIII introduced the 'great gun' afloat which revolutionised naval warfare, created the first 'standing' officers, and issued the earliest naval 'fighting instructions'.

The misguided efforts of Charles I to procure money from a reluctant nation to build more and better warships played no small part in his eventual downfall. Cromwell turned the navy into a truly national force and brought it under the direction of

Parliament, and with the restoration of Charles II it finally emerged as the Royal Navy.

But it had still not become a profession. Warships were not kept in permanent commission as they are today. There were thus no full time naval ratings, crews to man the ships being recruited either by financial inducement or other means as and when required. Nor, except for the 'standing', or warrant, officers created by Henry VIII, were there any permanent naval officers. When these were needed they were drawn from the nation's fighting leaders, usually noblemen or army officers and gentlemen volunteers, none of whom had any special sea training.

But when Charles II appointed the industrious Samuel Pepys as 'Clerk of the Acts', or secretary, to the Admiralty, the foundations of the administration of the Navy as it functions today were laid. One of Pepys's most important reforms was the creation of an 'establishment' of lieutenants. Since every candidate was required to produce evidence of sea service and pass an examination in seamanship and navigation, this meant that only professional seamen would be recruited instead of well-born amateurs. Youngsters who wished to make a professional career in the Navy could join as 'Volunteers' or 'Captain's Servants'. The upper age limit for their entry was 16, thus ruling out titled dilettantes and similar young men-about-town, and fixed numbers of midshipmen were established for each rate of ship.

Charles appointed his brother James, Duke of York, to be Lord High Admiral, and, although by no means a professional seaman, the latter commanded the English fleet at sea in person during the second and third Dutch wars with distinction. When he eventually resigned from the post because of his religious faith the office was placed 'in commission' and, except for two brief interludes, it was never again held by a single individual, either king or commoner. In fact, although the office still remained nominally vested in the monarch, executive power began to pass to the politically appointed Board of Admiralty. During the reign of William and Mary it was legally enacted that 'the Lord High Admiral's office has continued existence, and although ordinarily united to the Crown is never merged in the kingly office, never is dormant or in abeyance, and is capable of being conferred on a subject with equal authority to the Sovereign in the exercise of all its functions and attributes'.

The effect of this transfer of executive power from the Sovereign was strikingly demonstrated when in 1840 Queen Victoria wished her husband to be made Admiral of the Fleet. Since there was then only one holder of the rank, a professional sailor, the Board refused and the Prince Consort never held so much as an honorary naval title.

The Queen had her own back, however, when after the death of the Prince Consort the Admiralty suggested that the Prince of Wales should be given an appropriate naval rank. She refused, but in 1877 allowed him to take the honorary rank of captain in the Royal Naval Reserve. Ten years later he became an honorary Admiral of the Fleet. But except by special dispensation of the Admiralty Board, neither the Sovereign nor any member of the Royal Family can become a professional naval officer without undergoing the same training as anyone else.

By the time that George III came to the throne in 1760 the Navy had been turned into a strictly professional body. A permanent corps of naval officers had come into being with their own standard uniform. A Royal Naval Academy existed in Portsmouth naval dockyard for the pre-sea training of 'young gentlemen' desiring to become midshipmen. Sailors, however, were still paid off at the end of an emergency when the bulk of the fleet was laid up. When again required crews were obtained by means of alluring posters promising a bounty and liberal prize money, or through the agency of press gangs. Not until 1853 was continuous pensionable service introduced for the Lower Deck and impressment finally abolished.

English sailing warships were at the peak of their perfection. They could sail anywhere and keep the seas for long periods. First-rates of 100 guns and upwards displaced between 2,000 and 3,000 tons and carried a crew of close on 1,000 officers and men. Living conditions on board, however, were far from good. There was little room for comfort, even for officers, and the accommodation for the seamen was cramped and ill-ventilated. Messes were on the lower decks, which were dark and dimly lit and in heavy weather rarely dry. The midshipmen's berth was particularly small, noisome and overcrowded, and the wardroom not much better. When action was imminent all mess furniture and other gear was stowed in the hold or thrown overboard, and when battle was raging the gun decks became an inferno of slaughter, fire, smoke and uproar. Because food had to be kept in the hold much of it quickly went bad, and the fresh water soon became undrinkable. Punishments were severe — even midshipmen could be flogged — and leave, except in foreign ports, almost non-existent.

* * * * *

Although various early English kings had commanded a fleet at sea in war with considerable competence, the first Royal sailors in any professional sense were two brothers of George III. They were Edward Augustus, later Duke of York, and Henry Frederick, Duke of Cumberland.

Born in March, 1739, Prince Edward joined his first ship, the 64-gun third-rate *Essex,* at Portsmouth as a midshipman, in May, 1758, at the age of 19. In command of the ship was Commodore (later Admiral of the Fleet Earl) Howe who, since the young man arrived completely unprepared for naval life, was forced to kit him out at his own expense, and was never afterwards properly recompensed. Later he wrote to a friend:—

> I was not told how to provide for his Royal Highness, and all the answer I could obtain from ministerial authority respecting the treatment of, and conduct towards, the prince was limited to an instruction that I was to act respecting him just as if I had not any such person on board the ship. He came not only without bed and linen of almost every kind, but I paid also for his uniform clothes, which I provided for him with all other necessaries at Portsmouth. I made no inquiries how I was to be indemnified for every requisite attention to the then presumptive heir to the crown.

When the young man had been thus properly equipped, the other captains present in the port came on board the *Essex* to be formally introduced to him. One of the sailors watching the proceedings whispered to a companion, 'The young gentleman ain't over civil — look if 'e don't keep 'is 'at on before all the captains'.

'Why, you stupid lubber,' replied the other, 'where should 'e larn manners seeing as 'ow 'e never was at sea before'.

Despite the fact that he had received no sea training whatever, the prince was soon to be blooded in action.

Four years earlier hostilities had broken out between the French and English settlers in America over the ill-defined limits of their respective territories. As a result relations between England and France became increasingly strained until, in 1756, war was finally declared. While containing the enemy in Europe, Britain launched her main offensive against the French in America, which resulted in the fall of Quebec and the conquest of Canada. French naval squadrons which had been assembled to support a planned invasion of Britain were blockaded in Toulon and Brest by British warships. When the Toulon force did manage to slip out of harbour it was chased and smashed off Lagos by Admiral Boscawen. A few months later the Brest squadron ventured to emerge, only to be similarly destroyed amid the rocks and shoals of Quiberon Bay by Admiral Hawke.

But not all went successfully. In September 1758, a British amphibious operation was mounted against the enemy port of St. Malo. Howe was in charge of the covering naval force in the *Pallas*, but the troops were commanded by a general named Bligh who was really too old for active service.

At first the operation went well and, having driven off the defending enemy warships, Howe landed the soldiers in St. Lunaire Bay, some six miles west of St. Malo. Eager to see some of the fun at close quarters, Prince Edward volunteered and was permitted to go ashore with the troops. He attached himself to a reconnaissance party and, while scouting ahead of the main body, narrowly escaped being hit by an enemy ricochet. The French retreated without putting up much of a fight and, with his mission of destroying the port installations accomplished, Bligh signified his intention of re-embarking. But Howe had decided that the St. Lunaire anchorage was unsafe and moved his ships to the nearby Bay of St. Cas.

While Bligh's men were straggling along to the new embarkation point the general discovered to his alarm that a large French force was advancing on him. By the time his men began to arrive on the

B

beach the enemy had recaptured the village of St. Cas and were rapidly closing in. In the confusion of the hurried embarkation, horses and guns being ferried off before the troops, a third of the British force was trapped by the enemy and eventually compelled to surrender. Fortunately for young Edward, he was hustled back on board in the nick of time.

Nine months later, because he was a prince of the blood royal, the regulations were waived by the Admiralty and Edward was promoted to the rank of post-captain and to command of the 44-gun *Phoenix*. By then the immediate enemy threat at sea had been removed by our naval victories. For most of the year 1759, therefore, the *Phoenix* was employed on blockade duties in the Bay of Biscay. When the ship was finally driven from her station by an autumn gale and returned to Portsmouth for repairs, the Prince relinquished his command. There is no record of his receiving another appointment as a post-captain. But further honours were about to come his way during this temporary hiatus in his naval career. On April 1st, 1760, he was created Duke of York and a peer, and a year later promoted to the rank of Rear-Admiral of the Blue.

(In the early days of the Royal Navy the fleet was divided into three squadrons, Red, White and Blue, taking station respectively in the centre, van and rear, and each with its own admiral, vice-admiral and rear-admiral. Red was the senior, Blue the junior. Although the numbers of admirals was greatly increased, these 'coloured' squadrons were maintained up to the mid-nineteenth century, flag officers being promoted successively through the various grades.)

Early in 1762 the Duke of York hoisted his flag in the 80-gun *Princess Amelia* and spent the whole of that summer afloat as second in command of the Channel Squadron under Admiral Sir Edward Hawke, victor of the Quiberon Bay action. His flag captain was Earl Howe, under whom but a short time previously he had served as midshipman. The French fleet had still not recovered from its successive defeats and there was, therefore, comparatively little for British warships to occupy themselves with in home waters except to continue a desultory blockade of the French coast.

The Channel Squadron, comprising eleven sail of the line and three frigates, carried out two prolonged sorties in enemy waters, but when it returned to port in November of that year after the second cruise, peace terms had been agreed between the belligerents and active hostilities were at an end. Soon afterwards the Duke resigned his command. In more modern times he would probably have been placed on half pay, but in those days no such arrangement existed for the retention on the active list of temporarily unemployed naval officers.

In the following year the Duke, having been promoted to Vice-Admiral of the Blue in the previous October, hoisted his flag in the 50-gun *Centurion* and sailed for the Mediterranean to take up the post of Commander-in-Chief of that station. Since Britain was now enjoying a well-earned spell of peace there was nothing more important for our naval squadrons overseas to do than carry out a series of 'show-the-flag' cruises, often to the ports of our erstwhile enemies. The youthful admiral speedily tired of his sinecure post, however, and after a few months resigned his command and came home. It was the last time he would serve afloat. Nevertheless, in 1766 he was stepped up in rank to be Admiral of the Blue.

The spring of 1767 found the Duke spending a few days at the Hague on a visit to the Dutch Court. He then moved on to the south of France to enjoy a spell of sunshine. One August evening, after attending a ball given by a neighbouring French nobleman during which he had exercised his love of dancing to the full, he rashly decided to walk back to his lodgings, which were in fact some twelve miles away! In his overheated state he caught a chill, which he neglected in order to pay a visit to the theatre on the following evening. When he arrived back at his lodgings his condition had become considerably worse, but he insisted on travelling on to Monaco, whose prince he had met while serving in command of the Mediterranean station.

But, despite the improved accommodation and the assiduous attentions of his host's doctors, the Duke's illness had by now gone beyond their capacity to cure. Nevertheless, he remained cheerful and calmly made arrangements for an aide to travel back to England with the news of his death. He died on September 17th, 1767, and, after being embalmed, his body was brought back to this country in the frigate *Montreal*. Following a brief lying-in-state he was buried in the Henry VII Chapel at Westminister. He was only 28 years of age, and in less than four years naval service had risen in rank from midshipman to admiral and had flown his flag as Commander-in-Chief of an important naval station.

A few months after his death his brother, Henry Frederick, Duke of Cumberland, was entered on the books of the frigate *Venus* as a midshipman, Captain Samuel Barrington in command. Born on October 27th, 1745, fourth son of Frederick, Prince of Wales, and brother of George III, the Duke was then aged 23, at least seven years over the normal age of entry for the average run of 'young gentlemen' of the time. In view of the fact that he had been educated entirely by his doting mother and allowed to mix socially with no one save dependants, it is somewhat surprising that she should have been willing to allow her favourite child to be subjected to the rough and tumble of life in the midshipmen's berth of an 18th century British warship.

But life on board the *Venus* was to be made as comfortable as possible for the Royal Duke, for with him went no fewer than nine 'attendants'. The nation was still at peace, and between June and September, 1768, the *Venus* cruised no farther afield than the waters between Woolwich and Spithead. Even this, however, was evidently considered to constitute sufficient sea service to qualify the royal new entrant for promotion, and on October 28th, 1768, 'in pursuance of his Majesty's pleasure', Midshipman H.R.H. The Duke of Cumberland was appointed to be no less than captain of the *Venus* in supersession of the experienced Barrington!

Despite the fact that his command was still almost entirely non-seagoing, speedy promotion continued to come the way of Prince Henry Frederick. On March 10th, 1769, he was appointed Rear-Admiral of the Blue Squadron of his Majesty's Fleet, his commission as flag officer being signed by none other than that famous old seadog Admiral Hawke, who had now become First Lord of the Admiralty. Captain Barrington was re-appointed as his former midshipman's flag captain.

In June of the same year the Duke was appointed Commander-in-Chief of the Channel Squadron, 'to be employed as far westward as Scilly', and all captains, commanders, officers and ships' companies belonging to his Majesty's ships and vessels were ordered to be 'obedient to you, their Commander-in-Chief'.

Flying the Duke's flag, the *Venus* led her consorts of the Channel Squadron on a daring cruise as far distant as Gibraltar and back. It was probably just as well that England was not at war for, according to the Duke's naval contemporaries, he was not only a man of 'very small intellect' but short on seamanship as well. Once when paying an official visit to a warship in Portsmouth harbour as a senior admiral he actually asked her captain to point out to him which was the mizen mast!

After four months in command of the Channel Squadron the Duke struck his flag in October, 1769, and the *Venus* paid off. He seems not to have served afloat again but devoted the rest of his life to more pleasurable pursuits on shore, earning an unenviable notoriety on account of his excesses.

Nevertheless, he continued to hold naval rank and was moved steadily up the ladder of advancement on paper, being promoted successively to Rear-Admiral of the White in October, 1770, and Vice-Admiral of the Blue less than a week afterwards. In spite of the fact that his clandestine marriage to Mrs Horton in 1771 alienated him from the King, he was promoted to be Vice-Admiral of the White in February, 1776, an advancement which rendered such great sailors as Howe, Keppel and Rodney junior to him on the flag list. He was made Admiral of the Blue in 1778, and finally Admiral of the White, at that time the senior flag rank, in April, 1782. He died eight years later.

By then another Royal sailor had entered the Navy. But he and the royal youngsters who were to follow him were to receive very different treatment from George III's favoured brothers. He was the first really professional sailor.

CHAPTER II

YOUNG ROYAL TARRY BREEKS

One sunny June day in the year 1779 a little group of three people stood at the head of a jetty overlooking Portsmouth harbour. Youngest of the trio was a wide-eyed boy in his early teens who appeared fascinated by the noise, bustle and confusion which surrounded them. Screeching gulls wheeled and circled overhead; behind in the greasy cobblestoned street which led to the jetty slop-sellers, ship-chandlers and other shopkeepers loudly extolled their wares to reluctant customers; outside a tavern half a dozen drunken sailors exchanged bawdy badinage with a group of blowsy women; children played and squabbled in the overflowing gutters, and a brace of leather-aproned apprentices argued shrilly with each other as they trundled newly made barrels from a nearby cooper's workshop towards a carter's waiting dray.

The glittering waters of the harbour were equally alive with sound and movement. Rowing boats, their owners standing up to work their sculls against the push of the tide, were noisily plied for hire; crowded wherries ferrying foot passengers to and from Gosport, fishing luggers, and heavily-laden, bluff-bowed colliers, thronged the fairway; and here and there, nimbly threading a way through the clumsy sailing craft, a smartly rowed cutter or gig conveyed a uniformed naval officer on official business between the sloops of war and frigates in mid-stream.

But the main interest of the boy, who was dressed in a plain blue jacket and trousers such as those worn by ordinary sailors, with a low-crowned hat crammed down upon his fair curls, was centred on a single great line-of-battleship which, with sails neatly furled, lay at anchor farther out at Spithead. Now and again he would tug imperiously at the sleeve of the elder of his two companions, a middle-aged gentleman wearing gold-laced uniform, to point to this vessel and ask an eager question. The third member of the trio, a pale-faced individual dressed in clerical garb, stood slightly apart from the others regarding his clamorous surroundings with evident disapproval.

Presently a 12-oared naval cutter turned aside from the main stream of waterborne traffic and approached the steps above which they were standing, a youthful midshipman conning the boat beside the brawny coxswain. As she glided in oars were smartly tossed and bow and sternsheetmen stood up with raised boathooks. Gently the cutter bumped alongside, and as soon as she was secured the midshipman stepped ashore, mounted the steps and halted before the waiting group.

Facing the gold-laced officer, who was in fact Rear-Admiral Sir Samuel Hood, Resident Commissioner of his Majesty's naval dockyard at Portsmouth, he dragged off his hat respectfully and announced, 'Cutter from the *Prince George,* sir.'

After a brief word of acknowledgment the admiral turned and bowed formally to the boy beside him.

'Goodbye, your Royal Highness', he said. 'May I wish you the best of fortune in your new career.'

The lad smilingly shook hands with him, then, preceded by the midshipman and followed more sedately by the clerical gentleman, he ran down the steps and climbed aboard the waiting boat. At a word of command the cutter shoved off from the jetty, oars were lowered into the water, and a moment later she was being lustily rowed away in the direction of the distant man-of-war. A future monarch of England was about to join the Royal Navy.

* * * * *

Thirteen years before this scene was enacted a son had been born at Buckingham House to King George III and his consort, the former Princess Charlotte Sophia of Mecklenburg-Strelitz, the third male child in a row. Of this latest addition to the royal family Horace Walpole wrote, 'If it were not for the Queen the peerage would be extinct. She has given us another duke.' In fact, during the first twenty-two of their fifty years of married life Charlotte was to bear her husband nine sons and six daughters.

Christened William Henry, the new arrival was a bonny,

bouncing infant with fair hair and a fresh complexion, if somewhat squat-bodied and with a head shaped like a pineapple. Sensible and engaging as a child, he was brimful of vitality and constantly in scrapes with his elder brothers. As soon as he was old enough two tutors were appointed to take charge of his education; Colonel Bude, a Swiss who had served in the Sardinian army, and the Reverend Mr. Majendie, later to become Bishop of Bangor. His father, who had a great admiration for the Navy, decided that William should make that service his career, a decision which met with enthusiastic approval of his offspring, who was eager for adventure. The Queen, however, was not in favour of her young son being sent away from home so early but, during a visit to Portsmouth, the King arranged with Captain Robert Digby, an experienced officer commanding the 98-gun line-of-battleship *Prince George,* and Sir Samuel Hood, Commissioner of the dockyard, for his son's entry into the sea service. In due course he wrote to Hood to ask what clothes, necessaries and books the lad ought to take.

> He has begun geometry, and I shall have an intention to forward him in whatever you may hint as proper to be done before he enters into that glorious profession.

By May of 1779 William's preparatory education was considered sufficiently far advanced for him to be launched upon his new life, and arrangements were finalised for him to join the *Prince George* at Portsmouth. The King wrote to advise Hood that:

> I have sent a hair trunk, two chests and two cots done up in one mat to be delivered unto you for the use of my young sailor. I flatter myself that you will be pleased with the appearance of the boy, who neither wants resolution nor cheerfulness which seem necessary ingredients for those who enter into that noble profession.

The king also emphasised that 'not the slightest notice' was to be taken of William on his arrival on board and that he was to be treated exactly as any other midshipman. Then, with some sound advice from his father and the gift of a Bible, the boy was despatched to Portsmouth in the charge of Mr. Majendie, who was to attend to his classical studies on board. Like his two uncles, one of whom was still nominally serving, William had undergone no naval training whatever, yet, within a few months, he too would find himself in the thick of a sea battle.

His introduction to shipboard life needed the 'resolution and cheerfulness' of which the King had spoken, but it by no means dampened the spirits of the ebullient William. After a formal meeting with Digby, recently promoted to flag rank, who warned him, 'You are like a young bear – all your troubles are before you', he was taken below to the midshipmen's berth to be introduced to his messmates. This compartment, he noted afterwards, was:

> A small hole in the steerage about ten feet by six and some five feet four inches high, so that for some it was impossible to stand upright. An aperture cut into the ship's side about nine inches by six admitted a modicum of what we most needed, fresh air and daylight.

Most of the space in the compartment was taken up by a deal table covered with a cloth heavily spotted with wine and gravy stains, upon which stood a brass candlestick containing a 'purser's dip', or candle. The whole atmosphere of the place, which was thick with tobacco smoke, stank of bilgewater, gin, beer and frying onions.

Nor were the occupants of the mess whose life he was to share any more prepossessing in appearance, while they for their part were not prepared to be overawed by the Royal newcomer.

'By what name are you rated in the books?' demanded to know one tough looking youngster aggressively.

It was fortunate that William's boisterous childhood with his numerous brothers and sisters had effectively blunted any youthful inhibitions from which another boy might have suffered.

'I am entered as Prince William Henry,' he answered cheerfully, 'but my father's name is Guelph, and therefore, if you please, you may call me William Guelph, for I am nothing more than a sailor like yourselves.'

This reply disarmed his interrogators and, apart from the usual 'christening' ceremony of having a plate broken over his head and being made to take a drink of seawater for his temerity in bringing his name to sea, he was not made the butt of any special horseplay.

Though short in stature he was sturdily built and lacked nothing in the way of courage. Before very long he fell out with another midshipman named Sturt who threatened, 'If you were not the King's son, sir, I would teach you better manners.'

Retorted William cockily, 'Don't let that be any hindrance,' and offered to fight him over a sea chest, the accepted method of settling disputes among the young gentlemen.

But Sturt declined on the grounds that it would be unfair as he was the elder and stronger. Later on William did get himself into a fight, this time with a subaltern of marines. After it was over he shook hands with his opponent, remarking somewhat tactlessly, 'You are a brave fellow though you are a Marine!'

For the next few months after William joined the *Prince George* she cruised in the Bay of Biscay with the Channel Fleet, at that time under the command of Admiral Sir Charles Hardy. During this time the young Prince applied himself diligently to the business of learning all he could about his new profession. If he found the life hard he did not complain. And by modern standards hard it certainly was for a youngster scarcely in his teens. As well as being regarded as the slaves of the First Lieutenant, constantly at his beck and call as messengers and general dogsbodies, midshipmen had to work with the seamen in order to learn their job, were sent aloft with them for sail work, kept night watches, ran the boats in harbour, and were required to spend something like three hours daily studying under the Schoolmaster. And at any time of the day or night the drums might well have beat to quarters in real earnest on board the *Prince George* and her consorts, for Britain was at war.

A few years prior to William's entry into the Navy trouble had broken out in the American colonies when, rebelling against ill-considered taxation imposed from home, the angry colonists staged a number of riots. Troops were sent out from England to deal with the situation, but in 1775 the rebels decided to take up arms to defend their rights, their combined forces being commanded by George Washington.

Fifteen months later they issued a formal Declaration of Independence, to which the British replied by capturing New York and Rhode Island. But, badly handled by the British Government under the malign influence of George III, this purely domestic affair was to escalate into one of the most serious situations ever faced by this country. For in the following year France, eager to avenge the loss of her colonial empire during the Seven Years War, officially recognised American independence and began to send arms, troops and supplies to help the rebels. Two years later she declared war against Britain. Her example was quickly followed by Spain, hoping to recover Gibraltar, to which she at once began to lay siege, and in 1780 our enemies also included Holland. Our military resources were at once stretched to the limit, and the land campaign against Washington was now greatly hampered by the presence in American waters of a powerful French fleet under the Count de Grasse.

Soon after the declaration of war by France a squadron of 30 British sail of the line under the command of Vice-Admiral Keppel had sailed from Portsmouth, and in August 1778, encountered a slightly superior enemy fleet off Ushant. Keppel at once gave battle, but because of lack of co-operation by Vice-Admiral Palliser, his second in command, the action ended indecisively. In consequence of this failure Keppel was relieved of his command and superseded by Sir Charles Hardy. But the latter, finding himself menaced by growing enemy naval strength and, like Jellicoe centuries later, aware of the supreme importance of his ships to the defence of this country against invasion, took care to avoid action with the French.

Towards the end of 1779 Admiral Sir George Rodney was given command of a special squadron and ordered to the West Indies to take charge of that station and curb the activities of the French who were attacking our island possessions. On his way out he was to escort a relief convoy to Gibraltar whose hard-pressed garrison was in sore straits after being under enemy siege for six months. The *Prince George*, flying the flag of Rear-Admiral Digby was attached to Rodney's squadron for the relief operation.

Off Finisterre the British force encountered a convoy of

fourteen Spanish supply ships escorted by a 64-gun warship and six smaller armed vessels on its way to Cadiz from St. Sebastian. After a brief skirmish the entire convoy and escorts were captured and its supplies added to those intended for Gibraltar. The captured Spanish frigate was later taken into service in the British Navy and renamed *Royal William* as a compliment to the young sailor Prince who had taken part in the action.

A few days later this success was followed by one even greater when a Spanish squadron of eleven battleships and three frigates commanded by Admiral Don Juan de Langara was sighted off Cape St. Vincent. Despite the fact that the sighting took place on a gloomy afternoon which developed into a wild and stormy night, Rodney at once gave chase. By the early hours of the following morning six of the Spanish vessels including the flagship had surrendered and a seventh blew up. Only two managed to escape. When the action was over de Langara was eventually sent on board the *Prince George* as a prisoner of war, and expressed his astonishment and admiration when he found a son of the King of England serving as an ordinary midshipman and sharing the wretched accommodation of his messmates.

Relaxing with the rest of his companions in the taverns of Gibraltar after its garrison had been relieved, William indulged in the customary high-spirited escapades of any midshipman ashore. Like his brothers, whoe numerous love affairs were soon to scandalise their father, he was easily susceptible to female charms, and ogled the Spanish senoritas in the streets with precocious aplomb. Then while Rodney headed away westwards for the Leeward Islands, Digby returned to England with part of the fleet and the prizes they had taken. News that the King's sailor son had participated in these naval successes caught the fancy of the British public and brought him much personal popularity. The Poet Laureate composed a special verse in his honour, and Robert Burns dubbed him 'the young Royal Tarry Breeks'.

During the greater part of the summer of 1780 while the *Prince George* was refitting at Portsmouth William was given leave, which he spent in London enjoying himself in the company of his brothers. Fast becoming notorious on account of their dissipation and loose living, they exercised a bad influence on him, and all three were frequently in trouble with the authorities. On one occasion William himself was arrested for his part in a brawl during a masquerade at Vauxhall, only to find that his opponent was his brother George. When the affair came to the ears of the King he had the young midshipman's leave cut short and despatched him back to Portsmouth into the care of the resident Dockyard Commissioner, now a Captain Martin. The impressionable William promptly fell in love with Martin's daughter.

The war situation was still very grave. Gibraltar was again under siege and supplies once more running short. The *Prince George*, now back with the Channel Fleet, was detailed to accompany a special squadron commanded by Vice-Admiral George Darby to run another relief convoy to the defenders. On arrival off the Rock the squadron found itself opposed by a formidable flotilla of heavily armed enemy gunboats which had been assembled to prevent the supplies from being landed. Nevertheless, covered by a tremendous cannonade from the British warships, 7,000 tons of provisions and 2,000 barrels of gunpowder were successfully put ashore. Labouring alongside his sweating shipmates amid the deafening uproar on the *Prince George's* gundecks, Prince William Henry, still only a lad of 15, was fast becoming a hardened veteran.

On November 3rd, 1781, he was transferred to H.M.S. *Barfleur*, flagship of Admiral Hood, the former Commissioner of Portsmouth dockyard. The *Barfleur* was to proceed to American waters where, after the disastrous surrender of General Cornwallis at Yorktown, New York was the only British base left in the north. While the ship lay at anchor off Staten Island Prince William was allowed to go ashore in his regal capacity as the King's son, and much enjoyed taking sightseeing jaunts around New York accompanied only by Hood and his mentor, General Bude. His appearances were greeted by the inhabitants with surprising demonstrations of loyalty and esteem and, not for the first time, William found himself taking sides in opposition to his father, for he came to sympathise with the aims of the colonists.

Strange as it may seem, this easy-going, affable youngster might even have been accepted by them as the first King of America. But news that the King's son was in the habit of wandering about the streets of New York practically unguarded came to the ears of a Colonel Ogden, one of General Washington's staff officers.

The Colonel's eyes gleamed when he considered the possibilities, and he hastened to his chief with a plan to capture William and his companions. Washington approved the suggestion but cautioned his aide to be careful that neither insult nor indignity were offered to the persons of the Prince and the admiral. But whether the Colonel's nerve failed or the operation proved too difficult, in the event Ogden's plot came to nothing.

Speedily tiring of the monotony of harbour service, William applied for transfer to a cruising vessel, and was duly lent to the 50-gun frigate *Warwick,* commanded by the up-and-coming Captain Keith Elphinstone, later to become Admiral Viscount Keith. By doing so he missed taking part in one of the most decisive naval battles of the whole war. For in January 1782 Admiral Rodney, who had gone back to England in the previous autumn owing to ill-health, now returned to the West Indies station with a fresh fleet. Reinforced by Admirals Hood and Graves, he brought de Grasse to action off the Saints Islands on April 12th and inflicted a crushing defeat on the French fleet, capturing his opponent and his flagship.

But William had not been without his own share of excitement for, in a smartly fought action off the Delaware river, the *Warwick* captured the French 40-gun frigate *L'Aigle,* the 22-gun *Sophie* and the armed sloop *Terrier.* In November on the King's instructions William was transferred back to the *Barfleur,* once more anchored off Staten Island.

A few days after his return whilst on duty as midshipman of the watch he stood by the flagship's gangway to receive the *Albemarle's* gig bringing that vessel's captain, lately senior officer of escort of a recently arrived convoy, to pay an official call on the admiral. When the gold-laced visitor climbed on board Prince William gaped in astonishment at 'the merest boy of a captain I had ever beheld.' Shortly afterwards he was himself introduced by the admiral to Captain Horatio Nelson.

At that time the name meant nothing to the Prince, although he divined that this was no common being; nor did he have any inkling of their subsequent friendship which would last right up to that final tragic day in the distant future when, blinded with tears, he would attend Nelson's funeral in St. Paul's Cathedral. For his part Nelson approved of this fine looking lad, who had not then begun to show any signs of his later corpulence. Afterwards he was to write of the Prince:

> He is a seaman which you could hardly suppose with every other qualification you may expect from him – but he will be a disciplinarian and a strong one; with the best temper and great good sense he cannot fail of being pleasing to everyone.

Unfortunately this prophecy was not to be altogether fulfilled, although Nelson's enthusiasm for him never waned in later years.

* * * * *

The surrender at Yorktown, to which the naval blockade of de Grasse had greatly contributed by preventing the arrival of reinforcements for General Cornwallis, virtually ended the war as far as America was concerned. The French fleet in the West Indies had been destroyed, and it was time to show the flag around the islands.

Early in 1783 the *Barfleur* paid an official visit to Port Royal, in Jamaica, where William was received in his princely capacity. He was welcomed enthusiastically, and escorted everywhere by a corps of locally raised cavalry which became known as 'Prince William's Regiment'.

When hostilities with France and Spain came to an end a few months later the Prince also visited Cap Francois, in Hispaniola, and Havana, being warmly received by both French and Spanish authorities, our erstwhile enemies. At Cap Francois William's personal intervention was the means of saving the lives of a number of British prisoners, and they were duly collected by British warship. During the visit to Havana the Prince was accompanied by Captain Nelson who had been detailed to attend on him. At a ball given in his honour the impressionable young midshipman was greatly smitten by the charms of Dona Maria Solano, daughter of the Spanish Governor.

Fortunately, however, he could only carry on his flirtation in imperfect French, and any possibly embarrassing developments were nipped in the bud by the tactful intervention of Nelson, who whisked his young charge away as soon as he could. When the visits came to an end Admiral Hood was ordered home, and by the end of June the *Barfleur* and her 'young Royal Tarry Breeks' were once more back in England.

There now followed a lengthy break in the continuity of his naval service when, in order to complete his education, William was sent off to the Continent to make the Grand Tour. With him went the faithful General Bude and a naval aide, Captain Merrick, R.N. Temporarily freed from the restrictions of naval life and the hardships of the midshipmen's berth, William proceeded to indulge himself with gusto in all the pleasures open to a young man of wealth and position.

During his 2-year tour of Germany and Italy he got into a good many scrapes, which included landing himself in the hands of money-lenders in Hanover to obtain the wherewithal to settle the gambling debts he had incurred along with his brother Frederick. In Lunenburg he fell in love with the daughter of a German nobleman, who, however, decided that she preferred an older man and subsequently married Captain Merrick. William was by no means heartbroken and speedily solaced himself in willing arms elsewhere. But eventually the tour came to an end and he returned home to face his examination for lieutenant.

Although George III was remarkably indulgent in approving of the speedy and generally undeserved promotion of his brothers, he was adamant that the professional rules should be strictly adhered to in regard to his son, and would not permit William to be examined for promotion until he had completed the full six years' qualifying service. But Nelson had not erred in his judgment of William's quality as a seaman, and the young man passed his test with flying colours. Admiral Howe, who presided over the examining board, told the King that Prince William was every inch a sailor.

On June 17th, 1785, he was duly promoted and appointed to be third lieutenant of the 38-gun frigate *Hebe* under Captain Edward Thornbrough. Captured from the French in 1782, the *Hebe* was employed in home waters as far north as the Orkneys in operations against smugglers. She spent most of her time, however, patrolling off the south coast of England where smuggling was particularly rife. Whenever the frigate called in at Portsmouth her third lieutenant was a frequent, though by no means welcome, visitor at the house of the Dockyard Commissioner making love to

Prince Edward Augustus, Duke of York, younger brother of King George III
From an engraving after J. Macardell

Prince Henry Frederick, Duke of Cumberland, younger brother of King George III
From a portrait by Sir Thomas Gainsborough
Reproduced by Gracious Permission of Her Majesty the Queen

his daughter Sarah. Eventually the girl had to be sent off to stay with an aunt and uncle in London to remove her from his undesirable attentions!

Then Commodore the Hon. Leveson-Gower hoisted his broad pennant in the *Hebe* and her cruises round the coast took on more the aspect of ceremonial visits. For in every port at which she called the Prince was required to go ashore in his official capacity to be respectfully greeted by the local bigwigs and presented with loyal addresses. Thus being compelled to wear, as it were, two hats, one as the King's son and the other as a working naval officer, might have been expected to affect his efficiency adversely in the latter capacity.

But the easy-going William seems to have been able to combine the two duties satisfactorily, for in the following February he was appointed to be First Lieutenant of the 28-gun frigate *Pegasus*. Young Byam Martin, Sarah's brother, had recently joined that ship as 'Captain's Servant', and, during almost the whole of his junior service, he served under Prince William, and spoke highly of the latter's care and attention to the training of young officers.

Then, on April 10th, 1786, came the first relaxation in the rigid rules for the Prince's advancement in the Service. He was promoted to post-captain, thus skipping the intermediate rank of commander, and appointed to the command, no less, of the *Pegasus* herself. The ship was refitting at Plymouth at the time, and when the Port Admiral brought the news of William's promotion he added that all the other captains present wished to be officially introduced to their new Royal colleague. Accordingly William held what was described as a levee on board the *Pegasus*. Today this would have been a cocktail party.

Noticing that no lieutenants turned up at this function, although some were themselves in command of smaller craft and thus entitled to be addressed as 'captain', he asked the reason and was told it had been considered proper that only the more senior officers should be present at a royal occasion.

This would not do for the liberal-minded Prince, who thereupon arranged a special levee for the juniors, greeting his assembled guests on that occasion with the words, 'And now, my boys, we will have a jolly day together.'

Such an action might have been contrary to naval protocol but

c

it certainly helped to add to William's popularity in the Service at that time.

On completion of her refit the *Pegasus* was ordered to join the North America station, and duly sailed for Halifax early in June in company with two other vessels, one of them commanded by a senior captain. While his ship was at Plymouth William had been bombarded with requests from various noble families for him to take their sea-minded scions under his wing. But, showing that strong preference for his professional comrades he maintained all his life, he accepted only the sons of his old shipmates and other naval officers.

The first call made by the little squadron was at Guernsey in order to purchase stocks of wine for their captains' stores, since liquor was cheaper in the Channel Islands. In those days naval officers were permitted by the Admiralty to ship duty-free wine for their personal consumption on board in quantities which today appear staggering in their generosity. Thus admirals were allowed some, 1,260 gallons per annum, and even lieutenants in command could have 105 gallons a year. Captains of 'inferior rates' such as the *Pegasus* were entitled to embark twice the quantity allowed to a lieutenant in command. Since William's personal income was a mere £3,000 a year it behoved him to shop economically – and he was fond of a glass of wine.

When the *Pegasus* arrived at Halifax, headquarters of the station under the command of Commodore Elliott, he was greeted with royal ceremony, but hastened to ask that in future he should receive no special treatment. When some weeks later, as part of her normal cruise programme, his ship paid a routine visit to Plaecentia, in Newfoundland, William was able to enjoy the heady taste of power represented by the gold lace on his sleeves.

A riot had occurred on shore during which a local magistrate had been insulted. In those days prior to the grant of self-government it was customary for justice in the colony to be administered by the Captain of any visiting British warship, who thus became *ex officio* judge. When news of the disturbance was reported to him the captain of the *Pegasus,* accompanied by a file of marines and a couple of boatswain's mates, proceeded on shore.

The alleged ringleader of the riot was apprehended, hauled before the *ad hoc* court presided over by his Royal Highness in full fig, and sentenced to receive 100 lashes. But at 80 strokes the arms of the boatswain's mates grew weary, and the balance of the sentence was remitted. This was probably just as well, for next day it was discovered that the wrong man had been arrested!

In August William celebrated his coming of age by lunching in the wardroom when, according to Byam Martin, he got very drunk. He was crawling back to his cabin on all fours when he was spotted by some of the sailors. Although they were themselves the worse for wear, H.R.H's birthday celebrations having included permission for the men to splice the mainbrace, they decided that their captain could not be left to continue his journey in so undignified a fashion. They therefore heaved him on to their shoulders and at some risk of banging his head against the overhead deck beams ran him back to his quarters.

As the King had specifically forbidden William to enter any foreign port, although the French would have welcomed a visit, Commodore Elliott, with the concurrence of his Majesty and the Admiralty, decided to give his youngest captain a change from northern waters by temporarily transferring the *Pegasus* to the Leeward Islands station. Its Commander-in-Chief, Admiral Sir Richard Hughes, had returned to England and his successor had not yet arrived. The station was therefore in the charge of the next senior officer, who happened to be Captain Nelson in the frigate *Boreas*.

News that a prince of the blood royal was about to join the station caused considerable excitement in the islands, and invitations for him to attend a variety of functions poured in. All these had to be vetted by Nelson, who would himself be required to attend on his Royal Highness. The captain of the *Boreas* was in fact not very popular locally because of his strict enforcement of the Navigation Laws which forbade the carriage of goods in American ships, the many breaches of which had hitherto been winked at by Admiral Hughes.

But when the two young captains got together, for Nelson was still in his early twenties, William soon conceived a great admiration for his new friend. It was then, he noted:

that I particularly observed the greatness of Nelson's superior mind. The manner in which he enforced the spirit of the

Navigation Act first drew my attention to the commercial interests of my country. My mind took its first decided naval turn from this familiar intercourse with Nelson.

For almost two months the Prince and the senior officer of the station toured the islands, fulfilling many engagements, during which William earned considerable popularity and respect, not least for his efficiency as a naval officer. Commented one prominent merchant, 'The Prince is quite the officer, never wearing any other dress than his uniform and his Star and Garter only when receiving addresses or on any public occasion. He has not slept a night out of his ship since his arrival in these seas.'

Although he disliked the role of courtier, Nelson himself wrote:

Our Prince is a gallant man; he is indeed volatile but always with great good nature. There were two balls during his stay and some of the old ladies were mortified that H.R.H. would not dance with them, but he says he is determined to enjoy the privilege of all other men, that of asking any lady he pleases. He has his foibles as well as private men but they are far out-balanced by his virtues. In his professional line he is superior to near two-thirds, I am sure, of the list; and in attention to orders and respect to his superior officers I know hardly his equal. H.R.H. keeps up strict discipline in his ship, and without paying him any compliment she is one of the finest ordered frigates I have seen. He was more plagued with his officers than enough.

This last was a reference to certain difficulties which arose between William and some of his officers in the *Pegasus*. Unfortunately the early zeal the Prince had shown for the service had begun to wear off and deteriorate into what his later critics described as 'morbid official activity'. Opinionated and headstrong like his father, he was as fully conscious of his personal status as of his rank as captain. Thus instead of delegating normal responsibilities for the everyday running of the ship to his very efficient First Lieutenant, he ordered every aspect of the daily routine, even to calling away a duty boat, to be referred to him for prior approval.

Not surprisingly, Isaac Schomberg, his First Lieutenant, an older man with a distinguished service record whose appointment to the *Pegasus* had really been in the capacity of 'dry nurse' to the Prince, resented this niggling interference, and disagreements arose between them.

When H.R.H. finally accused Schomberg of neglect of duty the affair came to a head, and the aggrieved First Lieutenant officially applied for a court-martial. Nelson as senior officer had to take certain steps in support of his fellow captain, but managed to avert an actual court-martial. The Admiralty eventually superseded Schomberg in the *Pegasus*, but to soften the blow appointed him First Lieutenant of Admiral Hood's flagship. Even to this officer William pursued his vendetta, but eventually the whole thing blew over leaving the Prince bereft of some of the esteem with which he had been formerly regarded by his contemporaries.

Some time later there was a rather more serious occurrence on board the *Pegasus:* no less than an attempt to murder his Royal Highness. The affair took place while the frigate was at sea on a routine cruise between ports. One evening, according to Byam Martin, William was dozing on the settee in his cabin when he dreamed that the schoolmaster, a man named Mears, was going to kill him. He awoke with a start to find Mears actually bending over him clutching an open penknife in his hand.

'Good God, Mears', the Prince exclaimed, 'what are you about?'

The schoolmaster, who appeared pale and distraught, straightened up quickly and replied, 'I was merely going to warn your Royal Highness that you could lose your life by sleeping here with the windows open.' With that he turned and left the cabin, muttering beneath his breath.

The Prince immediately went up on deck and related the affair to the officer of the watch, adding, 'He is certainly mad.'

Some of the midshipmen, among them Martin, happened to be standing nearby and overheard the Prince's remark. They were not surprised; they all thought the schoolmaster was mad. But no one really supposed that he had serious designs on the captain's life. During the early hours of the following morning, however, Mears suddenly appeared on deck clad only in a shirt and begged the officer of the watch to take him at once to the captain so that he could tell him the ship's position, for, he said, if the present course was maintained the frigate would run aground within an hour. The nearest land was in fact some five hundred miles away. The lieutenant ordered Mears to go below, threatening to take a rope's end to him, and the man fled.

Shortly afterwards Martin, while making his rounds below, found Mears still wandering about and told him to go to bed. Instead the schoolmaster crept into the pantry belonging to the captain's steward and grabbed up a large carving knife. Then, waiting until the marine sentry patrolling outside the captain's cabin had turned his back, he hurled himself at the cabin door. But as a safeguard its latch had been additionally secured by a piece of rope. The marine sprang on the would-be assassin and during the struggle the schoolmaster's shrill screams woke all hands, and he was quickly seized and put under restraint. On the ship's arrival in port at Antigua he was discharged to hospital where he was certified to have been suffering from a fit of temporary insanity. Later he recovered and was sent back to England.

During their jaunts around the islands, dining with each other on alternate nights when in harbour, a close intimacy sprang up between William and Nelson which, as already mentioned, ended only with the latter's death. Nelson also had a profound reverence for royalty. The romantically inclined Prince soon discovered that his friend was engaged to be married. The bride-to-be was, of course, the attractive widow Mrs Frances Nisbet, niece of the President of the Council of the island of Nevis.

Somewhat to Nelson's embarrassment William insisted on acting as 'Father' of the bride so that he would be able to give her away at the wedding, although it was not his custom to attend private functions. On March 11th, 1787, wearing full dress uniform, he duly officiated in that capacity at the ceremony, which took place in the President's mansion.

'Poor Nelson is over head and heels in love,' he noted. 'I wish him well and happy and that he may not repent the step he has taken.'

Soon afterwards the *Boreas* sailed for England.

It was at this point in his naval career that William's self-assertive temperament impelled him to take certain actions which were to lead eventually to the frustration of his ambition to become professional head of the Service. Not only did he anger his father but he began to alienate his seniors in the Navy and others who were in a position to affect his professional future. Feeling low and depressed after Nelson's departure for home, he sailed for Halifax without first obtaining permission. As a punishment he was sent to winter at Quebec. But in flat defiance of orders he left the station altogether and sailed for England. When his unexpected arrival at Cork in December, 1787, was reported to the Admiralty the First Lord informed the King. His Majesty was furious and directed that the *Pegasus* was to proceed to Plymouth, the Prince to remain within the limits of that port for as long as he had been absent from his station, after which he was to return to Halifax.

The Prince of Wales, who was already at variance with the King over political matters, took advantage of William's disobedience of orders to go down to Plymouth along with his brother Frederick and pay a ceremonial call on the *Pegasus*. They followed this with a round of gaiety and festivities ostensibly to celebrate the royal sailor's safe return, but in reality to highlight the disagreement between the Sovereign and the heir to the Throne. Captain and Mrs Nelson were also invited down by William.

> They went gladly and found the West Country port en gala ... A perpetual crowd thronged Fore Street where Prince William abode with a wealthy merchant of the town. By day there were formal visits to the dockyard and marine barracks, which were beautifully illuminated every night, and at 1 a.m., the Sailor Prince and his brother officers were still lustily performing country dances in the Long Assembly Rooms. Nelson found his Prince 'everything I could wish — respected by all.' Certainly the *Pegasus* was said by every competent judge to be one of the best disciplined ships that ever came into Plymouth.*

The gentlemen with whom William had taken lodgings was a wealthy broker named Wynn whose daughter was the local reigning beauty. Needless to say the Prince fell for her charms and it was not long before their affair came to wider notice. In a story about Plymouth one journal wrote:

* *Nelson* by Carola Oman.

A town where, exiled by the higher pow'rs
the Royal Tar with indignation lours;
Kept by his Sire from London and from sin
to say his catechism to Mistress Wynn.

Meanwhile William had applied for command of H.M.S. *Melampus,* one of the latest and largest frigates, but the consequences of his recent misbehaviour now began to be felt and his request was turned down by Lord Howe.

Instead he was ordered to transfer with his crew to the *Andromeda,* a 5th rate of 32 guns. When she was ready for sea William was instructed to join up with the Channel Fleet, then under command of his ex-senior officer in the *Hebe,* Rear-Admiral Leveson-Gower. The fleet then put to sea on an evolutionary, or 'shakedown', cruise for the newly commissioned *Andromeda's* benefit.

By that time his love affair with Miss Wynn, which was still the talk of the town, had come to the ears of the King, who exclaimed, 'What, William playing the fool again? Send him off to America and forbid the return of the ship to Plymouth.'

Since he still stood in some awe of his father, the Prince dutifully sailed in July 1788 and such was the excellence of his navigation that the *Andromeda* made the 2,700-mile passage from the Lizard to Halifax in exactly one month from departure to landfall.

When she arrived there were only three other ships on the station, which was at that time under the command of Captain Charles Sanders, whom William described disgustedly as a 'vulgar drunken dolt'. For when the newly arrived captain went to pay his first official call on his senior officer he found the latter still in bed snoring off the effects of a carouse.

The Prince, however, ran his new ship as tautly as he had the *Pegasus,* as shown by the following extracts from his Order Book. In March, 1788, before the *Andromeda* left Plymouth he wrote:

From the shameful and un-officer like conduct of Mr. — towards Mr. — last night and from the very relaxed manner in which the service is carried on by the rest of the gentlemen it is my positive orders that none of the gentlemen sleep out of the ship till they behave themselves with diligence and obedience in their stations.

In August the officers of the *Andromeda* received another shake-up.

From the scandalous and disgraceful laziness of the gentlemen it is my positive orders and directions that the officer of the watch at sea and the officer carrying on the duty at an anchor do at six bells in the morning send down the day mate to have the hammocks of the gentlemen lashed up and taken down ready to be immediately brought up when they are piped up. In future the hammocks to be up in ten minutes from the first pipe up and down in five after being piped down.

Whenever he met officers ashore in improper dress he gave them a wigging on the spot. Those from his own ship received a more permanent reminder.

Andromeda. Halifax harbour. Sep. 1, 1788. From my having yesterday met in the town of Halifax several of the gentlemen belonging to his Majesty's ship under my command in shoes and stockings, who to my certain knowledge went on shore in the established dress of the ship, it is my particular orders and directions that every officer and gentleman belonging to his Majesty's ship under my command do appear when on leave on shore in their uniform as directed. It is with equal surprise and astonishment that I am under the necessity of giving this order, having already so repeatedly expressed my wish of uniformity and officer-like appearance in the officers and gentlemen. This order being particularly addressed to them, they are to remember that any person who has the honour to serve in his Majesty's naval service cannot distinguish themselves more properly than by a strict adherence to all written orders and verbal wishes of their commanding officer.

Hand salutes were then unknown in the Royal Navy. Seamen and junior officers always doffed their hats to a senior. William found it necessary to remind his younger officers of their duty in this respect. Thus:

All junior officers on shore meeting a superior officer are to show proper respect by taking their hats off.

These were the days before a standard uniform for the Lower Deck had been introduced. Ships' companies therefore dressed largely as dictated by their captains' personal whims. But an approved uniform for officers had been introduced as far back as 1746. William, as will be seen, had his own ideas on the form this should take for his juniors. Complained young Byam Martin, still serving as a midshipman with the Prince:

It was H.R.H's pleasure that there should be uniformity, but the dress was of his own imagination and quite at variance from that which the Service prescribed. Old and young, tall and short, all were to be alike; the boy of 12 years old was to be rigged out as a man and squeezed into a tight dress as to leave no chance of growing unless perchance nature's efforts should prove more than a match for the tailor's stitches. Only conceive a midshipman with white breeches so tight as to appear to be sewn upon the limb, yellow-topped hunting boots pulled close up and strapped with a buckle round the knee. A pigtail of huge dimensions dangling beneath an immense square gold-laced cocked hat; the tail was thickened by introducing between the hair a leather thong of the shape of a large carrot, and this ribboned over had a most formidable appearance. But to complete the headdress the side hair was allowed to grow to a great length and being frizzed down and well stuffed with powder and pomatum terminated with a large curl, leaving just room for it to work clear of the shoulder. Add to all this a sword about two-thirds the length of the little body that wore it — a boy of about 13 was four feet ten inches tall. Such was the dress conceived and adopted by our naval captain.

William was equally meticulous about the cleanliness and welfare of his ship's company. The men's clothes were ordered to be washed on Tuesdays and Saturdays; the hammocks and bags of the seamen were to be marked with their names in black, those of the marines in red; each seaman and marine was to have two hammocks and to be punished if their hammocks were not marked. Every morning the quarterdeck, main deck, forecastle and gangways were to be regularly washed; the quarterdeck scrubbed with holystone, the lower deck and gunroom washed every other morning, and occasionally with vinegar. When grog was served it was to be properly mixed, being 'four waters to one of spirit, and no boy to have his wine or grog'. No one to sit or sleep in the boats, no clothes to be spread or hung on the lower deck — orders which are equally relevant today in the 20th century Navy. 'At anchor a sentry to be constantly powdered and dressed in his full uniform on each gangway and the forecastle.' 'No person to presume to put a fishing line overboard without the captain's leave first obtained.'

Stickler for discipline he might be, but William also believed in relaxation of a different kind from that of normal recreational pursuits. Captain's order No.20 stated that the direction to the First Lieutenant to see all strangers out of the ship at gunfire (the evening gun, which was usually fired at 4 o'clock, or sunset in the tropics) was by no means to restrain the officers and men from having either black or white women on board through the night 'so long as discipline is unhurt by the indulgence'.

He also took care of the men's food. In August, 1788, he wrote to the senior officer at Halifax complaining that there was 'a quantity of bread, butter and cheese on board which is mouldy, rotten and rancid and unfit for the men to eat'. The Masters of H.M. Ships *Dido* and *Resource* were promptly ordered to repair on board the *Andromeda,* survey the provisions thus complained of, and if found as represented to have them thrown overboard and replaced.

During his time on the station William paid a number of duty visits to various islands in the West Indies in his official capacity and met with demonstrations of loyalty to the King, and expressions of affection for himself which took a gratifyingly tangible form. Thus when he called at Port Royal, in Jamaica, the whole House of Assembly waited on him with congratulations and voted 2,000 guineas for the purchase of a star ornamented with diamonds as testimony of their high respect and esteem and gratitude for his part in the defence of the British Empire and their island during the late war. The House of Assembly of Barbados likewise presented him with a gold-hilted sword valued at 300 guineas, and that of Dominica a watch to the same value. Eventually, after having completed almost twelve months on the station, the *Andromeda* was ordered home to pay off.

Shortly afterwards William was created Duke of Clarence and St. Andrews and Earl of Munster. With these titles went official quarters in St. James's Palace and an allowance of £12,000 per annum. A country home at Richmond, later called Clarence Lodge, was also allotted to him. But with the paying off of the *Andromeda* his sea time as a serving naval officer virtually ended.

To understand more fully how this came about it is necessary to take a brief look at the way the country was run and the part played in national affairs by the King. George III was a firm believer in autocratic rule; thus when he came to the throne he was determined to take the chief share in governing the country. Through the exercise of intrigue and the dispensation of royal patronage by way of pensions and titles he eventually built up his own party of followers. Known as the 'King's Friends', some were honest men, if political nonentities, wishing only to display their loyalty to the crown; others were corrupt and unscrupulous place-seekers. Unfortunately the King's private designs clashed with the best interests of the country. It was through his intervention that the American colonies were lost, and when the Treaty of Versailles which ended the Seven Years War was signed in 1783 Britain was actually forced to surrender possessions all over the world to her former enemies. The King's favourites either resigned or were superseded, and eventually a new government set about reducing his influence by cutting down the royal pension list and abolishing certain expensive and unnecessary 'grace and favour' offices.

But the King's intrigues continued until, in order to spite the government which sought to curtail his powers, he appointed William Pitt to the office of Prime Minister. An ambitious young statesman of spotless personal integrity, Pitt was precisely the man to spike his master's guns, and with skilful diplomacy proceeded to introduce a number of much-needed reforms which set the country once more on the road to prosperity and greatness.

Many of these measures the King disliked or only imperfectly understood, but he tolerated them, receiving in return Pitt's immense loyalty and personal regard. But the Opposition, which included such unscrupulous politicians as Fox, Burke and Sheridan, was factious rather than honest, and its leaders men of low moral reputation. Worse still in the eyes of the King, they were closely associated with the Prince of Wales, whose scandalous behaviour and unfilial conduct towards his father made him a byword among all decent-minded people. Indeed, the only hope of their return to power lay in the help of the Prince, who had promised to dismiss Pitt and call Fox to office when he should be in a position to do so. In 1788 when the King suffered a bout of temporary insanity it seemed that this might be possible, but fortunately George recovered before his son could formally be proclaimed Regent.

Although its senior officers had little time for politics, the Navy, too, had been affected by the King's conduct of affairs during the early years of his reign. Sons of some of the most powerful political families were serving in the Navy, and strong social ties bound leading flag officers to the Opposition Party. The 'King's Friends', however, had few adherents in naval circles.

But as time went on and world-shaking events in Europe began to unfold, loyalty to the person of the Sovereign replaced the ties of service to a political party in the Navy. Foolishly, the newly created Duke of Clarence allied himself with the Prince of Wales and his cronies, and by doing so finally put an end to his own naval career. Not for nothing had he been described by the wits as 'a bon enfant with a weak head', and 'a good egg but cracked'.

For the next few months after paying off the *Andromeda* he busied himself with domestic affairs on shore, settling into the new house at Richmond, taking his seat as a peer in the House of Lords, and campaigning for appointments for his naval friends, including Nelson. But his applications did more harm than good, and Nelson himself remained unemployed for five years. For relaxation he disported himself in the company of his brothers in London and at Brighton. Together with their dissolute companions they drank, gambled and womanised, William further shocking the censorious by his use of the raciest nautical language. He fell in love again and this time contracted a liaison which was to last for 20 years.

His inamorata was a buxom Irish stage beauty named Dorothy Jordan who was noted for her silvery voice, infectious laughter and winning ways. Leading actress of the day, she was appearing at a London theatre when William first saw her, starring as 'Little Pickle' in a farce called *The Spoil'd Child*. When the play moved to Richmond the fevered attentions paid by 'a certain exalted youth' to its leading lady speedily became headline news. Eventually the two set up house together at Bushey Park where, over the years, Dorothy bore him 10 children, all of whom received the surname of Fitzclarence. At the age of 42 she finally left him to return to the stage.

But the shadow of war was again looming. In 1790 Spain, ever ready to irritate her old enemy where she could, provoked an incident which brought the threat of hostilities. A squadron of Spanish warships appeared off an English settlement at Nootka Sound, in Vancouver Island, bombarded the place and treated the settlers with barbarous cruelty. A partial mobilisation was ordered in Britain, and among the ships being prepared for service was the 74-gun line of battleship *Valiant*. William was nominated for command of this vessel, but the power and reputation of the Royal Navy proved too formidable for the Spaniards, who climbed down, and the *Valiant* paid off. A month later, on December 3rd, 1790, William was promoted to the rank of Rear-Admiral of the Blue.

In 1789, however, revolution had broken out in France, and for a time it seemed that this would result in the establishment of a limited constitutional monarchy in that country. There was even admiration and approval for the reformers in Britain, especially among the Parliamentary Opposition party. But the excesses of the revolutionaries grew progressively worse until finally they culminated in the brutal execution of King Louis XVI and his Queen. Less than a month after the King had been guillotined, in February 1793, the new rulers of France, declaring themselves to be champions of universal liberty and equality, and that 'all governments are our enemies, all peoples our friends', attacked Holland and declared war on England.

Fortunately we had a strong Navy ready. Powerful British naval squadrons were at once despatched to blockade the great French arsenals of Brest and Toulon.

William, who had been promoted a further step, to Rear-Admiral of the Red, on February 1st, naturally desired to get back to sea, and a ship, the 98-gun first-rate *London,* was already being tentatively fitted out at Portsmouth to take his flag. But he was still a friend and ally of Fox and his shrinking party of supporters and had taken a stand against the government's war measures in Parliament. Pitt could not overlook this, and complained to the King who, although he would have preferred to send his son back to sea in order to remove him from the baleful influence of his political cronies, felt compelled to back up his Prime Minister, and refused permission for William to serve afloat.

As time went on William continued to bombard the Admiralty with requests for active employment. Finally, on March 15th, 1794, he addressed the following appeal to the Board, whose chief naval member was his former senior officer Hood, now ennobled and an Admiral of the Blue. First Lord was the Earl of Chatham, Pitt's brother.

My Lords. At a time when this country is engaged in a war with a powerful and active enemy whose great aim appears to be the subversion of all the ancient monarchies of Europe, it behoves every man who values the constitution under which he enjoys so many blessings to rally round the Throne and protect it from the dangers by which it is so imminently threatened. Conscious that during my naval career I never committed an act which could tarnish the honour of the flag under which it was my pride and glory to fight, I solicit in this hour of peril to my country that employment in her service which every subject is bound to seek, and particularly myself, considering the exalted rank which I hold in the country and the cause which it is my duty to maintain and defend. I regard a refusal of that employment as a tacit acknowledgement of my incapacity and which cannot fail to degrade me in the opinion of the public, who from the conduct which has been pursued towards me are justified in drawing a conclusion unfavourable to my professional

character on account of the very marked neglect which has
been shown towards every application on my part which has
been transmitted to your lordships to be employed in the
service of my country. If the rank which I hold in the Navy
operates as an impediment to my obtaining the command of
a ship without that of a squadron being attached to it, I will
willingly relinquish that rank under which I had formerly
command of a ship and serve as a Volunteer on board any
ship to which it may please your lordships to appoint me. All
I require is active service and that when my gallant
countrymen are fighting the cause of their country and their
sovereign I may not have the imputation thrown upon me of
living a life of inglorious ease when I ought to be in the front
of danger.

Their lordships did not even acknowledge receipt of this
heartcry and, nine days later, William took the matter to his
father. 'Sir,' he wrote:

on the 15th of this month I addressed a letter to the Lords of
the Admiralty, of which I transmit a copy, soliciting from
them that employment in the service of my country to which
my rank and character entitle me. To neglect they have
added insult inasmuch as they have withheld from me even
that courtesy which is due to every individual who makes a
respectful tender of his services at a momentous period like
the present when everything that is valuable to an English-
man is at stake, and the Throne on which you sit is
endangered by the machinations of regicides and revolution-
ists. As in this treatment of the Lords of the Admiralty my
character as a naval officer becomes seriously implicated I am
emboldened to make this request to my royal father,
soliciting from him that he will be pleased to issue his
commands to the Lords of the Admiralty to grant me that
employment which I desire, or publicly to state the grounds
on which their refusal is founded.

But Pitt still refused to yield and the King was disinclined to
overrule him. There was to be no sea command for William. As a
sop, perhaps, he was promoted in April, 1794, to be Vice-Admiral

King William IV
From a portrait by Sir Martin Archer Shee

King William IV, when Duke of Clarence
From an engraving by Cook after a drawing by Skelton

of the Blue, and three months later to the rank of Vice-Admiral of the White. Against the implacable hostility of the Prime Minister and the unwillingness of the Admiralty to run counter to the wishes of his Majesty there was little now that William could do. But he never forgot the treatment he had received at the hands of the Board. He took up farming at Bushey, immersed himself in the study of naval history, and the promotion of such reforms as were not completely condemned by the Admiralty, and paid frequent visits to Portsmouth to see how the Navy was getting on.

During his service afloat he had noted the general superiority of French ships to our own and knew that the French maintained schools of naval architecture in all their principal ports. No such school existed in this country, and William tried to form a society under his own patronage for the improvement of British ship-building. But the Admiralty remained indifferent to this laudable scheme, and it was not until 1810 that a School of Naval Architects was set up in Portsmouth dockyard under the direction of the Admiralty itself.

He corresponded regularly with Nelson, Collingwood who had been a station-mate of his in the West Indies and who held an equally high opinion of the Prince's professional ability, and other naval friends.

One of these, Captain (later Admiral) the Hon. William Cornwallis, had earlier written of William:

> Our royal duke is tired of the shore. It would be a pity if any of the zeal and fondness he has so evidently shown for the service should be suffered to abate, as there is every reason to believe that with his ability he will one day carry its glory to a greater height than it has yet attained.

But he was not among those who were earning the glory. How he must have writhed under the jibes of the squib writers who called him, who was a trained seaman 'an armchair sailor'. How also must he have regretted his misguided essays into politics which had brought him to his present condition of inactivity.

Great events came and went without his own participation in them. Off Ushant in 1794 while William was having the gold lace of his rank changed on his uniforms Admiral Howe won the

D

resounding naval victory over the French, known as 'the Glorious First of June'. Two years later Britain found herself almost encircled by enemies when both Holland and Spain joined France against her. In due course the naval power of these formidable foes was to be crippled by Admiral Jervis at the battle of Cape St. Vincent; Admiral Duncan at Camperdown; and Nelson himself at the battle of the Nile. In 1801 the Treaty of Amiens brought hostilities to an end with Britain once again triumphant at sea.

But the peace was only a breathing space, for Bonaparte, France's new supreme ruler, was determined to crush once for all her ancient enemy. So in 1803 war was again declared and, while the British Navy once more took up its ceaseless vigil outside enemy ports, defensive measures were stepped up at home, for the menace of actual invasion of these islands had become very real. But there was still no job for the languishing Duke of Clarence. On June 1st, 1795, he received another step in rank, this time to Vice-Admiral of the Red, or senior, Squadron; and on February 14th 1799, to Admiral of the Blue. On January 1st, 1801, he was promoted to be Admiral of the White, thus passing Nelson and other worthies on the flag list; and on November 9th, 1805, in the general wave of naval promotions that followed the great victory at Trafalgar, to Admiral of the Red, a new and senior rank created by the grateful King.

But now William's best friend and former comrade was dead and, apart from letters, all he would have by which to treasure the latter's memory was the musket ball that killed him.

Following the destruction of his fleet at Trafalgar, Napoleon finally abandoned all idea of invading England, and proceeded to make himself master of Europe. But his old enemy was still in the ring against him, at first alone, then with allies. By the unprecedented use of sea power, under cover of which she was able to land an army on the Continent commanded by Wellington, which eventually fought its way into France and joined up with newly heartened allies from the east, she finally brought about the downfall of the dictator. In April, 1814, Napoleon abdicated.

Pitt died in 1806 but his policy was maintained by his successors. Four years later the King's recurring fits of insanity became permanent, and the Prince of Wales assumed the duties of Regent. But he was now so hedged about with checks and restrictions that he could do little harm. Fox, his political crony, was also dead.

In December 1811, on the death of Sir Peter Parker, William was promoted by seniority to be Admiral of the Fleet, and thus became the senior flag officer in the Navy, since there could be only one holder of the rank at that time. After the battle of Trafalgar he had applied to the Admiralty to be appointed Commander-in-Chief in the Mediterranean.

But the Board's veto on his active employment remained, and in order to bar his way their Lordships privately asked Collingwood, who had taken over on the death of Nelson, to continue in the post. Despite the fact that he had been continuously at sea ever since the outbreak of war in 1803, Collingwood agreed, but early in 1810 he was taken ill and died soon after embarking for home.

But at last, in 1814, the royal Admiral of the Fleet was able to hoist his flag afloat. With the banishment to Elba of Napoleon, Louis XVIII could now safely return to his own country from his exile in Britain. He duly embarked in the yacht *Royal Sovereign* at Dover and was ceremonially escorted across the Channel to Calais by a squadron of British warships commanded by the Duke of Clarence, flying his Union flag in the frigate *Jason*. The Prince Regent himself accompanied Louis as far as Dover and stood on the jetty to wave him farewell.

William had forgotten none of his seamanship, and when the squadron arrived off Calais the royal yacht hove to while the *Jason* led the escorting ships past her with yards manned and the crews giving three cheers. Ten days later William struck his flag and the *Jason* reverted to her normal duties.

But there was more ceremony to come. Two months later, in June, 1814, the Emperor of Russia and the King of Prussia paid an official visit to this country for the purpose of celebrating the allied victory over Napoleon. The royal visitors and their suites landed at Dover and later travelled down to Portsmouth for a naval review at Spithead. The last such event — and the first of its kind to be held — had taken place in 1773 when George III himself had inspected the fleet and distributed promotions to the officers and largesse to the poor of Portsmouth with an equally generous hand.

William now hoisted his flag in the *Impregnable,* a 98-gun

first-rate commanded by Captain the Hon. Henry Blackwood, one of Nelson's captains. Other flag officers present with the fleet for this glittering naval occasion were Admiral Sir Richard Bickerton, who had originally been knighted by George III at the previous review, Vice-Admiral Sir George Martin, Vice-Admiral Sir Francis Laforey, Rear-Admiral Sir Harry Neale, Rear-Admiral Edward Foote, and Rear-Admiral Sir Thomas Byam Martin, William's former midshipman in the *Pegasus* and *Andromeda.*

Martin's flag captain in the *Montague* brought along a whiff of a different kind of history, for he was Peter Heywood who, as a midshipman, had been condemned to death and later pardoned for his alleged part in the *Bounty* mutiny.

But Admiral Martin had grown to be rather more censorious of his old commanding officer. In his recollections of the review he wrote:

> The yards of the *Impregnable* were manned on the arrival of some personage or other when something real or imaginary struck the Duke as wrong by one of the men of the fore t'gallant yard. H.R.H., who was pretty vehement in the use of a speaking trumpet, sent forth at the unfortunate man the most tremendous volley of oaths I ever heard — it quite made one shudder to hear such blasphemy. But it was taken in a different light by the Prince Regent, who turned to Lord Melville, the First Lord, and said, 'what an excellent officer William is'.
>
> But the first Article of War says that all officers in or belonging to the fleet who shall be guilty of profane oaths, cursing, execrations or other scandalous actions in derogation of God's honour, and corruption of good manners shall be punished as a court-martial may inflict.

No court-martial, however, awaited the titular head of the Navy, who expressed his approval of the efficient show put up by the fleet in the following order issued at the end of the visit of the allied monarchs:

> H.R.H. The Duke of Clarence cannot quit this anchorage and resign the command of the distinguished officers, seamen and

Royal Marines he has had under him on this particular and very flattering occasion without expressing his entire approbation of the attention that has been shown by all descriptions of officers and men whilst under his orders. If H.R.H. does not particularise individuals it is only because he has every reason to be most perfectly satisfied with the conduct of all; but H.R.H. must nevertheless express his particular thanks to Admiral Sir Richard Bickerton, Bart., and also to Rear-Admiral the Hon. Henry Blackwood, Captain of the Fleet, for their marked attention and great assistance on this occasion.

For the next thirteen years following the review William reverted again to being an 'armchair sailor'. Although there would be no major war for forty years after the final defeat of Napoleon at Waterloo there was plenty of work for the Navy to do. One of the first tasks which devolved upon Britain as mistress of the seas was to rid them of the pirates that preyed on merchant shipping from the Mediterranean to China, and to suppress the slave trade. Permanent British naval stations were established in the Mediterranean, North America and West Indies, at the Cape of Good Hope, in the East Indies and South America.

As well as policing the seas the Royal Navy also began making them safe for navigation. A Hydrographic Department had been set up at the Admiralty, and systematic marine surveying began. Attention was also turned to exploration and a number of expeditions were sent out from this country, chiefly in search of the elusive North-West Passage. The usual post-war reductions took place in the fleet. Most of the ships scrapped were battle-scarred veterans due for replacement, and the new building programme emphasised the Navy's growing role of commerce protection and peacekeeping.

In 1822 George Canning, the wisest disciple of Pitt, became, first Foreign Secretary, then Prime Minister. George III had died hopelessly insane two years before and the former Regent was now King. Through Canning's efforts William's annual allowance was increased from £12,000 to £21,000 and, perhaps as some form of recompense for his years of naval unemployment, Canning proposed that William should assume the rank of Lord High

Admiral. He meant, of course, that this should be only a titular appointment, the normal administrative and executive duties of the Admiralty Board being carried on by a Council, or, in other words, the Board with a new name.

But this having been done, William soon showed that he was putting up with no more inactivity. Remembering how he had been made to suffer by past Lords of the Admiralty, he was determined to demonstrate that he was no mere figurehead. He moved into Admiralty House, gave a series of receptions for all the naval officers who had ever come to his notice, and launched a campaign for the early promotion of deserving young officers and the pensioning off of the older ones. Then he hoisted the famous red and gold anchor flag of the Lord High Admiral at the masthead of the yacht *Royal Sovereign* and sailed off on a cruise.

But Canning died after only five months in office as Prime Minister and was succeeded by the Duke of Wellington. William cut short his unauthorised cruise and, once back on shore, proceeded to deal high-handedly with his Council, now headed by Vice-Admiral Sir George Cockburn, the effective First Sea Lord. Without consulting them he set up a commission of enquiry into the state of gunnery in the fleet, at which in the following order he peremptorily commanded the out of Town attendance of its members:

> It is my directions that the members of the Committee on gunnery now sitting at the Admiralty proceed to Portsmouth ready to wait upon me there by Monday morning, 14th inst., and that they be prepared to remain at Portsmouth if I shall think proper. Given under my hand on board the *Royal Sovereign,* yacht, this 10th day of July, 1828.

Following this he set off on another unauthorised cruise.

When Cockburn ventured to write in protest at his behaviour William replied:

> Sir, your letter does not give me *displeasure* but *concern* to see one I had kept when appointed to this situation of Lord High Admiral constantly opposing what I consider good for the King's service. In this free country everyone has a right to have his opinion and I have therefore to have mine which

differs totally from yours. The only point of your letter
which I can approve is where you mention expense, and
being now under weigh I have only to say I shall for the
present leave the order you so improperly object to in your
hands till I return when I shall talk the matter over with you
deliberately. But I cannot conclude without repeating my
Council is not to dictate but to give advice.

Sir George was inclined to give way, but the other members of
the Council were thoroughly affronted and took the matter to the
Prime Minister. When he learned of their action William wrote
direct to Wellington to demand that Cockburn be relieved and
another admiral appointed in his place. The Prime Minister passed
this on to the King, who himself wrote to his brother to point out
that he was exceeding his duty. But William persisted in his
demand, and finally the Council threatened that if Cockburn went
they would resign *en bloc*.

William then put to sea again without seeking approval, and this
time took with him a squadron of warships from Plymouth in
order to exercise them at manoeuvres. Not surprisingly, the
officers and men of the squadron were tickled to death to be
sailing under the command of one who was deliberately flouting
the stuffed shirts at the Admiralty. Meanwhile Wellington had
referred the Council's threat to the King, who was by now growing
tired of William's antics, and decided to put his foot down.

'I am quite aware that I am fast drawing to the close of my life,'
he wrote to the Prime Minister. 'A month, a week, a day may call
the Lord High Admiral to be my successor . . . the Lord High
Admiral shall strictly obey the laws enacted by Parliament . . . or I
desire immediately to receive his resignation.'

Faced with this ultimatum William resigned in August, 1828,
after 15 months in the ancient office of England's Lord High
Admiral – the last single individual to fly his flag as such afloat.
Two years later he himself became King. Of nearly half a century
in the Royal Navy he could claim to have spent 10 years, 9
months and 3 weeks on active service afloat in peace and war. He
was, on the whole, entitled to be called 'the Sailor King'.

CHAPTER III

AFFIE

Queen Victoria was furious. The cause of her anger was a leader article in *The Times* which ventured to criticise at length and with considerable outspokenness certain events which had taken place on the arrival in Malta of her son, the 14-year old Prince Alfred. The Prince had recently joined the Navy as a cadet and his first seagoing ship, H.M.S. *Euryalus,* sailed from Portsmouth in October 1858, to join her consorts on the Mediterranean station.

When the ship entered Valetta's Grand Harbour however, she was greeted with a royal salute fired by the assembled warships and Fort St. Angelo, and even before she had cleared quarantine the Governor, General Sir John Pennefather, hurried on board in cocked hat and full dress to bend the knee before the royal cadet and invite him to attend a grand banquet to be held in his honour at the Auberge de Castille that same evening.

In due course the Prince was conveyed ashore in the Governor's barge to the accompaniment of more gun salutes from the garrison and driven along streets lined by the cheering populance to preside somewhat nervously over a glittering assembly, which included the Island's Council, the Bishops of Malta and Gibraltar, judges, magistrates and foreign consuls.

Commented *The Times* acidly, which a month or so earlier had approved of the Prince's entry into the Navy as a wise step:

We want him to learn his profession, but not in a vapid, half and half, Royal Highness kind of way. He was sent out to be trained to salt water, and it is upon rose water that his first lesson in navigation is taking place. What has a middy [he was a cadet] to do with royal receptions and royal salutes and royal fiddle-faddles of every description?

After listing the ceremonial which followed the arrival in Malta of the *Euryalus,* fully described in a despatch from their own correspondent, the leader-writer went on:

Prince Alfred might just as well be tempting the perils of Virginia Water. He was greeted by the slogan 'Viva Alfredo' by the Maltese. But why not 'Viva Midshipman Easy?'

Wrote the angry Queen to her favourite daughter, Princess Victoria:

We had long and detailed accounts of Affie from Malta. The impudent *Times* thought fit to disapprove of his being properly and loyally received.

But in spite of this somewhat less humble commencement of his naval career compared with that of his great-uncle William nearly eighty years before, Prince Alfred was nevertheless, and in due course, to rise to the top of his profession largely through his own ability.

* * * * *

When George IV died in 1830, worn out, it is said, by evil living, he left no legitimate heir to the throne. The Duke of Clarence, therefore, became next in line of succession, for his elder brother the Duke of York had died three years before the King. By his marriage to the Princess Adelaide of Saxe-Meiningen in 1818 William had two daughters, but both died practically in infancy. He, too, thus left no heir, and was succeeded in 1837 by his niece Victoria, only daughter of the already defunct Duke of Kent. In 1840 the young Queen married Prince Albert of Saxe-Coburg and Gotha, and in the following year their first child was born, eventually to become King Edward VII.

In August, 1844, a second son was born and christened Alfred. But to the end of his life Queen Victoria always referred to him by the affectionate diminutive 'Affie', and, during the boyhood of the two, frequently compared his character and industriousness to the detriment of his elder brother. Blame, however, was not entirely to be laid upon Prince Albert Edward, usually known as 'Bertie'. Rather it was his strict and narrow upbringing which was directly due to the influence of Baron Stockmar, the German physician who was friend and counsellor of both the Queen and the Prince Consort.

For the good Baron attributed to defective education the sins and errors committed by the sons of George III. This fault, he emphasised, must at all costs be avoided, and the Heir to the Throne moulded into a moral and intellectual paragon. Stockmar also criticised in detail the shortcomings of William IV who, he said, had been anything but a moral and wise man, yet towards the close of his reign went under the endearing appellation of 'the good old Sailor King'.

Queen Victoria, however, would not accept this outright condemnation of her uncle. 'And not without reason,' she added in a footnote to Stockmar's critical letter.

> Whatever his faults may have been, it was well known that he was not only zealous but most conscientious in the discharge of his duties as king. He had a truly kind heart and was most anxious to do what was right.

Thus Prince Albert Edward was not allowed to go to a public school, and for most of his early years was privately educated by a tutor whom he hated.

His sailor great-uncle had declared, 'There is no place in the world for making an English gentleman like the quarterdeck of an English man of war.'

But Albert had no liking for the Navy; he wanted to join the Army. 'I must be a soldier,' he said. 'There's no life like a soldier's.'

When he was 18, therefore, his parents had him gazetted lieutenant-colonel in the 16th Hussars. But this initial launch so high up the rungs of the military ladder only made him indignant; he wanted to start at the bottom. Before that, however, he, too, for a brief spell was borne on the books of a British warship as a sailor, albeit the vessel in question was merely the Royal Yacht.

At the age of 7 he accompanied his parents on an extended voyage to visit a number of places on the Devon and Cornish coasts and the Channel Islands. After a few days at sea the Queen wrote in her journal:

> It became quite smooth and then Bertie put on his sailor's dress which was beautifully made by the men on board who make for our sailors. When he appeared the officers and sailors, who were all assembled on deck to see him, cheered and seemed delighted with him.

Although the 'sailor's dress' was in fact a miniature suit of bell-bottoms, the young Prince was rated as a midshipman for the period of the cruise.

The return of the Royal Yacht to Portsmouth at the end of the voyage was greeted by a signal from the naval Commander-in-Chief: 'The Navy is delighted. God bless our little Admiral!'

But even if Prince Albert was not to embrace the sea as a profession he at least popularised the sailor suit, which for many years afterwards remained the *de rigueur* party and Sunday-go-to-meeting dress for small boys of all classes — and even for some girls.

William, too, had perpetuated his memory in the Navy, although not sartorially, for it is said that the term 'snotty' for a midshipman dates from the habit of the 'young Royal Tarry Breeks' during his early days as one of the 'young gentlemen' of wiping his nose on his sleeve! He is also commemorated in more solid form by the Royal Clarence victualling yard at Portsmouth, and the Royal William Yard at Devonport.

Prince Alfred, however, unhesitatingly plumped for the Navy as his chosen profession. His father, who had been worrying over the kind of training he should receive, whole-heartedly agreed and told his brother, the Duke of Saxe-Coburg — whom Alfred was eventually to succeed — 'Some time ago you wrote to me about Alfred and you expressed your astonishment at his having hardly any knowledge of his original Saxon ancestors, and of his wish to enter the Navy. That this may make him disinclined to become sovereign of Coburg-Gotha. As regards his wish to enter the Navy, this is a passion which we his parents believe not to have the right to subdue. It is certainly not right to break the spontaneous desire of a young spirit.'*

* *A Century of British Monarchy* by H. Bolitho.

Accordingly, when he reached the age of 13 Alfred was provided with a separate establishment away from home where he could pursue his studies uninterruptedly in order to fit himself for entry into the Navy in due course. The 'establishment' was a cottage at Alverbank, near Portsmouth, formerly the property of Sir John Wilson Croker, a Secretary of the Admiralty; and Lieutenant John Cowell of the Royal Engineers was appointed to be the boy's 'Governor'.

Cowell, who later became Master of the Queen's Household, was a man of the highest scientific training, and had served as adjutant to Sir Harry Jones, the Army's Chief Engineer at the assaults on Bomarsund and Sebastopol during the Crimean war. Prince Alfred's special tutor was the Reverend William Rowe Jolley, a chaplain and naval instructor. Dartmouth Naval College did not exist in those days, although the groundwork for this establishment had been laid, and on passing his entry examination the Prince would go straight to sea.

In 1806 the Royal Naval Academy, which had functioned in Portsmouth dockyard ever since its opening in 1733, was reorganised and renamed the Royal Naval College. The total number of pupils it was able to accommodate was increased to seventy, forty of whom were to be the sons of officers, noblemen or gentlemen 'who are found to be qualified'.

The age of entry was fixed at between 13 and 16, and the training course lasted three years. Included in the curriculum were geometry, navigation, writing and arithmetic, French and drawing, and fencing and dancing – but these last two subjects were abolished by William IV. Seamanship and ship construction were taught by the Master Attendant of the dockyard and the Master Shipwright. Marine sergeants instructed the young gentlemen in the use of the firelock. On passing out successful trainees were awarded a certificate of qualification. In 1837, however, the college was closed to new entries, its facilities being utilised instead for training older officers, such as mates, and for the next twenty years naval cadets were sent straight to sea.

In 1854 Sir James Graham, then First Lord of the Admiralty, conceived the idea of establishing at Portsmouth a training ship for young seamen – a project, incidentally, dear to the heart of the Prince Consort who took a great interest in the welfare of the country's first line of defence. They were called 'Jemmy Graham's Novices'. A 2-decker, the *Illustrious,* was set aside as a training ship and Captain Robert Harris, a first-class officer and fine seaman, appointed in command.

Before very long Harris was urging that similar instruction should be given to young officers, and in fact trained his own son in the *Illustrious* before sending him to sea as a midshipman. His advice was taken by the Admiralty, and in 1857 all new entry cadets, after taking a preliminary examination at the R.N. College, were required to undergo a 3-month course in the *Illustrious* prior to going to sea.

The ship was moored off Haslar Creek with its own playing fields nearby, and a brig and other small craft were attached as tenders so that brief cruises could be undertaken by the cadets. The scheme was a success, and at the end of that year the ship was entirely given over to the training of cadets, and 'Jemmy Graham's Novices' had to find other quarters. Although he did not live on board, Prince Alfred became one of Harris's pupils, attending daily for instruction in seamanship and navigation.

By the middle of August, 1858, he was considered sufficiently far advanced to take the naval entry examination. This ordeal lasted three days and his parents, who had been out of the country on a visit to Germany, were able to learn the result for themselves at first hand. After landing at Dover on their return they drove along the coast to Portsmouth where 'Sir George Seymour [Commander-in-Chief] gave us the delightful news that Affie had passed an excellent examination and received his appointment. He had just gone to report himself on board the *Euryalus* and would meet us at Osborne.'

Alfred duly met his parents when they disembarked at their private pier 'in his middy's jacket, cap and dirk, half blushing and looking very happy. He is a little pulled from these three days hard examination which only terminated today,' commented his fond mother.

'We felt very proud,' the Prince Consort informed his brother, 'as it is a particularly hard examination.'

Indeed, Prince Albert was so impressed that, writing to the Prime Minister, Lord Derby, a few days later on other matters, he added:

I send you also Prince Alfred's examination papers which may perhaps interest you. He solved the mathematical problems almost all without fault, and did the translations without a dictionary.

Derby was obviously equally impressed, for in his reply he wrote:

As I looked over them I could not but feel very grateful that no such examination was necessary to qualify Her Majesty's Ministers for their offices, as it would very seriously increase the difficulty of framing an Administration!

Alfred's first seagoing ship had already been selected. She was, as mentioned earlier, the screw steam frigate *Euryalus* of 400 horsepower and armed with 50 guns. She was commanded by Captain John Walter Tarleton, 'a good and careful officer' who, as a commander, had served in the East Indies in H.M.S. *Fox* under Commodore Rowley Lambert during the second Burma campaign. After promotion to captain he had commanded the *Euryalus* on the North America station. At that time the Navy was entering upon a prolonged period of transition, from sail to steam, from wooden wall to ironclad, from muzzle-loading guns to shell-firing breech-loaders.

Experience gained in the Crimean war helped to bring about the demise of the wooden warship, for duels between ships and shore batteries against the Russians had effectively demonstrated that wooden vessels could not stand up to the destructiveness of shellfire, shell-firing guns having appeared some years earlier.

The French were the first to appreciate the value of armour plating for warship protection, but in 1860, two years after Prince Alfred joined the *Euryalus,* Britain herself launched the world's first ironclad warship *Warrior.* Although propelled by steam she was still, however, rigged for sails.

During his tenure of office as Lord High Admiral, William IV had seen the necessity of keeping up with the times; and it was solely due to his progressive ideas that the Navy's first steam vessels were purchased and put into commission in 1828. The first engineer officers were entered in the Royal Navy in 1847, but for a long time steam was applied only to smaller naval craft, and it was not until 1852 that the first steam line of battleship was launched in this country. Paddles were first used for steam propulsion, but after a specially staged tug-of-war between the screw steamer *Rattler* and the paddle vessel *Alecto* had decisively proved the superiority of the former, the screw propeller was adopted by the Admiralty. Nevertheless for sixteen years after Prince Alfred's entry into the Service sails remained the Navy's principal means of propulsion.

Following his examination and initial appointment to the *Euryalus* the Prince was given six weeks' special leave, which he spent with his parents at Balmoral. But at last the day of parting came, and his father went with him down to Portsmouth to see him safely embarked. On October 25th, 1858, the latter had written to Baron Stockmar, 'The day after tomorrow I take Alfred to his ship at Spithead. That same evening he goes to sea. His departure will be another great trial for us.'

The Queen was even more anguished at the thought of parting with her 'dear, good, clever, promising child, whom God may bless'. On October 1st she had written indignantly to the Princess Royal:

> I have been shamefully deceived about Affie; it was promised me that the last year before he went to sea he should be with us, instead of which he has been taken away and I saw but very little of him, and now he is to go away for many months and I shall not see him God knows when! And Papa is most cruel upon the subject. I assure you it is much better to have no children than to have them only to give them up! It is too wretched.*

And again on October 27th when the boy had departed:

> Dearest Affie is gone, and it will be ten months probably before we shall see his dear face which shed sunshine over the whole house from his amiable, happy, merry temper. Again he was much upset at leaving and sobbed bitterly, and I fear the separation from dear Papa will have been equally trying.*

* From *Dearest Child,* Roger Fulford (Ed)

In these circumstances it was probably as well that the *Euryalus* was due to sail immediately. Once the final farewells had been said the Prince was taken out to his ship by pinnace, and soon afterwards the frigate hoisted her anchor and headed down Channel on the first leg of her voyage to the Mediterranean. She called in at Gibraltar to land mails for home, and on December 8th the Queen noted:

> From Alfred we have heard from Gibraltar; he arrived there on the 27th and had had very bad weather. He is quite well but his letters, of which he has given us only three specimens, are too shockingly and disgracefully written. Strange that both the boys should write so ill and all the girls so well. But Affie's is very much worse than Bertie's!*

While the midshipmen's berth on board the *Euryalus* was probably a little less primitive than that of the *Prince George* in which William IV had first gone to sea, it would still have appalled the Queen had she seen it. Writing of conditions in the gunroom of a British warship as much as ten years later, another young naval officer – a relative of Prince Alfred's – noted that this compartment was just abaft the men's quarters on the lower deck, with chests and hammocks stowed outside. The food was dreadful. Bread being practically unknown at sea they lived, like the ship's company, on hard tack. But before the biscuits could be eaten maggots had to be knocked out of them. Kept in pill-boxes and specially fed and trained, however, these creatures were raced along the mess table by the irrepressible young gentlemen in the weekly 'Maggot Derby'.

Small scuttles were let into the ship's side to provide air and daylight, but because these were small and grimy it was so dark in the mess that lamps or 'purser's dips' stuck in the tops of gin bottles had to be kept on all day. It was little wonder, therefore, that Prince Alfred's handwriting was so bad!

Blissfully unaware that such conditions could exist in her warships, the Queen comforted herself that all would be well with her boy. On Christmas Day, 1858, she wrote:

* From *Dearest Child,* edited by Roger Fulford.

Poor dear Affie is all alone amongst strangers — in the midst of life of no easy kind — but he has a most kind friend [Major Cowell] near him whom he dearly loves — and he has a Father in Heaven who never leaves us.*

Instructions had been given by the Admiralty to Captain Tarleton and Admiral Fanshawe, the Commander-in-Chief, Mediterranean, that at the wish of his parents the Prince was to be given no special treatment except when he went ashore. Unfortunately, it is extremely difficult to maintain a clear line of demarcation between the exalted status of a royal personage and his lowly Service identity as a very junior naval officer. This was especially so in the case of Prince Alfred.

The *Euryalus,* although nominally a unit of the Mediterranean Fleet, had been ordered to carry out a special programme of visits to foreign ports, partly to educate the young man and partly to show him off as the Queen's son. At the same time he was required to work hard learning his job as a naval officer. Thus during 1859 the ship visited Marseilles, Algiers, Tunis, Alexandria and various other ports in the Levant, including a short tour of the Holy Land, at all of which Alfred was received, noted the Prince Consort approvingly, 'with great cordiality'. In between these ceremonial cruises the *Euryalus* exercised with the fleet.

To add to the Queen's worries over the welfare of her sailor son there was even a threat of war during the year. In April she wrote to the Princess Royal:

I don't know when Affie will return. Possibly in July — but only of course for a short time. Should there be war he must remain and do his duty like every other officer. I should not wish him to do otherwise . . . the poor dear boy may see fire before long.*

The trouble into which it was feared that Britain might be drawn that year stemmed from the struggle of Italy for freedom and the schemes of Napoleon III for the aggrandisement of France.

On the pretext of aiding the liberation of northern Italy, which

* From *Dearest Child,* edited by Roger Fulford.

E

was under Austrian rule, Napoleon declared war on his fellow Emperor Francis Joseph and, with the assistance of Sardinian troops, defeated the Austrians at the battles of Magenta and Solferino. But instead of helping his allies to set up a united country he proceeded to make peace with the enemy and annexed Nice and Savoy.

Thus abandoned the Italians managed to liberate themselves and created their own kingdom in 1861.

For a time relations between England and France were severely strained, but at the urging of the Queen the British government maintained a policy of non-intervention. Eleven years later, as she had foreseen, Napoleon was to have his wings clipped by Prussia.

The *Euryalus* was due to return to England early in 1860 when, after passing his examination for midshipman, Alfred was to be prepared for confirmation at Easter. 'The service is really very hard,' noted his father, 'but he continues to take great pleasure in it.' Towards the end of February, therefore, the *Euryalus* sailed for home, and must obviously have been urgently in need of a refit, for on the 29th the Queen wrote to her daughter:

> You will know, I think, very much of us now and have a very real longing to be with us here now that darling Affie is back again. If possible, the joy is greater than usual this time, as I was very anxious about him all Monday when it blew a perfect hurricane and knowing the ship was not in a good state it kept me in a fever till in the evening the happy news of his safe arrival came to relieve our anxiety and gladden our hearts. Papa will have told you of his brilliant examination etc. He looks well though rather tired from his broken nights. Dear Child, I feel so proud of the hardship he has endured, the way he has worked. I feel truly happy and grateful to have this darling boy – always so great a favourite with his dear handsome good face – back again for a time. He is much improved and very clever and intelligent and talks so sensibly and pleasantly about all he has seen ... Faults he still has, but with God's blessing and the care of our invaluable Major Cowell I trust they will be got rid of and his excellent qualities – affection and great intelligence and cleverness will

make him very distinguished some day I hope . . . His hands are very clean, a great improvement, but so rough and hard from work.*

In March the young midshipman was duly confirmed, and the Queen again went into transports of delight over her darling Affie, whose head, fortunately, remained unturned.

Affie is, I think, really beautiful (excepting Papa who is much more so) but it is such a darling handsome round face. Bless him, he is such a dear, dear boy, and I must say we have not had a single fault to find with him since he has been here. The ceremony went off extremely well. Affie was much impressed, cried and was much moved when I kissed his dear handsome face. To see the young sailor, inured to life, its trials and hardships, its dangers and temptations, who had been in foreign lands and to the Holy Sepulchre itself, standing there before the altar was very moving to a fond mother's heart.*

One of the dangers to which he had had no chance to become inured, however, was smoking – unlike his brother Bertie, who had recently been accorded grudging permission to indulge in this undesirable habit on condition that he never did so in public or indoors!

A longer voyage was now planned for Prince Alfred. It was time for him to see something of the great Empire over which his mother ruled. Accordingly arrangements were made for the *Euryalus* to proceed by way of South America to the Cape of Good Hope so that Alfred could visit Cape Colony, Natal, and the recently created Orange Free State. On April 27th, 1860, the Prince Consort wrote to the King of the Belgians:

Alfred leaves on Thursday next to make his long voyage to the Cape of Good Hope by way of Rio de Janeiro. It will be a strange and note-worthy circumstance that almost in the same week in which the elder brother is to open the great bridge across the St. Lawrence in Canada the younger will lay

* From *Dearest Child*, edited by Roger Fulford.

the foundation stone of the breakwater for the harbour of Capetown at the other end of the world.

Since he was to be treated in his royal capacity only when away from the ship, Alfred was worked hard like any other midshipman during the voyage, performing the traditionally humble duties of a 'snotty'. In addition to his continuing instruction in seamanship he was learning a little more about the mysteries of marine engineering. Like most British warships at that time which were fitted with both steam and sails, however, the propeller of the *Euryalus* was lowered into the water and her engines used only during periods of calm weather. In common with most of his fellow captains when it came to the matter of ship propulsion Tarleton preferred sail to steam, but he nevertheless saw to it that the royal trainee was properly instructed in new-fangled techniques.

Simons Bay was reached on July 24th, and on boarding the frigate soon after her anchor was dropped the harbour-master was astonished to discover that the duty midshipman waiting at the head of the gangway to receive him was none other than His Royal Highness himself. But ceremonial was soon to begin, for next day the prince landed in his best Number One uniform and was driven to Capetown, there to be greeted by the Governor, Sir George Grey, amid great enthusiasm.

He remained on shore attending various official functions until August 2nd when, accompanied by the Governor, he re-embarked and the *Euryalus* cruised along the coast to enable visits to be made to Algoa Bay, Port Elizabeth, Natal and the Orange Free State, where various sightseeing excursions and hunting expeditions had been laid on. He was received everywhere, in Grey's words, with 'transports of delight'. That he was not entirely overwhelmed by so much adulation is evident by the Governor's comment that 'Prince Alfred is a noble young fellow, full of life and fun.'

But what most impressed the colonists and others was the fact that his rank in the Navy was but that of a midshipman — 'the lowest form of naval life.' In his introductory speech at the opening of Capetown's public library by the Prince, Sir George said that, 'In their eyes the most admirable of all the many things they saw was the sight of a number of hardy barefooted lads assisting at daybreak in washing the decks, foremost among them in activity and energy was the son of the Queen of England.'

The humble naval status of Prince Alfred also powerfully impressed the native chiefs who visited the *Euryalus*. One of them wrote to Captain Tarleton:

> One thing we understand, the reason of England's greatness. When the son of her great Queen becomes subject to a subject, that he may learn wisdom; when the sons of England's chiefs and nobles leave the homes and wealth of their fathers, and with their young Prince endure hardships and sufferings in order that they may be wise and become a defence to their country, when we behold these things we see why the English are a great and mighty nation.

Finally, on September 17th before a huge crowd of spectators, the Prince performed the principal ceremony of his visit. Staggering along unaided, he tilted into the sea the first wheelbarrow-load of stones which were to form the breakwater in Table Bay.

Two months later the *Euryalus* arrived back at Portsmouth with her young royal midshipman, who had not only thoroughly enjoyed himself but performed a first-class job of public relations for his mother by which loyalty to the crown had been enormously stimulated. As usual, she was delighted to have her Affie home again. On November 13th she wrote to the King of the Belgians:

> Here we have the happiness of having our dear Alfred back since the 9th, who gives very interesting accounts of his expedition and has brought many interesting trophies. He is grown, though very short for his age . . . he is really such a dear gifted handsome child that it makes one doubly anxious he should have as few failings as mortal men can have.*

A week later Alfred was transferred from the *Euryalus* to the books of H.M.S. *Victory*, the port guardship.

* From *A Century of British Monarchy* by H. Bolitho.

On January 8th of the following year he was appointed midshipman of the *St. George,* a 90-gun screw steamship classed as a second-rate. In command was Captain the Hon. Francis Egerton. She left Devonport a week later for what was then called 'particular service', a term applied to certain seagoing ships not attached to any specific naval station. For a time she cruised in the Channel, then proceeded westwards to join the North America and West Indies station. Commander-in-Chief of the station was Rear-Admiral Sir Alexander Milne with 27 vessels under his command.

Although the station had lost much of its former importance compared with, say, the Mediterranean, the Prince was fascinated to find himself cruising in the same historic waters which in the past had known so many of Britain's most famous sailors, from Drake to Nelson himself. In May, 1861, he was granted a brief spell of leave and returned home to spend this with his parents.

Life in the Navy was obviously continuing to have a beneficial effect on his character and outlook. In July the Prince Consort wrote to his brother:

> Alfred could have only four weeks leave of absence, and then he returns to his ship for a year. He had grown. His hair has become darker. He is a dear fellow and very agreeable in society, and always ready to learn and get on. He may become a very excellent man, but he will have to go through a hard school if he is not to perish in spite of all his good qualities.*

This was to be the last time that father and son would meet. In November the Prince Consort was taken ill, although thought to be suffering from little more than a feverish cold. It was a time of great national anxiety. The Northern and Southern States of America were engaged in the fierce quarrel over the question of slavery which would eventually develop into civil war. Britain found herself becoming involved when a Union warship stopped the British mail steamer *Trent* and forcibly removed two Confederate envoys who were sailing in her as passengers.

There was great indignation in Britain over this high-handed action, but a peremptory demand for apology drafted by

* From *A Century of British Monarchy* by H. Bolitho.

Palmerston's Cabinet was considerably watered down on the advice of the Prince Consort, and the danger of war thereby averted. By then the Prince had become so weak that he could scarcely hold a pen. He grew steadily worse, and towards midnight on December 14th, 1861, he died. Prince Alfred was already on his way home.

After the funeral of his father the Prince remained at Osborne to comfort his stricken mother, being borne for this period on the books of the *Victory.* But his naval duties were by no means neglected. For much of the time he was lent to H.M.S. *Rolla,* a 6-gun brig commanded by Lieutenant Charles Nelson (no relation of the famous admiral) which was used as a boys' training ship. Later on he returned to the *St. George* which had now become a unit of the Mediterranean Fleet.

Then in the closing months of 1862 there came an unexpected threat to his continuance in the service he loved. The Greeks deposed King Otho who had ruled their country for thirty years, and asked that Prince Alfred should become their new monarch. Britain, France and Russia were the three Protecting Powers of the Greek State and, although Queen Victoria was not averse to the idea of her son becoming its new king, Palmerston and his Foreign Secretary knew that this would contravene the agreement that no prince of the Protecting Powers could take the Greek throne.

Accordingly Prince William George of Denmark, then a naval cadet of 18, was suggested. He was willing and found acceptable, and in 1863 became King George I of Greece. Subsequently he married Princess Olga, daughter of the Grand Duke Constantine of Russia, and their youngest son Prince Andrew of Greece became the father of Philip, the present Duke of Edinburgh.

Although Alfred would normally have been permitted to take the examination for lieutenant at the age of 18, his absences from the service brought about by his royal duties and responsibilities seemed likely to extend unfairly that qualifying period. On January 9th, 1863, therefore, an Order-in-Council was made allowing him to pass for lieutenant irrespective of age and regulations. A week later the Admiralty informed the Commander-in-Chief, Mediterranean, Vice-Admiral Sir William Martin, that on passing his examination for lieutenant Prince Alfred was to be appointed Acting Lieutenant of H.M.S. *Marlborough,* Martin's flagship, and then to be sent home on leave overland via Marseilles.

His commission was to be prepared but left undated and delivered to him on the day after his passing. The reason for his being given leave at such a time was in order that he could attend the wedding of his brother, the Prince of Wales, to the Princess Alexandra of Denmark, which was due to take place in London on March 10th. H.M.S. *Magicienne,* a corvette commanded by Captain His Serene Highness the Prince of Leiningen, the Queen's half-brother, who would travel to London with him, stood by to take him to Marseilles as soon as the examination was over.

But Alfred unwittingly threw a spanner in the works by suddenly going down with a bad cold which developed into a severe attack of Malta fever. On February 19th he had to be sent to hospital. But he was not to be done out of promotion through illness. Before being carried from the ship on a stretcher he insisted on taking the examination. As required by the regulations, this was duly conducted by three senior officers, Captain Egerton of the *St. George,* Captain Stewart of the *Marlborough,* and Commander Marsoll of the *Firefly,* and Alfred passed brilliantly.

'It is strange', commented the *Times of Malta* somewhat inaccurately, 'that he should have passed his first step to promotion in a hospital.'

When the result of the examination was communicated to the Admiralty the Prince was promoted Acting Lieutenant, appointed to H.M.S. *Racoon,* and ordered to be sent home to join that ship as soon as he was fit. The *Racoon* was a 22-gun steam corvette of 1,476 tons and 400 horsepower, refitting at Chatham. Early in May Alfred arrived back in England and was ordered to be examined in gunnery and navigation for confirmation in the rank of lieutenant. Because of his severe illness the examination was to be confined to inspection of the work previously performed and a *viva voce* examination.

The tests were conducted by Captain Richard Hewlett of H.M.S. *Excellent,* the naval gunnery school, Captain Henry Broadhead of H.M.S. *Asia,* the port guardship, and Professor Main of the Naval College, and once again the Prince passed with flying colours. He was accordingly confirmed in his new rank and duly joined the *Racoon.* She was commanded by Captain Count Gleichen, later Admiral Prince Victor of Hohenlohe, a nephew of

Queen Victoria, and as junior lieutenant Alfred shared duties with his three senior colleagues, Henry Miller, Hugh Campbell and George Trefusis.

For the next three years the *Racoon* was employed on particular service, cruising in the Mediterranean and visiting Spain, Italy, Greece and other countries. During this period Prince Alfred was given several spells of leave, but these were by no means all holidays. He attended a course of study at Bonn University, and whenever able to take a break from lectures went to stay with his sister Princess Alice, who had married Prince Louis (afterwards reigning Grand Duke) of Hesse. The visits of this handsome and agreeable young naval officer to Darmstadt were to inspire a certain growing lad to join the Royal Navy as soon as he was old enough and, incidentally, to become in his turn a famous British admiral.

* * * * *

Britain was at peace but the Navy was kept busy dealing with brush-fire wars and minor campaigns in various parts of the world which arose from her peacekeeping role and the need for safeguarding the Empire. Thus between 1845 and the close of the century British sailors and marines, both ashore and afloat, fought in India, China, Burma, New Zealand, Abyssinia and West Africa. Meanwhile the Navy continued to progress through the various stages of transition towards the twentieth century. More ironclad warships were launched; guns were improved in accuracy and penetrative powers; and other additions to the armoury of naval warfare such as the mine and torpedo were also developed.

In 1864 squadronal colours were abolished – which meant the end of admirals of the Red, White and Blue – and directions issued that the White Ensign should be used only by the Navy, the Blue Ensign by the Naval Reserve, and the Red Ensign as the national flag by all other ships. In 1852 the problem of manning the Navy was examined by a special committee. Their recommendations led to the introduction of pensionable continuous service for the Lower Deck in the following year with all-round increases of pay, and impressment was finally abolished. Barracks were built on shore to replace the rotting hulks formerly used as depot ships, and the ration scale expanded to include fresh meat and vegetables, sugar, chocolate and tea. Four years later a standard uniform was approved for the sailors, similar to that worn today. In order to form a pool of trained seamen which could be called upon in time of war, a project which had been mooted by the late Prince Consort, the Royal Naval Reserve was created.

Like his great-uncle William, Prince Alfred was required to work hard at his dual role of naval officer and son of the sovereign. In February 1866, came his first – unwelcome – jump in promotion. His mother was due to celebrate her 47th birthday on May 24th of that year, and she had plans for her dearest Affie. On February 3rd she signed an Order-in-Council authorising the Admiralty to promote Prince Alfred direct to captain, and subsequently to flag rank, without passing through the intermediate rank of commander. Doubtless the similar leap in promotion which had been accorded to the Duke of Clarence provided the necessary precedent. The promotion was gazetted three weeks later.

Alfred was also granted a personal income of £15,000 per annum. Then on the Queen's birthday her favourite son was literally loaded with honours. In addition to being created Duke of Edinburgh and Earl of Ulster and Kent, he was made a Knight of the Garter and the Thistle, awarded the Grand Crosses of the Orders of St. Michael and St. George, the Star of India and the Indian Empire, and presented with a host of foreign orders. In March, 1866, Trinity House made him its Master, and the Lord Mayor of London presented him with the freedom of the City.

Somehow he came through this glittering ordeal comparatively unaffected, and on January 22nd of the following year received an appointment which pleased him far more, command of the 3,227-ton screw frigate *Galatea*. But this was in fact to bring with it further royal chores. For, after a brief shakedown cruise in the Mediterranean, the *Galatea* was to proceed on a world tour, with special attention being paid to Australia and New Zealand.

Built at Woolwich and launched in 1859, the *Galatea* had previously been commanded by Captain Rochfort Maguire, and for four years had served in the Baltic during the Crimean war, the Mediterranean and the West Indies. She measured 317 feet in length overall with a 50-foot beam, and could develop 800 horsepower to drive her along at a top speed of 13 knots. She mounted eighteen 10-inch, 86 cwt. guns on the main deck, two 10-inch, 6-ton guns forward and aft, and four 64-pounders. She also carried 700 tons of coal. It took three weeks to prepare the ship for sea, after which she went round to Plymouth to embark ammunition and carry out speed and other trials.

Then, after formal inspection by the Commander-in-Chief, she sailed for Lisbon and the first of her ceremonial duties when the King of Portugal came on board to dine with His Royal Highness. After carrying out gunnery exercises off Gibraltar, the *Galatea* then sailed on to Malta. The Mediterranean Fleet, at that time commanded by Vice-Admiral Lord Clarence Paget, was anchored in the Grand Harbour, and comprised in addition to the flagship *Victoria*, the *Royal Oak*, *Prince Consort*, *Endymion*, *Arethusa*, *Enterprise*, *Racer* and *Psyche*. But there was none of the ceremonial which had attended the first arrival of His Royal Highness as a blushing young cadet in the *Euryalus*.

After anchoring under the critical gaze of his fellow captains in the billet allocated to a junior private ship, the *Galatea* was formally inspected next day by the Commander-in-Chief. This was followed by the usual evolutionary drills and fleet exercises to accustom the new arrival to the high standards maintained by the Navy on its senior station.

On her first independent cruise away from the main fleet the *Galatea* visited Marseilles, where her captain was able to give further proof that he was no mere Royal dummy but a skilled professional seaman. A gale blew up while she was there, and just as the French passenger steamer *Dauphine* was entering harbour under these difficult conditions her engines broke down. Heavy seas swept the helpless vessel against a jetty and she was soon in danger of capsizing. Quickly assessing the situation, the Duke sent his boats and working parties of sailors to her aid. By their efforts the steamer was saved from almost certain destruction.

The French authorities were so appreciative of his prompt and successful actions that the provincial governor himself came on board the frigate to thank the Duke in person and offer him the freedom of the city. He also brought with him several cases of champagne for distribution to the *Galatea's* crew.

Later the French Government sent an official letter of thanks to the British Admiralty, which was duly added to the Duke's personal dossier. Soon after this episode, unfortunately, fever broke out on board the *Galatea* and one boy died before the epidemic could be mastered.

At the beginning of June the frigate left the Mediterranean to start her world cruise. The first call was made at Tristan da Cunha where the Duke went ashore and at the wish of the islanders named their settlement 'Edinburgh'. The ship then went on to the Cape where the Duke was required to attend a number of public functions in his official capacity. His former ship, the *Racoon,* was now attached to the station, and he went aboard to renew old acquaintanceships, and also visited H.M.S. *Peterel* which had just returned from landing the Livingstone search party at the mouth of the Zambesi.

Soon after leaving the Cape the *Galatea* ran into heavy weather, but apart from the ship's pet monkey being washed overboard, the voyage to Adelaide was completed without serious incident. The Duke was given a great welcome when he landed, and the first Royal tour of Austrialia had begun. Like his brother the Prince of Wales, whom he closely resembled in appearance, Prince Alfred was enormously popular everywhere he went, not least for the nautical forthrightness of his language.

The *Galatea* called in due course at Melbourne, Hobart, in Tasmania, and finally Sydney. A stickler for naval etiquette, Prince Alfred invariably called on the senior naval officer present in each port in his capacity as a junior captain before assuming his second hat as a Royal Duke. It was at Sydney, however, that the *Galatea's* world cruise came to an abrupt end.

One of the official functions the Duke was called upon to attend in Sydney was a fete and picnic held to raise funds for the local Sailors' Home. Also present in port at the time were H.M. Ships *Challenger* and *Charybdis* under the station's Commander-in-Chief, Commodore Rowley Lambert, whose crews were taking part in the events. The day of the fete was fine and sunny, and the launch from Government House took the royal party, which included the Earl and Countess of Belmore, Sir William Manning, a local magnate, and the Governor himself, Sir Alfred Stephen, over to Clontarf where fete and picnic were being held.

After lunch the Duke and Sir William Manning, deep in conversation, were taking a stroll towards the beach when a man suddenly pushed through the spectators, drew a pistol and shot the Duke in the back at close range.

Crying, 'Good God! I am shot – my back is broken!' the Duke collapsed on to his face.

Manning turned on the assailant, who promptly covered him with his gun and ordered him to stand back. Manning, however, lunged at the man, who thereupon pulled the trigger. But the weapon misfired and before he could re-cock it a coachbuilder named Vial sprang on him. During the struggle the pistol went off again, the bullet hitting one of the horrified bystanders in the foot. But the gunman was quickly overpowered and disarmed.

Meanwhile the Duke had been picked up and carried to a nearby tent where doctors examined him. They found that the bullet had penetrated his back, traversed the ribs and lodged within two inches of the breastbone. Miraculously no vital organs had been hit. The Duke in fact had literally been saved by his braces, the bullet having passed through the thick rubber join at the back which thus absorbed much of its force.

The would-be murderer was almost lynched on the spot by the infuriated sailors, but somehow the police managed to get him to jail in one piece. He was a Fenian terrorist named Henry James O'Farrell who said he had been allotted the task of executing the Duke, and only lamented having made a mess of the job. He declared that he would have shot the Duke again and then turned the gun on himself. When news of the outrage became known there was immense indignation throughout Australia. O'Farrell was duly brought to trial and subsequently hanged.

The Duke, who was fortunately young and healthy, made a fairly speedy recovery. While he was lying in his sick bed at Government House, Commander Hugh Campbell, his executive officer and an old shipmate from the *Racoon,* called one day to see him and brought the following 'memorandum' which had been drawn up by the crew of the *Galatea*:

To our beloved captain, H.R.H. the Duke of Edinburgh.
May it please your Royal Highness, we the petty officers and n.c.o's of the *Galatea* on behalf of the ship's company desire

to express to your Royal Highness, our beloved captain, our heartfelt sympathy with you in your sufferings consequent from the wound recently inflicted by the hand of an assassin, and we all desire to express our deep-felt thankfulness for your providential escape from the assassin's deadly intent. We pray that the same good Providence may soon restore you to perfect health and strength and that your Royal Highness may in God's good time be enabled to resume the joyful command of your most obedient servants, the *Galatea's* ship's company.

The Duke was most touched by this spontaneous expression of sympathy and goodwill by his crew, and excused any defaulters who were awaiting trial and remitted all punishments which had already been awarded. When he finally rejoined the ship he was given a tremendous ovation.

Despite the attempt on his life he continued fearlessly to appear at various public functions which had been postponed from his original programme. But Commodore Lambert was only too well aware that there was a good deal of Fenian activity in New Zealand as well as Australia. Accordingly, although the *Galatea* had been scheduled to visit not only New Zealand but Tahiti, Honolulu, Callao, Valparaiso and the Falklands, the worried Commander-in-Chief cancelled the tour and ordered the frigate to proceed direct to the United Kingdom.

She sailed for home on April 6th, 1868, and, after rounding the Horn arrived back in Portsmouth on June 26th. Here she was formally inspected by the Commander-in-Chief who, in his report to the Admiralty, stressed his approval of her efficiency. The interrupted world cruise was completed in the following year without incident.

Afterwards the *Galatea* continued in commission under the Duke's command, mostly on particular service. But when she came into Portsmouth in August 1870, for Commander-in-Chief's inspection, this revealed that her former efficiency had begun to slip from its former high standard. The state of her gunnery, reported the admiral, was not as satisfactory as it might have been, and officers' mess bills were too excessive. By the following May, however, discipline had been tightened up, and when she was again inspected, this time by the Commander-in-Chief, Plymouth, he was able to forward a highly satisfactory report, which also showed that she had regained her former efficiency in gunnery.

The *Galatea* duly paid off at the end of her commission early in 1872, after which the Duke attended a two month course in the naval gunnery school. The big gun had now become the principal weapon afloat, and the notion of grouping a number of them together in central batteries led to the invention of revolving turrets and brought about the final abolition of sail in the Royal Navy. At the end of his course the Duke went on half pay. He had already fallen in love, and was soon to marry.

* * * * *

His bride was the Grand Duchess Marie Alexandrovna, only daughter of the Tsar Alexander II of Russia, and the wedding took place on June 23rd, 1874. Oddly enough, this event was to have an effect upon the uniform regulations for British naval officers. Following the Duke's bethrothal he had been given by the Tsar the honorary rank of captain in the Russian Navy, and made Chief of the Second Division of the Russian Black Sea Fleet. Commented the English press upon this appointment, 'The Duke would be in a singular position if war suddenly broke out.'

When in due course he was issued with his Russian naval uniform he discovered that a greatcoat was included in the outfit. Up to then such a garment did not form part of the uniform kit of an officer in the Royal Navy. Prince Alfred thought it should, and in due course the addition of an overcoat was made to the British naval uniform regulations. He also noticed that, as a special mark of honour and distinction, certain of the Russian grand dukes were appointed to be personal aides-de-camp to the Tsar, and wore large gold aiguillettes which bore not only the cypher of the present Tsar, but also former Tsars whom they had similarly served.

Alfred liked the idea, and eventually persuaded Queen Victoria to replace the crimson and gold sash worn over the left shoulder by aides-de-camp to her Majesty by a gold aiguillette worn over the right shoulder. On May 26th, 1876, he was himself appointed personal aide-de-camp to his mother — unpaid!

In February of that year he had been appointed to the command of H.M.S. *Sultan*. She was an interesting vessel – a curious hybrid, illustrative of the changing era through which the Navy was passing. Built at Chatham and launched in 1870, she was a broadside ship, one of a class of twelve. She carried a complement of 600, displaced 9,290 tons, was protected by a belt of 9-inch armour plate, and mounted eight 10-inch R.M.L. (rifled, muzzle-loading) guns, and four 9-inch. She was fitted with an engine and a screw propeller with which she could attain a top speed of 14 knots, and carried 740 tons of coal in her bunkers. Nevertheless, she was barque rigged, with three masts and two funnels.

The Admiralty has often been blamed by modern historians because sail was retained for so long in the Royal Navy. But they overlook one of the most important reasons, which was that it took a considerable time to establish adequate coaling stations around the world. Since British warships were required to cover vast distances on their trade protection duties, their own coal stocks carried on board would quickly have run out, without sails they would have been left with no means of propulsion at all!

The *Sultan* spent the first few months of her commission in home waters as a unit of the Channel Fleet, and was then transferred to the Mediterranean Fleet. At that time the Mediterranean was considered to be a British lake, and our strongest fleet was based on Malta. When the *Sultan* joined up the station was commanded by Vice-Admiral the Hon. Sir James Drummond with his flag in the *Hercules*.

Together with his flagship the fleet consisted of eight great ironclads, which included the world's most powerful warship, *Devastation,* a sailless, double-turreted fighting machine; four powerful cruisers — although that term had not come into general use for warships of lesser size and gun power than capital ships; and a number of smaller steam gun vessels.

In 1877 Drummond was relieved by Vice-Admiral Geoffrey Phipps-Hornby, who brought out from England the newly completed *Alexandra* of 9,400 tons, the first big warship in the Navy to be fitted with compound engines and twin screws. Phipps-Hornby was the first British admiral to introduce steam manoeuvres, and his skill at fleet tactics was said to be unrivalled — except in due course for that of one other individual, the Duke of Edinburgh himself.

Prince Alfred, Duke of Edinburgh, younger son of Queen Victoria, as a midshipman
From an engraving by D. J. Pound after a photograph by Mayall

King Edward VII as a boy in naval uniform
From a lithograph after a photograph taken in 1858 by Lake Price

Trouble had been brewing in the Balkans for some time and was now about to erupt. In 1875 a revolt against the oppressive rule of their overlords, the Turks, broke out in the Slavonic provinces of Bosnia and Herzegovina, which spread rapidly to Montenegro, Serbia and Bulgaria. During their brutal repression of the rebellious peasantry the Turks massacred thousands of Christians. Russia, which for long had cherished designs on Constantinople with the aim of obtaining an ice-free port and a window on the Mediterranean, took up the cause of the down-trodden Slavs in the Balkans, and in 1877 declared war on Turkey.

The Russian armies carried all before them, and early in 1878 the Turks were compelled to sign a treaty at San Stefano under which, inter alia, a free Bulgaria was created, to be garrisoned for two years by Russian troops. These aggressive moves caused alarm and indignation in Britain, especially as it seemed likely that the Russian victories would imperil Britain's position in the Middle East.

Fanned by memories of the Crimea, a warlike spirit sprang up in this country, extending even to the music-halls where the song 'We don't want to fight, but by jingo if we do'. became wildly popular. In February, 1878, the Reserves were called up and the British Mediterranean Fleet was ordered to Constantinople. In India native troops began to embark for Malta ready to take over from the garrison troops in that island, who would be formed into an advanced striking force in the event of hostilities. The world, it seemed, stood on the brink of war.

In those days the British Mediterranean Fleet frequently visited Besika Bay, on the coast of Anatolia close to the ancient plains of Troy, the ships bringing along with them their own recreational facilities for use when anchored in the bay. The most novel of these was a pack of beagles, which had been specially sent out from England, and with ponies hired from local villages hare hunts and paper chases were organised. Collapsible stables and kennels were constructed on board by the ships' carpenters and set up on shore whenever the ships were using the anchorage.

In fact, one of the standard Mediterranean Fleet evolutions was for the ships to embark ponies, hounds and stables at short notice. When the order to proceed to Constantinople was received, Phipps-Hornby happened to be at Besika Bay with his ships and a

F

hunt was actually in progress. The embarkation evolution moved smoothly into action, and in short order the hunt, complete with animals and buildings, was neatly stowed on board H.M.S. *Agincourt,* flagship of Rear-Admiral Commerell, V.C., the second in command. The smartness of this manoeuvre was, however, somewhat blunted when the fleet flagship herself ran aground in a snowstorm en route. Despite the fact that the British had arrived to protect them against further Russian aggression, the Turks nevertheless protested at the presence of foreign warships anchored so close to their capital!

While negotiations between Russia and the Great Powers to try to persuade the former to modify her demands were taking place in Berlin, the British Mediterranean Fleet remained strategically poised in the Bosphorous. It was then by an innocent-seeming act of hospitality during their stay that Prince Alfred became the centre of a storm of disapprobation, bringing down upon his head the wrath even of his august mother.

Serving on board his ship as a lieutenant was Prince Louis of Battenberg, a nephew of the Empress of Russia. The Prince's brother 'Sandro' (Alexander), who later became the ruling prince of Bulgaria, was at that time serving as an officer in the Russian army. The two brothers met, and with his captain's approval Prince Louis invited Alexander to visit the *Sultan.* The latter in fact stayed on board for two days, during which time he met Admiral Phipps-Hornby and was allowed to witness some fleet exercises.

But when news of this got out a first-class 'spy' story burst in the British press. This took the form of accusations that during a delicate period of strained relations between Britain and Russia, a Russian officer had actually been entertained on board the British fleet flagship, allowed to visit other warships in the squadron and been let into some of our most jealously guarded naval secrets!

A full Admiralty investigation was demanded. Queen Victoria, who wholeheartedly condemned Russian aggression against the Turks, accused her son of nothing less than treason. Press reports stated that he was to be relieved of his command and Lieutenant Battenberg sent back to England in disgrace.

Wrote the Tsaritsa to her brother, Prince Alexander of Hesse, about 'Sandro' when she heard of the affair, 'the poor boy is beside himself that Queen Victoria, that crazy old hag, made him a pretext for persecuting Alfred and, more especially, Louis.'

Although certain coincidental moves did in fact follow this episode, there is little doubt that 'Affie' was able to satisfy the Queen that no harm had in fact been done.

Battenberg was transferred out of the *Sultan* in April, 1878, but after a short spell on the books of the depot ship at Malta he was appointed to the *Agincourt* and, in the following year, to the royal yacht *Osborne* herself. The rest of his story is told elsewhere.

As for the Duke himself, the affair and its repercussions are perhaps best summed up in the following extracts from the *United Services Gazette,* the first showing how the initial incident was reported by most organs of the press.

> 16 March, 1878. We have received a communication from Pera dated 28th February commenting in no measured terms on an incident which has aroused feelings of extreme indignation among both officers and men in the fleet now anchored near Constantinople. The incident referred to is that a German prince who is attached to the Russian army, together with another officer, both attired in Russian uniforms were on board H.M.S. *Sultan* for two days as guests and during this time witnessed all sorts of operations for the defence of the ships against night torpedo attacks which were being carried out on board the various vessels.

But editorially the *Gazette* declared that it did not believe anyone had played the part of a spy.

The next extract was published on 6th April, 1878, and reported that:

> H.M.S. *Sultan* is ordered home forthwith to be paid off. Captain H.R.H. the Duke of Edinburgh will rejoin the *Sultan* at Malta and will pay her off at Portsmouth where she will be immediately taken in hand to receive new boilers and to be brought forward for further service. The *Sultan* was to leave the Sea of Marmora Wednesday. The Duke and Duchess of Edinburgh arrived at Malta on Wednesday from Smyrna in H.M.S. *Antelope.*

By then Admiral Phipps-Hornby had left Turkish waters with the bulk of the Mediterranean Fleet, leaving a small 'squadron of observation' at Suda Bay under command of Vice-Admiral Lord John Hay.

On April 24th, 1878, the *Gazette* announced that:

H.R.H. The Duke of Edinburgh has transferred from command of the *Sultan* to that of the *Black Prince,* the latter ship also taking over the majority of the officers and crew of the former. Captain Howard of the *Black Prince* is transferred to the *Sultan*, which ship will hoist the flag of Rear-Admiral Dowell, C.B., and proceed to England, as the Rear-Admiral will complete the usual period of one year's service as second in command of the Channel Squadron on the 16th prox. It has been generally supposed that the Duke of Edinburgh, having more than completed his six years' period of qualifying service as a captain would have been promoted to flag rank and relieved Admiral Dowell.

The *Black Prince,* larger and more heavily armed than the *Sultan,* was, incidentally, the first British armour-plated steam warship to be fitted with watertight compartments.

Although the affair of Prince Louis of Battenberg and his brother was eventually settled to the satisfaction of the Queen and the Admiralty – in fact, in the following year Sandro, now the reigning Prince of Bulgaria, paid an official visit to Queen Victoria in London and was warmly received – it is evident that some sections of the British press were reluctant to let go of a good story, for on June 1st, 1878, the *United Services Gazette* commented:

It is to be regretted that a certain class of our contemporaries should take the liberties they do with the name of the Duke of Edinburgh and his reputed doings, but it is more to be regretted that they should find it necessary to indulge in statements to which one might apply a stronger term than misleading. H.R.H. is on one side attacked in language which nothing – even truth itself – would justify; on the other side he is as unjustifiably made the victim of 'penal' treatment by the Admiralty. The following explains our meaning. 'Without enquiry by the Admiralty, however, and without the shadow of a pretext the Duke was treated as though he was almost guilty of high treason, and he was with all his officers and crew penally removed from the *Sultan* to the *Black Prince*.' Now this is all wrong and displays an utter want of knowledge of facts. The Duke desired to retain a command in the Mediterranean. The boilers of his ship the *Sultan* were in such a bad state – the two years for which she had last been made efficient having expired – that it was imperative she should return home for repair and refit. What was to be done to meet the wishes of the Duke? A transfer of himself and officers to the *Black Prince,* a more efficient ship than the *Sultan,* suggested itself and was acted upon, thus meeting the desire of his Royal Highness not to return home while there was any probability of England coming to blows. Such a procedure can hardly be made to bear the interpretation of himself, officers and crew being 'penally removed' from the *Sultan,* but quite the reverse. In addition, however, we might add, that even had the Duke not been consulted no possible blame could attach to the Admiralty.

Before he did sail for home at the end of the year after the Russo-Turkish crisis had passed the Duke was to earn a useful encomium from his senior officer. In November, 1878, Vice-Admiral Lord John Hay informed the Admiralty that the captain of the *Black Prince* was deserving of the highest praise for his services during the difficult disembarkation at Cyprus of the Indian troops who had been sent to take over in Malta during the recent emergency. And on December 30th the following memorandum from the Lords Commissioners of the Admiralty was published:

Whereas by Your Majesty's Order-in-Council of 3rd February, 1866, we were empowered to promote Lieutenant H.R.H. Prince Alfred, K.G. (now Captain H.R.H. The Duke of Edinburgh, K.G., K.T., K.P., G.C.S.I., G.C.M.G., Personal A.D.C. to Your Majesty) to the rank he now holds without requiring him to pass through the intermediate grade of Commander, and whereas by the said Order-in-Council it was laid down that H.R.H. should be held in all respects eligible for advancement to the various grades on the flag list of Your Majesty's Navy. H.R.H. having now served at sea as captain in command of three of Your Majesty's ships for a period exceeding that required to qualify an officer for advancement to flag rank we are of opinion that it is desirable to advance him to the rank of Rear Admiral, such promotion being additional to the authorised numbers as established by Your Majesty's Orders in Council of 22nd February, 1870, and 5th August, 1875, until the time arrives at which he would be entitled to such promotion by seniority when he should be considered as absorbing a vacancy. And we would further submit that such promotion shall not entail the resignation by His Royal Highness of the appointment he now holds as personal Naval A.D.C. to your Majesty.

The Queen approved and the Duke thus attained flag rank entirely by his own endeavours.

On November 21st, 1879, he was appointed Admiral Superintendent of Naval Reserves, to hold this appointment during her Majesty's pleasure for not more than three years. Accordingly he hoisted his flag in H.M.S. *Penelope,* an 11-gun, armour-plated iron corvette of 4,394 tons. She was the flagship of the First Reserve and Coastguard and Drill Ship of the Naval Reserves, stationed at Harwich. In addition to the *Penelope* the Navy's First Reserve consisted at that time of the armour-plated ships *Warrior, Hector, Valiant, Resistance, Lord Warden, Hercules, Belleisle* and *Audacious;* also the gunboats *Britomart, Cromer, Cherub, Netley, Firm, Merlin, Ariel* and *Nimble.* Stationed around the coast were nine more Coastguard and Reserve drill ships.

Although, perhaps, not a particularly arduous post, the Duke, who had already attained something of a reputation for his skill in the conduct of fleet manoeuvres, worked hard and conscientiously at the task of bringing the Reserves to a high state of efficiency. Each year he took his ships to sea for exercises with the Channel Squadron and for cruises as far afield as the Baltic. Four years later he published a paper for the International Fisheries Exhibition in London on sea fisheries and the fishing population of the United Kingdom which was compiled entirely from information and experience gained during his command of the Naval Reserves when he regularly visited all the fishing ports in the country.

At that time fishermen were recruited into the second class of the Naval Reserves, which became in later years the Royal Naval Reserve Trawler Section, and subsequently the Royal Naval Reserve Patrol Service. These were the men who, after the sea mine had been developed into a potent weapon of naval warfare, swept up the deadly eggs assiduously sown around these islands by the enemy in two world wars.

In November 1882, the Duke was promoted vice-admiral, and in December of the following year appointed Vice-Admiral Commanding the Channel Squadron, hoisting his flag in the armour-plated ship *Minotaur*. This vessel and her sister ships *Agincourt* and *Northumberland* were among a number of particularly good ironclads which had been built some fifteen years previously. Not only were their hulls protected throughout by thick armour, their big guns were for the first time also mounted behind armour. In addition these ships were fitted with steam steering gear, at that time a new innovation. The Channel Squadron also included one of the newer turret ships which carried four 80-ton guns mounted in pairs in barbettes. The squadron spent most of its time in manoeuvres and exercises and especially the practice of defensive tactics against torpedo attack. Overseas the Navy continued to be kept rather busier. In Africa the Zulu war was fought and won with the aid of a naval brigade, and in 1882 when rebellion against the Khedive's rule in Egypt menaced the Suez Canal, opened some years earlier, British warships bombarded rebel-held forts at Alexandria, and naval gunboats operated against the enemy on the Nile. During these operations a certain Captain John Fisher and Commander Lord Charles Beresford, whose feuds in later life would split the Navy into two camps, greatly distinguished themselves.

At the end of 1884 when the Duke hauled down his flag and relinguished command of the Channel Squadron, their Lordships of the Admiralty expressed their complete satisfaction with the efficient performance of his duties.

During the greater part of the following year the Duke chaired a committee appointed to consider the desirability of organising a scheme for granting pensions or gratuities to the widows and children of seamen and marines. He brought his usual talents to bear on the committee's deliberations, as a result of which an insurance fund for the payment of pensions was recommended. Then, in February 1886, he was given the Navy's plum appointment, that of Commander-in-Chief, Mediterranean, in succession to Admiral Lord John Hay who was to assume the post of First Sea Lord.

On the 20th of the month he duly hoisted his flag in H.M.S. *Tamar* and she sailed for the Mediterranean on the same day. On March 5th his flag was hoisted in H.M.S. *Alexandra* and he formally assumed supreme command of the station which he had first joined more than a quarter of a century earlier as a shy and blushing young naval cadet. It was a proud moment for him.

But this was no sinecure post. Problems crowded in daily on the new Commander-in-Chief. For even at that late stage in the Navy's changeover in ships and material his fleet was nothing if not polyglot, and he was required to be familiar with all the various peculiarities of its different units. Thus there were the broadside ships *Sultan* and *Superb;* the barbette ship *Temeraire;* the turret ships *Dreadnought* and *Agamemnon;* the armour-plated twin-screw ironclads *Neptune* and *Thunderer;* the armoured broadside corvettes *Orion* and *Carysfort;* the torpedo depot ship *Hecla;* the torpedo ram *Polyphemus,* the sloops *Gannet* and *Dolphin;* the gun-vessels *Condor* and *Falcon;* the gunboats *Grappler, Albacore, Coquette, Cygnet* and *Starling;* the steam vessels *Imogene* and *Cockatrice;* the sailing sloop *Cruiser;* and, foreshadowing the shape of things to come, Torpedo Boats Nos.21 and 22.

Although this was an era of magnificent seamanship the Navy was still in a very backward state, changes rendered inevitable by the march of science coming about only gradually. Officers in general had but a scanty knowledge of the tactics and strategy of the new era, drills and evolutions being devised less for their war value than their competitive value, with ship pitted against ship.

This state of affairs stemmed, of course, from the fact that for nearly a century Britain's title as Mistress of the Seas had not been seriously challenged. But in less than twenty years the whole character of the Navy would be drastically altered by the dynamic little Captain Fisher who now occupied the post of Director of Ordnance at the Admiralty.

Soon after the Duke assumed command of the station his Duchess came out again to Malta with their children and they took up residence in San Antonio Palace. Thus whenever the fleet was in Malta the Duke was able to live ashore with his family, being conveyed to and fro between ship and shore in a magnificent 10-oared *dghaisa* he had had specially built for use as a harbour galley. Serving under his command in more lowly surroundings as a young lieutenant on board the *Thunderer* was another budding royal sailor, whose story will be told later.

For much of the Duke's three years of service in the Mediterranean there was comparatively little excitement. But soon after his arrival on the station trouble again blew up in the Balkans. It was in fact an extension of the former pan-Slav disturbances which had led to Russia's attack on Turkey in 1877. For in revising the Treaty of San Stefano in 1878 the Congress of Berlin had confirmed the independence of Rumania, Serbia and Montenegro, but divided Bulgaria into two automonous provinces called Bulgaria and Eastern Rumelia.

In 1885 the Bulgars declared their independence and the union of both provinces. Emulating their example, the Greeks decided in the following year to re-draw their frontiers with Turkey, and mobilised their army with the object of accomplishing this by force. Hostilities were, however, averted when the Great Powers presented an ultimatum to the Greeks and brought about their submission by ordering a blockade of their coasts to be carried out by an Allied Fleet in the Mediterranean. In September of that year when calm had once more been restored the Duke, accompanied by his young relative from the *Thunderer* (later to become King George V), paid a ceremonial visit to the Sultan of Turkey whose bacon had been saved yet again by the British.

Towards the end of April, 1889, on the expiration of the term of his appointment, Prince Alfred struck his flag as Commander-in-Chief and returned to England in the *Alexandra,* which paid off at Portsmouth. Their Lordships of the Admiralty again expressed their approval of the conduct of their royal flag officer — he had been promoted to full admiral in October, 1887 — not only for his efficient blockade of the Greek ports during the Balkan crisis, but also for 'the able, zealous and efficient manner in which he discharged on all occasions the many anxious and responsible duties devolving on him as Commander-in-Chief, Mediterranean'.

In 1890 he was appointed chairman of a committee on naval officers' uniforms. As a result of their recommendations new uniform regulations were issued in the following year. The principal changes were that the number of buttons on the full dress coat was reduced from ten to eight, and the gold lace on the skirts, formerly worn by flag officers, removed. There were alterations to the cocked hat, the frock coat modified and the monkey jacket made the normal undress rig for a naval officer. The device used on the epaulettes of admirals of the fleet was changed to a crown above crossed batons surrounded by laurel leaves, and a wide variety of other dress reforms were introduced, including the provision of a boat cloak.

The committee also recommended that admirals of the fleet should wear an aiguillette and receive a baton the same as a field marshal. But despite the fact that certain former admirals of the fleet had received batons this last was not approved. However the Duke himself was eventually to be given this unusual honour.

On August 4th, 1890, he was appointed Commander-in-Chief, Plymouth, and remained in that command until June 2nd, 1893, being promoted on the following day to admiral of the fleet. He had thus reached the top of the tree, and the end of his active service in the Navy, for on August 22nd, 1893, he succeeded his late uncle as reigning Duke of Saxe-Coburg and Gotha. Three months later the question was raised as to whether he could retain his privileges as an English peer and his rank of Admiral of the Fleet. The Queen decided that he should retain the honorary rank of Admiral of the Fleet (unpaid) but was to have no voice in the Lords.

And now she was about to clash, not for the first time as titular Lord High Admiral, with the Board of Admiralty. On the occasion of her approaching Jubilee she proposed to give a special present to her dear Affie. On May 31st, 1897, therefore, Colonel Sir Fleetwood Edwards, private secretary, wrote to the Right Honourable George Goschen, First Lord of the Admiralty, to say that her Majesty desired to present a baton to her son, the Duke of Edinburgh, and asked if the whereabouts were known of the one given to the Duke of Clarence in 1821. On June 2nd Goschen replied referring to the batons given to the Duke of Clarence and Admiral of the Fleet the Earl of St. Vincent in 1821, and suggesting that St. Vincent might have received the award as Colonel of Marines and not Admiral of the Fleet. In any event the Board, he said, would have no objection to the Queen's proposal, although they did not say where Clarence's baton had got to. Next day Edwards wrote suggesting that the Admiralty should pay for the baton now to be presented.

But this brought an immediate protest. The Admiralty, wrote Goschen, did not approve of batons being carried by Admirals of the Fleet. Also since the first two had been personal gifts the King must have paid for them. As this, too, was to be a personal gift it was suggested that the Queen should pay for it — the Treasury would be certain to object.

In fact four batons had previously been presented to Admirals of the Fleet; the first in 1821 by George IV to the Duke of Clarence, and the second in the same year by George IV to the Earl of St. Vincent; the third by William IV who gave his own baton to Admiral of the Fleet Williams-Freeman in 1830; and the fourth, also by William, to Admiral Gambier in 1832. Garter King of Arms gave it as his opinion that the first two should not be considered as establishing a precedent or as a right of appointment. It was never the custom, he said, for an admiral of the fleet to receive a baton by virtue of his rank as for field marshals. Nevertheless the Queen was determined that Alfred should have his baton and on her own terms. She ordered one to be made by the Court jewellers and paid for it herself.

In due course she presented it to him, and as to the capacity in which the gift was made she defied the Admiralty in the following Supplement to the London Gazette issued on June 22nd, 1897, which stated that 'On the occasion of her Jubilee Queen Victoria was pleased to present to her dear son, H.R.H. The Duke of Saxe-Coburg and Gotha, Duke of Edinburgh, K.G., a baton *as Admiral of the Fleet.*'

On July 30th, 1900, the sailor Duke died suddenly of a heart attack. He had spent 35 years in the Royal Navy and was a real professional.

CHAPTER IV

OLD SOUL

Shortly after dawn on a September morning in 1914 Kapitan-leutnant Otto Weddigen, commanding the German submarine *U.9*, gazed through his periscope at three British cruisers steaming abreast on a steady course towards him. He had sailed from Heligoland three days earlier with orders to attack transports reported to be conveying British troops across the Channel to Ostend.

In fact the German report was incorrect. No troops were crossing the Channel, and the cruisers were on normal patrol in an area off the Dutch coast known as the Hoofden, unaware of the presence of any enemy submarine. At that time the submarine was a comparatively new weapon of war, sonar was unknown, and anti-U-boat measures had not been developed.

At first Weddigen thought that the cruisers formed part of the screening force of a larger fleet. But when no other ships appeared he decided to attack the targets thus presented to him. Closing to within 500 yards, he fired his first torpedo at the centre ship of the three. This exploded just abaft her foremost funnel, causing her to list over, and in less than half an hour she capsized and sank. The second cruiser hove to nearby and sent away boats to rescue survivors. Weddigen calmly put two torpedoes into her, and in a few minutes she, too, capsized and sank.

Meanwhile the third cruiser, after briefly opening fire at what her gunners took to be a periscope, closed her stricken consorts. Weddigen fired two more torpedoes at her. One missed but the other struck home amidships. The cruiser listed over, but as her watertight doors had been closed and she seemed likely to remain afloat, the work of saving the crews of the other two ships was resumed. Weddigen closed in and fired a third torpedo at this vessel, and she then turned over and sank rapidly, leaving the sea covered with wreckage and drowning sailors.

Of a total of more than 2,000 officers and men of the three torpedoed ships, which were in fact the armoured cruisers *Aboukir, Hogue* and *Cressy*, only 28 officers and 258 men were subsequently picked up by a passing Dutch steamer and two Lowestoft trawlers. This disaster and the heavy loss of life was one of the worst suffered by the Royal Navy in the first world war. In due course heads rolled and two British admirals were ordered to strike their flags. But Kapitanleutnant Weddigen's torpedoes struck an even more fateful blow at the Royal Navy, for just over a month later the First Sea Lord, Admiral His Serene Highness Prince Louis of Battenberg, sat down at his desk in Whitehall and wrote the following letter to the First Lord of the Admiralty:

Dear Mr. Churchill, I have lately been driven to the painful conclusion that at this juncture my birth and parentage have the effect of impairing in some respects my usefulness to the Board of Admiralty. In these circumstances I feel it to be my duty, as a loyal subject of His Majesty, to resign the office of First Sea Lord, hoping thereby to facilitate the task of the administration of the great Service to which I have devoted my life, and to ease the burden laid on his Majesty's Ministers.

What had driven Battenberg to this 'painful conclusion' was the growing anti-German feeling in this country, fanned by reports of German atrocities in Belgium and, in particular, a virulent press campaign directed against him personally. The stunning news of the loss of so many sailors in the sinking of the *Aboukir, Hogue* and *Cressy*, the majority of them naval reservists with wives and families, and a number of young naval cadets, whipped up the campaign to fever pitch.

Who better for a scapegoat than the First Sea Lord, himself a 'German prince' (he was in fact a British subject), upon whom lay the ultimate responsibility for sending these ageing and unprotected vessels into a U-boat infested area? On October 28th, 1914, therefore, Battenberg decided to bow out of the Service he loved.

News of his resignation came as a shock to the Navy, and Admiral Sir John Jellicoe, Commander-in-Chief of the Grand Fleet, sent the following message to his chief:

Have received with the most profound sorrow the information contained in your telegram. The whole fleet will learn the news when published with the deepest posible regret. We look to you with the greatest loyalty, respect and gratitude for the work you have accomplished for the Navy.

Thus came to an end forty-six years professional service of a brilliant royal sailor who had done much to modernise the fleet and enable it to face with confidence the greatest threat since Napoleon. That legendary character, Admiral Fisher, recalled from retirement to take the place of his own protégé as First Sea Lord had called Battenberg one of the two best officers in the British Navy — 'What they don't know no one call tell them.'

Today his grandson is Prince Philip, another royal sailor.

* * * * *

In the year 1841 the daughter of the Grand Duke Louis II of the small but important Prussian State of Hesse married the eldest son of the Tsar Nicholas I of Russia. Since the bride was a young and rather shy girl, her brother Alexander went along also to live at the Russian Court and was given a commission in the Russian army. He was a handsome young man with a roving eye and speedily fell in love with the Tsar's daughter, the Grand Duchess Olga. The Tsar, however, had other plans for her, and he wished Alexander to marry his sister, the Grand Duchess Catherine.

But Alexander found that lady unattractive and finally turned his attentions to the Countess Julie von Hauke, Olga's lady-in-waiting, whose father had been the Polish War Minister. In November 1851, the couple eloped and were married in Breslau. The Tsar was furious and expelled him from the Russian army, and Alexander's brother, now the reigning Grand Duke Louis III of Hesse, was extremely annoyed when he learned of the morganatic marriage.

Nevertheless, he created Julie Countess of Battenberg, a small district in the State of Hesse, with a seat at the Schloss Heiligenberg in Darmstadt, the capital. In 1858 she was given the rank of Princess of Battenberg and her five children were permitted to be styled Princes and Princesses of Battenberg.

Eldest of these was Louis Alexander, born at Graz, in Austria, on May 24th, 1854. When the boy was eight years old his cousin, also named Louis, married Princess Alice, second daughter of Queen Victoria. Thereafter, as already recounted, Prince Alfred was a frequent visitor to Darmstadt when he came to stay with his sister and her husband.

'Affie' thus became well acquainted with the family living at the Schloss Heiligenberg, and young Louis was thrilled by his stories of life afloat. Although he had only once seen the sea, while on holiday at Venice, the boy decided that he wanted to join the Navy. There was at that time no unified Germany and the few Prussian warships in service belonged to the navy of the North German Confederation. When Prince Alexander suggested that he should join the Austrian Navy Louis turned this down with youthful scorn.

The British Navy, he said, was the largest and most advanced and for him there could be no other service. His father gave way, and two tutors were brought over from England to coach the young prince for his entry examination. He spent the whole of the summer of 1868 swotting hard, and in September was taken to England by his father and entered in Dr. Burney's school at Alverstoke for a final brush-up. On October 4th Burney took him to a public notary at Gosport where Louis swore an oath of allegiance to Queen Victoria and became a British subject. Under the auspices of Lord Henry Lennox, Parliamentary Secretary to the Admiralty, he was duly entered as a naval cadet on the books of H.M.S. *Victory*.

In December he took the entry examination and passed easily. As a child he had shown great intelligence, and at the age of four could read and write German and draw well. He had a gift for languages and could speak English, Russian, French and Italian. The only thing that worried him about the examination was that his eyesight might not be good enough. He knew that at a certain point in the ordeal his examiners would ask him to read the time by the clock on the dockyard tower. He therefore carefully set his watch by this clock beforehand, and when the inevitable request came managed to steal a furtive glance at his watch as he turned to the window!

Prince Alfred had suggested to the Admiralty that after passing the entry examination young Louis should join his ship, the *Galatea,* of which he was about to take command, and thus undergo his early training in a fully commissioned ship. Normally new entry cadets were required to undergo a year's training in H.M.S. *Bristol,* a seagoing training ship. Unfortunately the new royal sailor suffered from a plethora of friends in high places. For the Prince and Princess of Wales were about to start on a cruise round the Mediterranean in the screw frigate *Ariadne* and, thinking to do his young relative a kindness, the Prince asked the Admiralty to appoint Louis to that vessel.

The youngster was not too pleased with this arrangement as he feared that his instruction would suffer on board a ship being used as a royal yacht. However, there was nothing he could do about it. He was given leave to spend Christmas in Darmstadt and ordered to join the *Ariadne* at Trieste. This he did on January 15th, 1869, in a howling gale, and when he was conducted below to her dark and smelly gunroom he felt very lonely and forlorn.

This was in fact the midshipmen's berth upon whose mess table the 'Maggot Derby' was regularly held, and there were the usual hardships inseparable from life at sea in a 19th century British warship to be endured. But Louis quickly conquered his home-sickness and buckled down to learn all he could about his new career. In his spare time he took up boxing, singlestick and fencing, and learned how to play whist and chess. Because of his royal status there were additional privileges to be enjoyed which were denied to his messmates.

The tour of the Prince and Princess of Wales took the *Ariadne* to Alexandria from whence the Royal party visited Cairo and went on sightseeing tours up the Nile with the Khedive; to Suez to meet De Lesseps and inspect the then uncompleted Canal; to Constantinople to visit the Sultan and wander over the battlefields of the Crimea; and to Athens to call on the King and Queen of Greece. Midshipman Battenberg was included in all these expeditions. At the end of the tour, in June, 1869, the *Ariadne* returned to England to pay off.

Artist's impression of King Edward VII bringing his two sons, Prince Albert Victor and Prince George (later King George V), aboard the *Britannia* at Dartmouth, October, 1877

Prince Louis of Battenberg, later 1st Marquess of Milford Haven

After a brief spell of leave which enabled Louis to rush home and show himself off to his family, he and the majority of the 'young gentlemen' from the *Ariadne* were appointed to H.M.S. *Royal Alfred,* flagship of the North America and West Indies station. There were in fact twenty-six of them crammed into the mess, and conditions were almost as bad as they had been in the *Ariadne.* But two or three times each week they were able to enjoy at least one civilised meal, for the admiral issued a standing invitation to those midshipmen and cadets who had kept the morning watch each day to take breakfast with him.

The *Royal Alfred* was an old line-of-battleship which had been converted to an ironclad while still in the building stage. She carried ten 9-inch guns and eight 7-inch, all of which were fitted with rope breechings like those of Nelson's day and had to be worked by hand. She was equipped with an 800-horsepower engine which drove a single screw, and when not in use her single funnel could be closed down like a telescope. But the principal means of propulsion was still sail, for which the *Royal Alfred* was fully rigged, and when all her 29,000 square feet of canvas were spread in a spanking breeze she was a fast sailer.

As with most British naval stations during those transition years the North America and West Indies command comprised the usual polyglot collection of warships. Thus, in addition to the *Royal Alfred* and her consort the *Defence,* there were three 6th rates, or corvettes, fitted with steam and sail, 4 sloops, 5 screw gun vessels, 4 gunboats and a floating battery.

The *Royal Alfred's* commission lasted for 4 years and 7 months, during which Louis was promoted to midshipman and eventually attained the position of senior member of the gunroom. The squadron spent a great deal of time cruising, much of it hard, all-weather sailing, but to break the monotony periodical visits were paid to various ports around the station at which dances and picnics were held. When reports of these junketings appeared in the local newspapers the presence on board the flagship of the young royal sailor was given special prominence. Louis thoroughly enjoyed naval life. He learned to handle boats and men and was never seasick. One of his fellow midshipmen later recorded:

From the very date of his joining the *Ariadne* in 1869 Prince

G

Louis was remarkable for his zeal and diligence which few British-born youngsters showed in those days. His log was full of charts and sketches, all a model of neatness. He showed indeed all the qualifications which gave the promise he so amply fulfilled of becoming a great sea officer in his ability, character and temperament. He secured a warm feeling towards him of all ranks and ratings that he served with. His nickname of 'Old Soul' shows the cordial feeling felt on both sides. This came from his remarking of his friends 'He's a dear old soul', one of the first pieces of English slang that he picked up.*

On one occasion Louis was invited to accompany the Commander-in-Chief on an official visit to Demerara in the frigate *Sirius*. While on board he saw for the first and last time in his life a sailor being flogged. 'It was a gruesome sight,' he wrote, 'especially as the second three dozen lashes were laid on by a left-handed boatswain's mate.' The punishment had been awarded by the captain because the man refused to obey an order.

'Yet,' commented Louis, 'the *Sirius* was the smartest and happiest ship in the squadron.'

Another aspect of the times was the excessive drinking which took place on board, even in junior officers' messes. One evening the midshipmen of the *Royal Alfred* invited the gunroom messes of the ships of a visiting squadron which called at Halifax to dinner on board. Louis was midshipman of the watch, and by the time the lights had been put out in the gunroom and the squadron's boats were alongside to collect the guests most of these were so stupefied with drink that they had to be carried bodily over the gangway!

He was allowed to take one short break during this lengthy commission. This was in June 1870, when his father obtained Admiralty permission for him to come home to be confirmed in the Lutheran church at Darmstadt. But the visit had to be cut short when the Franco-Prussian war broke out and Louis was hurriedly sent back to rejoin his ship. One significant result of the war which ended in France's defeat and cast the first small shadow over Europe was the unification of all the petty States of

* *Prince Louis of Battenberg*, by Mark Keer.

Germany, including Hesse, into a German Empire and the proclamation of William I of Prussia as its first Emperor.

In December 1873, a new Commander-in-Chief arrived in a new flagship to take over the North America station, and the *Royal Alfred* sailed for home to pay off. Louis was now due to take his examinations for sub-lieutenant, in all of which he obtained first-class certificates, the results of his gunnery examination being the best ever recorded.

He was duly promoted in April, 1874, and then took a refresher course at the recently opened R.N. College at Greenwich to brush up in classics and languages. Once again he obtained top marks, except, surprisingly, in French. But the reason for this was that although he was more than proficient in the language, his French professor was still resentful over the outcome of the Franco-Prussian war and chose to regard Louis as one of the 'enemy'. Thus unfairly the accident of his birth was to go against him.

In 1875 the Prince of Wales paid a State visit to India. He and his suite were to travel in H.M.S. *Serapis* escorted by a squadron of warships. The Prince now asked Louis if he would like to serve in the *Serapis* for the period of the tour. Louis accepted, although with some misgivings, and was duly appointed to the Royal tour ship. She was in fact an old trooper specially fitted out with royal apartments for the accommodation of the heir to the throne, but Louis found his own quarters anything but sumptuous. As senior sub-lieutenant he was president of the gunroom mess, which was the usual dark and overcrowded compartment well below decks, but he did manage to obtain a tiny cabin to himself.

The tour was an affair of great splendour and ceremonial and, since Louis was attached to the royal suite while in India, he was privileged to be present at all the magnificent State occasions and to participate in the many sporting events provided for the Prince's relaxation, which included tiger and elephant hunts.

When the *Serapis* returned to England in the spring of 1876 the Prince of Wales invited Louis to spend the rest of the season at Marlborough House. But the latter, having now been promoted to lieutenant, was eager to get back to sea. He was accordingly appointed to H.M.S. *Sultan,* whose captain was H.R.H. The Duke of Edinburgh.

Once again he was made aware of the disadvantages of his royal status. For no sooner had he arrived on board than the Duke asked him to become his equerry. Louis knew this to be a great mistake, but again he had no option. He was allotted a small, rat-ridden cabin, and required to stand in as spare lieutenant for any unpleasant job that might be going. He also had to mess with the Duke instead of in the wardroom as he would have preferred. However, there were some compensations, not least of which was being able to live ashore in some comfort with the Duke's family whenever the fleet was in Malta.

When the Russo-Turkish crisis developed in 1878 he became involved in the affair over the invitation to his brother Sandro (Alexander) to visit the *Sultan,* already related, which brought down the wrath of Queen Victoria on the heads of himself and his captain. Then when the Bulgars won their freedom at the Congress of Berlin they invited him to become their ruling Prince. But the Navy was his first and only love, and he turned down the offer in favour of Alexander.

When the Duke of Edinburgh and his officers transferred from the *Sultan* to the *Black Prince,* Louis was appointed to the *Agincourt,* flagship of Rear-Admiral Commerell, V.C., second in command of the Mediterranean Fleet, and he remained in that ship until April, 1879. Subsequently he was appointed to the royal yacht *Osborne.* The Prince of Wales tried to persuade him to remain in this sinecure appointment, but Louis was determined not to become a mere courtier and firmly declined the invitation. After twelve months in the yacht he was appointed to H.M.S. *Inconstant.*

At that time British naval stations overseas included the Mediterranean, North America and West Indies, the Pacific, China, the East Indies, Australia, Cape of Good Hope and West Africa. Between them they absorbed more than 130 warships in full commission, from ironclads to small gunboats. There was also a Flying, or Detached, Squadron, comprising half a dozen fully commissioned vessels employed partly as a training squadron and partly as a special reinforcement which could be speedily despatched to any station where extra warships were needed to cope with an unexpected emergency.

The *Inconstant,* an iron screw frigate cased with wood, of some 5,800 tons, was flagship of this squadron, then under the command of Rear-Admiral Lord Clanwilliam. Other ships of the squadron were the 14-gun screw corvettes *Carysfort* and *Cleopatra,* and the composite screw corvette *Tourmaline.* All the ships carried sail as their principal means of propulsion, the *Inconstant* being a particularly fast vessel under sail or steam.

When Louis joined her, along with another young lieutenant named Percy Scott, later to become a famous gunnery expert, he found that the squadron was about to set out for no less than a world tour. For a fifth ship, the *Bacchante,* another screw corvette, was to be temporarily attached to the squadron, and the world cruise was being undertaken chiefly for the benefit of two young midshipmen she had on board. They also were royal sailors.

But this was to be no 'banyan' cruise, for much of the voyage was to be carried out under sail, with the ships being regularly exercised at evolutions, including gunnery and ship towing. Clanwilliam was not fond of steam and used engines only when absolutely necessary. After leaving England the squadron headed south-westward, calling at Madeira and the Canary Islands en route to Montevideo.

At a ball in the Uruguyan capital attended by the squadron officers on January 8th, 1881, a telegram was brought to the British Minister, the Hon. Edward Monson. It so happened that at that particular moment he was about to propose marriage to a young lady, so he stuffed the envelope in his pocket and forgot about it.

Next morning it was discovered by his valet who brought it to him. When Monson opened it he was horrified to find that the telegram contained orders for the Flying Squadron to proceed with all despatch to the Cape of Good Hope as war had broken out with the Boers in South Africa. But by then the squadron had already sailed for the Falkland Islands!

The worried Minister hastily despatched the gunboat *Swallow* in pursuit, but she was delayed by a gale and only just managed to catch the squadron at Port Stanley. Clanwilliam at once headed eastwards at top speed, while officers and men practised landing party drills and the *Inconstant's* maintopmast staysail was cut up to make gaiters for them. After 23 days hard steaming the squadron arrived at the Cape.

But the naval brigade was not required after all, for the shooting war had ended — in defeat for the British forces on the spot — and the affair had moved into the realms of higher diplomacy. The trouble had originated when the predominantly Boer colonies of Natal, the Orange Free State and the Transvaal were annexed to the British Crown.

In June 1880, Gladstone had taken office at the head of a Liberal Administration pledged to cancel annexation of the Transvaal. But as the months went by and the Home Government took no action the Boers revolted and set up a provisional government of their own. When the small British army in South Africa moved in to crush the rebellion it was disastrously defeated at the battle of Majuba Hill. Instead of sending out powerful forces to smash the rebels, an armistice was arranged by Gladstone's Cabinet, peace terms agreed and a measure of self government eventually granted to the Transvaal Republic.

But while these negotiations were going forward the Flying Squadron was ordered to remain at the Cape ready to land its sailors if required. In March 1881, Louis' uncle, the Tsar Alexander II, was assassinated by Nihilists, and when a Russian corvette arrived at Simons Bay a few days afterwards Louis was given the task of going on board to break the news to her captain.

In April, after settlement had been reached with the Boers, the squadron resumed its interrupted voyage to Australia. But in the Roaring Forties they ran into a severe gale and the ships became separated. Despite shortened sail the *Inconstant* continued to make 18 knots and quickly lost sight of her consorts.

One by one the battered ships managed to reach Albany, in western Australia, but for several days the *Bacchante* was almost given up for lost. She had to go into dock at Melbourne for repairs, and the two royal midshipmen were temporarily transferred to the flagship in order to pay a scheduled visit to the King of Fiji. Escorted by their cousin Louis, they duly met that jovial monarch who had originally been a cannibal and confided to the young officers that he still preferred babies' legs to modern dishes!

After visiting Japan and China and calling at Singapore and the Cape, the squadron had reached the Cape Verde Islands on its way home when the *Inconstant* was ordered to proceed at top speed for Egypt where an insurrection had broken out.

This was yet another of the 'brush-fire' wars in which Britain was embroiled during the latter half of the 19th century in the consolidation of her empire. In 1879 Britain and France had established a dual control over bankrupt Egypt in order to safeguard their interests in the Suez Canal. While the young Khedive Tewfik Pasha raised no objection, a revolt against foreign domination broke out headed by a Colonel Ahmed Arabi. France refused to join in active measures against him, but the British Mediterranean Fleet was ordered to Alexandria which Arabi was fortifying. When hundreds of Europeans were massacred in anti-foreign riots the fleet began bombarding the forts.

The *Inconstant* and her three consorts of the Flying Squadron ferried troops from Malta to Egypt, and kept the bombarding British warships supplied with shells and ammunition. Keen to get closer to the fighting, Lieutenant Battenberg was landed in charge of a naval detachment armed with half a dozen Gatling machine guns to guard the young Khedive in his palace. Gunnery expert Percy Scott obligingly mounted the weapons on special carriages so that they could be used as 'mini' field guns.

Eventually the army arrived in force to take over from the sailors, and the Flying Squadron returned home to pay off. Louis now went on half pay, and while staying in Darmstadt became engaged to Princess Victoria of Hesse, daughter of the reigning Grand Duke and grand-daughter of Queen Victoria.

Then followed another spell of service in a royal yacht, this time the *Victoria & Albert,* although Louis would have preferred a more active appointment. But at least it enabled him to take time off to visit his fiancée at satisfyingly frequent intervals, and on April 30th, 1884, the two were married in Darmstadt. The wedding was attended by Queen Victoria and her youngest daughter Princess Beatrice, who in the following year married Louis's brother Prince Henry of Battenberg.

In August 1885, Louis was promoted to commander, but as there was no immediate seagoing appointment available he underwent a series of courses in gunnery, torpedo, signals and the study of manoeuvres. This was an exciting period in our naval history for young officers of vision, drive and ambition, and Louis possessed all three. Larger and more advanced types of warship were emerging from the building yards, constructed almost wholly of the newly invented steel instead of iron, with increased boiler power, higher speeds, and carrying breech-loading guns of greater muzzle velocity.

The weight-saving property of steel enabled secondary batteries of smaller destructive weapons to be mounted in addition to the central grouping of big guns which had previously comprised almost the sole fire power of the older ironclads. Self propelled torpedoes had been developed, capable of travelling some 2,000 yards at a speed of more than 20 knots, which could be launched from tubes mounted below the waterline.

New theories of fleet tactics were evolving, one of the most important of which – subsequently proved to be erroneous – was that armoured ships were now becoming impregnable to gunfire, and in a fleet action would have to ram their opponents. Steel rams were therefore provided, and gunnery standards began to fall off. But men like Fisher, Wilson, Jellicoe and Louis himself held different ideas.

After almost two years of alternate study courses and brief spells of half pay, Louis was finally appointed to be executive officer of the battleship *Dreadnought* on the Mediterranean station. Launched in 1875 and of 10,820 tons displacement, she was the most heavily armoured ship in the Navy and the first to have artificial ventilation and longitudinal bulkheads. 8,200 h.p. engines drove her twin screws at a top speed of 14½ knots, and she carried a complement of 406 officers and men. That the job of executive officer of a 19th century coal-burning ironclad was no easy one is shown by Battenberg's description of an all too frequent but necessary evolution of those days.

'We have had a heavy job of coaling from a collier alongside,' he wrote to a friend:

From Saturday at 4.30 a.m., until Monday forenoon I was in my clothes, having my meals almost always standing, and only lying down on the deck all dirty and greasy for an hour's sleep at a time. It was very hard on the men who worked incessantly, two halves relieving each other every two hours night and day and, having to work all through Sunday, they required a good deal of humouring. The heat was intense and with a burning sun. On the third day I was so worn out that I could hardly drag myself along. We hoisted in close on 1,000 tons, that is, 1100 bags which had to be filled, then hoisted in, emptied and sent back for refilling. I wonder what a lieutenant-colonel in the British Army would say if he was expected to do that in time of peace and as a matter of ordinary routine?

But his hard work and conscientious attention to duty paid off, for in July 1887, Louis obtained his first independent command. She was the twin-screw torpedo cruiser *Scout* of 1,580 tons. Armed with four 5-inch guns and seven torpedo tubes, she carried a complement of 145 officers and men. Louis was delighted and at once set to work to make her the most efficient ship on the Mediterranean station. Since smaller units of the fleet had more of a roving commission than their larger sisters, which included routine patrol of the Red Sea to check the activities of slavers and gun-runners, Louis was able to enjoy a wider freedom of action.

It was while the *Scout* was engaged on a stint in the Red Sea that history repeated itself with astonishing fidelity. One day while the ship was anchored off an Arabian port a slave swam out, clambered on board and claimed protection. Soon afterwards a boat came alongside bringing the local British consul who demanded that the man be returned. Louis refused, and the indignant official sent off a strongly worded complaint to the Foreign Office in London.

In due course Commander Battenberg received an official reproof from the Admiralty, but soon afterwards the system was altered to free naval officers from consular interference. A hundred and twenty years earlier, at Genoa in 1769, two Turkish slaves jumped into a boat belonging to H.M.S. *Alarm* commanded by Captain John Jervis, later Admiral of the Fleet the Earl of St. Vincent, and wrapped themselves in her ensign, claiming that by so doing they were free. They were dragged away by the Genoese authorities, but later returned at Jervis's peremptory demand together with a piece of the boat's ensign which had been torn in the struggle. He, too, was officially reprimanded by the Admiralty, but knew that in fact his action met with Their Lordships' full approval.

In December, 1891, Louis was promoted to captain, and almost at once invited by the Second Sea Lord, Vice-Admiral Sir

Anthony Hoskins, to become his chief of Staff, an appointment which carried with it the posts of Assistant Director of Naval Intelligence and Head of the Mobilisation Department. Hoskins, who for three years had been Battenberg's Commander-in-Chief in the Mediterranean, had noted his ability and marked him down as the man to improve the Navy's inefficient Intelligence Service.

Because of his drive and capacity for hard work, Louis soon found himself given the tasks of Naval Adviser to the War Office and Chief Secretary of the Joint Naval and Military Committee of Defence in addition to his other departmental duties. Thus, although only a junior captain, he handled top secret War Office and Admiralty papers and could confer direct with the First Lord and the Adjutant-General of the Army. He also served on important committees dealing with armaments and the defence of this country against invasion.

Under his guidance the Naval Intelligence Division began to develop into a useful department. When he left at the end of three years to take up another seagoing appointment he received the high praise of both the Commander-in-Chief of the Army and the First Lord of the Admiralty.

His new command was H.M.S. *Cambrian,* a second class cruiser, one of a class of eight launched in 1893. She displaced 4,360 tons, was armed with 6-inch guns as well as torpedo tubes, and her forced draught engines gave her a top speed of 20 knots. It was back to the Mediterranean Fleet again, and although one of the smallest ships on the station the *Cambrian* speedily became the smartest, topping the records for every drill and evolution. Her crew also carried off most of the regatta cups, and even won the field gun trophy previously always held by the Marines from the battleships. More important, perhaps, the *Cambrian* boasted the lowest percentage of punishments of any ship on the station.

So meticulously was she run, her decks snowy white, paint spotless and brightwork gleaming, that she became known as 'Prince Louis' yacht'. But Battenberg knew how to get the best out of his ship's company. Said his officers of their royal captain, 'He lived so much for those who had the honour of serving under him and who in turn did their best to serve him.' And the ratings, 'On the lower deck he was always highly thought of and men were willing to follow him anywhere.'

On one occasion when the *Cambrian* was acting as guardship at Villefranche while Queen Victoria was staying at an hotel above Nice, Louis persuaded her to come out and inspect his ship's company whom he had lined up along the road below. This 'beau ideal of a naval officer,' as Winston Churchill called him, was frequently consulted by his seniors about naval affairs and, on a higher plane, because the Empress of Russia happened to be his sister-in-law, his diplomatic services were called upon to smooth matters between Russia and Egypt over use of the Suez Canal.

During his service in the Naval Intelligence Department Louis had discovered that most of the British consuls in foreign ports were not of British nationality yet could handle secret documents in time of war. He brought this fact to the notice of the Prime Minister, with the result that the system was altered and only British born individuals appointed to consular posts overseas. In his spare time Louis invented a navigational instrument known as the Battenberg Course Indicator, which was adopted by the Admiralty and became standard throughout the Navy. The Russians also used it, and in World War I the instrument was adopted for the Air Force. Not surprisingly, Battenberg incurred the jealousy of some of his contemporaries, but those with vision divined that he was a man destined for high office, not because of his royal birth but in spite of it.

Having turned the *Cambrian* into crack ship of the Mediterranean Fleet, Louis was next appointed flag captain to the Commander-in-Chief of the Channel Squadron. He found this very differently run from the Mediterranean command. For one thing, the admiral suffered from dyspepsia and, apart from being difficult to get along with, spent much of his time ashore. In spite of having to shoulder many of the duties of his absent chief, Louis stepped up the flagship's coaling time to the unprecedented level of 162 tons an hour!

Early in 1901 Queen Victoria died, and as His Serene Highness Prince Louis of Battenberg and husband of the dead queen's grand-daughter he took his official place amid the impressive gathering of European royalty who attended her funeral. When the cortege was about to leave Windsor station for St. George's Chapel one of the artillery horses drawing the gun-carriage plunged and reared, breaking the traces. Louis promptly suggested to King

Edward that the restive animals should be removed and that the naval guard of honour should take over. The King agreed, and the traces and chains were turned into drag-ropes and the gun-carriage drawn the rest of the way by the sailors.

Ever since then the Royal Navy has performed this duty at the Sovereign's funeral.

As a result of the Navy scares of 1884 and 1888 huge shipbuilding programmes had been put in hand, and between 1886 and the turn of the century no fewer than 42 battleships were added to the British fleet. Each new class embodied improvements of one kind or another, adding to speed, armour and fighting capability. In 1898 a number of new battleships of a class known as the *Formidables* were laid down, and attracted more than usual popular attention, if only because they were the first British warships which cost £1 million to build. With a displacement of 15,000 tons and a speed of 18 knots they were the largest and fastest capital ships yet to appear. Their main armament comprised four 12-inch guns mounted in hooded barbettes, and they carried a powerful secondary battery of twelve 6-inch guns besides a large number of smaller weapons and four submerged 18-inch torpedo tubes.

One of the earliest of the class to be completed was the *Implacable,* and in September 1901 Louis was appointed in command, destined once more for the Mediterranean. Vice-Admiral Sir John Fisher had now become Commander-in-Chief and he re-vitalised the station. At his direction manoeuvres were carried out at full speed and under battle conditions, more attention was paid to gunnery with firings taking place at longer ranges, and war games introduced. Louis greatly admired the dynamic little admiral even if he did not agree with all Fisher's ideas.

Under Battenberg's magic touch the *Implacable* quickly climbed to the eminence of crack ship in the fleet, carrying off all the records for cleanliness, drills and evolutions just as had the *Cambrian.* She topped the other ships in gunnery firings, obtaining eleven hits out of thirteen rounds from her 12-inch turrets and ninety per cent of hits with her secondary armament. Louis also had the chance to show that he was an excellent tactician. On one occasion during combined manoeuvres with the Channel Fleet the admiral commanding the squadron to which the *Implacable* was attached for the exercises went sick. Louis was ordered to take over as Commodore, and at a crucial point in the exercise cleverly extricated his ships from a tight corner.

At Fisher's invitation he wrote a series of memoranda on a variety of professional subjects, which included the organisation of naval staffs ashore and afloat, naval preparations for hostilities at short notice, and technical changes in engines and propulsion machinery. One of his suggestions was for the formation of an Admiralty staff, hitherto non-existent.

In 1902 Fisher became Second Sea Lord, and soon afterwards Louis was again appointed to the Admiralty, this time as Director of Naval Intelligence. The post then covered a wider field than its title suggests, and among the reforms and innovations Fisher introduced and in which Louis played no inconsiderable part were the creation of a nucleus crew system to enable the Reserve Fleet to be kept in being, with its own admiral; a new educational system for naval officers, extending their training to four years; up-dated methods of commerce protection and the defensive arming of merchant ships in war; better conditions for the lower deck; the formation of 'flying squadrons' of armoured cruisers; and an improved naval intelligence service. He also helped to prepare the groundwork for the formation of the future Imperial Defence College. Since there was then no Naval Secretary to the First Lord, Louis was consulted on officers' appointments and always tried to get younger men promoted.

By his marriage to Princess Victoria he became the father of two sons and two daughters, and in October 1903 took time off to visit Darmstadt for the wedding of his eldest daughter Alice to Prince Andrew of Greece. This was a glittering royal occasion and many European crowned heads attended the ceremony.

On July 1st, 1904, Louis was promoted to rear-admiral. He was now fifty years of age, a big handsome man with a piratical looking torpedo beard and up-curling moustaches. He had spent thirty-six years in the Navy, and even his detractors had to concede that he had gained every step of the way to promotion by sheer ability and driving ambition.

'I hate the idea of getting anything as regards naval work at the hands of the King,' he wrote to a friend. 'I want to get it on my own merits – if I have any.' Far from his exalted rank having helped him it had hindered his career.

The fast armoured ships he had suggested should be built were now coming into service, and in November 1904 he was appointed Rear-Admiral Commanding the Second Cruiser Squadron, and hoisted his flag in H.M.S. *Drake*. One of a class of four, she was a heavy armoured cruiser of 14,100 tons armed with two 9.2-inch guns and twelve 6-inch. The other five ships of the squadron, all designated 'County' class and bearing such names as *Cornwall, Berwick, Essex, Cumberland* and *Bedford,* displaced 9,800 tons apiece and were armed with fourteen 6-inch guns. All were fast vessels, capable of speeds of up to 24 knots.

The King himself inspected the *Drake* soon after she commissioned, and the squadron then sailed for Gibraltar to join the Channel Fleet. While they were anchored off the Rock the royal yacht arrived with Queen Alexandra on board, and she, too, came to look over the new cruiser flagship. Another royal caller was Kaiser William II of Germany who, lacking a proper yacht of his own, was cruising in a converted mail steamer. Since the Emperor held the honorary rank of Admiral of the Fleet in the British Navy, Louis delighted him by flying his Union flag at the masthead during the time he was inspecting the cruiser.

Early in the following year the squadron was ordered to carry out a special cruise to Canada and the United States with the object of creating good feeling and cementing the friendship between the three countries. During the visit Louis was not to be treated as a royal sailor but as an ordinary naval officer. The cruise was an enormous success, not least because Battenberg was in command, the ships being enthusiastically received everywhere they went, both in Canada and the United States. Of their dashing admiral the *Washington Post* wrote:

> All those who have seen Prince Louis of Battenberg are delighted with him . . . he is not the kind of man to whom salaams are agreeable. He is clean cut and every action denotes virility.

The one discordant note came in a letter from an Irish-American in Chicago who hoped Prince Louis would 'come to our fair city so I can plaster your royal puss with rotten eggs!'

He met President Theodore Roosevelt, and so impressed the American Navy chiefs by his brilliant handling of his squadron in the Chesapeake at manoeuvres and gunnery that they sent Commander (later Admiral) William Sims over to England to study his methods. The cruise was appropriately rounded off by the squadron making the 3,300-mile return passage to Gibraltar in the record time of 7 days 7 hours.

In February 1907 Louis was advanced to the acting rank of vice-admiral and appointed second in command of the Mediterranean Fleet with his flag in the 15,000-ton battleship *Venerable*. He was given a tremendous send-off when he left the cruisers, and the Mediterranean Fleet was delighted to welcome the sailor prince back to the station. His exploits had become legendary, not least of these being his practice of leading his squadron into Malta's Grand Harbour at speed, dropping anchor checking cables, then going astern to bring it into position with almost pinpoint accuracy.

On one occasion when the *Venerable* called at Villefranche two of her midshipmen visited nearby Monte Carlo and lost most of their money at the gaming tables. They then went into a restaurant for a meal and, horrified at the prices, ordered the cheapest food they could find on the menu. As they waited to be served the admiral, accompanied by his flag captain and a number of friends, entered the restaurant. A few minutes later the captain came across to their table with a message from Louis to say that the midshipmen were probably unaware that they were in one of the most expensive hotels in Europe and they might therefore find it difficult to meet the bill. They were, however, to order anything they liked and the charge would be added to the admiral's bill!

In November, 1908, Battenberg was confirmed in the rank of vice-admiral and appointed to command of the Atlantic Fleet with his flag in the battleship *Prince of Wales*.

More great changes were in progress in the Navy consequent upon the rise of a menacing naval rival. From being a minor sea power, Germany in less than two decades had moved up into second place.

'Every German vessel launched,' declared the Kaiser as the Imperial Navy increased in size, 'is a guarantee for peace on earth.

Every new warship makes it impossible for our enemies to attack us. We are the salt of the earth.' Arrogantly, he even styled himself 'Admiral of the Atlantic.' Profound disquiet arose in England. What did Germany want this great Navy for, and against whom, except Britain, could she intend to use it?

At the Admiralty Fisher had now become First Sea Lord. Regarding war with Germany as inevitable, he worked and planned to bring the Royal Navy to a high state of efficiency and preparedness. One of his early moves was to concentrate two large squadrons of warships in home waters. The Home Fleet was therefore renamed the Channel Fleet and strengthened by the addition of a number of capital ships withdrawn from the Mediterranean. The old Channel Fleet became the Atlantic Fleet and, composed of vessels of the latest class, was strategically based on Gibraltar so that it could speedily reinforce either Home or Mediterranean Fleets if required.

Numerous technical and other developments were also crowding on to the naval scene. Thus came the invention of wireless telegraphy to revolutionise naval communications; the advent of the submarine; improved types of shells, gunnery control and rangefinders; the coming of steam turbines; the introduction of oil fuel in place of coal; and, Fisher's masterstroke, the appearance of the all-big gun battleship. Since the Wright brothers in 1903 demonstrated the practicability of powered flight in heavier-than-air machines interest grew in the possibility of applying mastery of the air to naval purposes, and in 1908 an Air Department was set up at the Admiralty.

In 1910 Fisher retired and was succeeded as First Sea Lord by Admiral Sir Arthur Wilson. But Fisher's influence was still strong in Whitehall, for the new political head of the Navy, the ebullient Winston Churchill, leaned heavily upon the old admiral for advice on naval affairs. Disagreements soon arose between Churchill and his First Sea Lord and, since their ideas proved incompatible, Churchill decided to create a new Board of Admiralty.

Fisher suggested Prince Louis as the man to take Wilson's place.

'He is the ablest admiral that we possess,' he told Churchill, 'the most capable administrator *by a long way.*'

But at a Cabinet meeting Lloyd George, Chancellor of the Exchequer, expressed horror 'at the idea of a German in the supreme place.' Admiral Sir Francis Bridgeman therefore took over from Wilson and Battenberg became Second Sea Lord.

Prior to this Louis had been commanding the 3rd and 4th Divisions of the Home Fleet with his customary brilliance, testing out new ideas in tactics and manoeuvres. Until the future formation of the Grand Fleet under Jellicoe this was probably the largest and most important command to be held by one admiral. The two Divisions comprised no less than 20 battleships, 30 cruisers, 87 destroyers and torpedo boats, 43 submarines and a large number of auxiliary vessels. Except for a brief period in command of the Blue Fleet during manoeuvres in 1912, it was to be Battenberg's last seagoing appointment.

'He had a far wider knowledge of war by land and sea and of the Continent of Europe than most of the other admirals I have known,' wrote Churchill in *The World Crisis 1911-1918*.

> He was deeply versed in every detail, practical and theoretic, of the British Naval Service. It was not without good reason that he had been appointed under Lord Fisher to be head of the British Naval Intelligence Department, that vital ganglion of our organisation. He was a thoroughly trained and accomplished staff officer, with a gift of clear and lucid statement.

The two men worked well together on the task of preparing the fleet for the war that both now felt to be inevitable. Among their innovations was the creation of a naval war staff — the idea originally suggested by Battenberg while a captain in the Mediterranean Fleet; a new warship building programme with larger calibre guns; the formation of three separate fleets in home waters — one fully manned and operational, the second at sixty per cent of full strength, and the third ready to be manned by the Reserves at the outbreak of war; the formation of a 'fast division' of battleships; and the changeover of all ships from coal to oil. In 1912 Bridgeman was retired due to ill health, and Battenberg, now a full admiral, moved up to the post of First Sea Lord.

Although the spring and summer of the year 1914 were marked by an exceptional tranquillity, storm clouds were gathering fast. Churchill had suggested that the naval manoeuvres for that year

H

should be omitted as an economy measure and a test mobilisation of the Third Fleet substituted. This meant that the entire strength of the Naval Reserves would be called up for a period of ten days beginning in July. Prince Louis agreed, and the huge concentration of the three fleets duly assembled at Spithead and was inspected by the King.

But on June 28th an assassin had fired his fatal shots at Sarajevo and the world was steadily moving towards war. While the diplomats played their deadly chess game in Europe, Louis took the first steps to place the Royal Navy on a war footing.

Following the Spithead review the Third Fleet would normally have reduced to skeleton crews, the Second Fleet to its nucleus strength, and the First Fleet dispersed to home ports to give leave. But all these moves were cancelled and the First and Second Fleets ordered to remain at full strength. Only the Reservists were dispersed.

On July 28th when Austria declared war on Serbia, Prince Louis despatched the signal which sent the fleet to its war station at Scapa Flow. Nothing could now check the march of events, which for the First Sea Lord would culminate in his own resignation within three months as a result of the venomous campaign conducted against him because of his Teutonic birth.

Wrote Churchill in *The World Crisis:*

The uncomplaining dignity with which he made this sacrifice and accepted self effacement as a requital for the great and faithful service he had rendered to the British nation and to the Royal Navy was worthy of a sailor and a Prince.

Battenberg quietly retired to the Isle of Wight, and in 1917 was created Marquess of Milford Haven. When King George V changed the name of the Royal Family from Guelph to Windsor, Louis changed his to Mountbatten, a literal translation of Battenberg.

In January, 1919, he was placed on the retired list at his own request, and two years later specially promoted to Admiral of the Fleet. He died a few weeks after the promotion was gazetted.

CHAPTER V

THE RIGHT ROYAL PICKLE

To the shrilling of boatswains' pipes a portly bearded gentleman clad in the full dress rig of a captain in the Royal Naval Reserve stepped on to the quarterdeck of the training ship *Britannia,* moored in the river Dart. Trailing behind him came two small, fair-haired boys wearing the uniform of naval cadets. Normally the visit of an R.N.R. officer would have called for comparatively little ceremony on the part of Captain Henry Fairfax, Royal Navy, who commanded the *Britannia.*

But his present visitor was very much more important than his gold lace proclaimed; no less exalted a personage in fact than His Royal Highness the Prince of Wales, and the two apprehensive looking youngsters he had in tow were his sons, the Prince Albert Victor, more usually known as 'Eddy', and Prince George, who were about to be inducted into their new life in the Royal Navy.

Therefore the entire ship's company of the *Britannia* had been fallen in on deck in their best uniforms for the occasion. Quizzed by dozens of pairs of critical teenage eyes as they climbed aboard, the two embarrassed princes devoutly wished their august father elsewhere and themselves at the bottom of the Dart.

One of the youthful onlookers recorded that:

Prince Eddy was rather tall for his age, which was nearly 14, slight and good looking. Prince George, was some 18 months younger, very fair and small but also very nice looking. They seemed a bit shy and quiet at first, which was not surprising when you come to think of it. Two youngsters like that being suddenly pitchforked into a den of about two hundred ravening wolves such as we were. For these were no soft days. The *Britannia* was a hard school, though a splendid one. It made very little difference whether you were prince or commoner — you had to take what was coming to you and, believe me, it came pretty often during the first two terms on board.*

The decision that his sons must leave home and serve on board a training ship if they were to have the education, proper discipline and undisturbed studies they needed was that of the Prince of Wales himself. When he discussed the matter with his mother, Queen Victoria, she agreed that Prince George should make the Navy his career as the boy ardently desired, but was not enthusiastic about his elder brother being included.

'The very rough sort of life to which boys are exposed on board ship is the very thing not calculated to make a refined and amiable prince,' she demurred, a sentiment somewhat at variance with her previously expressed feelings about 'Affie's' early days in the Navy.

Canon Dalton, who had been the boys' tutor since they emerged from the nursery stage, allied himself with their father. The princes, he had earlier reported to their parents, were below the standard of education of average private scholars of their respective ages and would make a poor showing among their contemporaries at a public school. Prince Albert Victor, he added, should accompany Prince George to the *Britannia* to improve his moral, mental and physical development. Queen Victoria eventually agreed on condition that Dalton went along too.

Accordingly, in April 1877, arrangements were made by the Admiralty for the two boys to sit the entry examination for naval cadet at the Royal Naval College, the usual certificate of qualification being dispensed with. After all, their grandmother was titular Lord High Admiral, even if their father held only honorary rank in the Royal Naval Reserve. Prince Albert Victor was then thirteen years of age, and his brother would reach his twelfth birthday on June 3rd. Because of his mischievous ways when a child the latter had been dubbed by the Palace staff 'the Right Royal Pickle'.

The examination, which included arithmetic, algebra, geometry, dictation, 'reading English intelligently', French translation, the Scriptures, geography, and English history, was duly

* From *King George V — A Personal Memoir* by J. Gore.

undergone, and the President of the College was able to report satisfactory results. It was decided that the new cadets should join the training ship on June 5th, two days after Prince George's birthday.

Certain changes had been made in the training arrangements for naval cadets since their uncle, Prince Alfred, now a serving captain, had entered the Service in 1858. The old *Illustrious* had been replaced in Haslar Creek by the three-decker *Britannia,* formerly the flagship of Admiral Dundas in the Crimean war. In 1861 the ship was moved to the Portland Roads. But this berth proved unsatisfactory, and after two years she was shifted to the river Dart, off the town of Dartmouth.

In 1864, in order to increase the living and instructional acommodation, the two-decker *Hindostan* was added, being moored ahead of the *Britannia* and connected to her by a bridge. The establishment was now able to take some 217 cadets for 12 months training before being sent to sea. Then in 1868 the steam frigate *Bristol* was attached as seagoing training ship in which the cadets were required to spend a further 12 months instructional period before joining the fleet. A year later the entry examination was made more competitive; more nominations could be given, although entry was limited, and 13 became the lower age limit. Finally the original *Britannia* was scrapped and replaced by the ex-screw ship *Prince of Wales,* which was renamed *Britannia.*

The daily routine of the cadets verged upon the spartan. They slept in hammocks, from which they were roused each morning at 6.30 to plunge into a bath of cold water as part of their daily toilet before assembling for drill at 7.15. Breakfast was at 8, and studies commenced at 8.50 and continued until ten minutes after noon when the mid-day meal was served. Studies were resumed at 1.40 p.m., and lasted until 4. At 4.20 all fit cadets were landed for physical and recreational exercise, which included football, or cricket and tennis in the summer, and general athletics, returning on board shortly before 7 p.m.

Tea, the last meal of the day, was at 7.15, after which the cadets were required to occupy themselves with further studies until prayers at 9.15. Half an hour later all were turned into their hammocks. In winter 'pipe down' was at 9.30 and there were other slight variations in the daily timetable.

The cadets received one shilling a week pocket money, cadet captains two shillings, and cadet chief captains two shillings and sixpence. No boy was allowed to have more than ten shillings in his possession at any one time, nor were they permitted to bring sweets, fruit, or other eatables on board, or to receive food parcels from home. The reason for this latter veto was that envy should not be aroused among boys whose parents might perhaps prove less generous than others.

A fellow cadet of the two princes, recorded that they:

> were treated exactly the same as all the rest of us. Their sole privilege was a sleeping cabin to themselves under the poop. They soon settled down and after a time, I believe, they enjoyed the life. It was hard certainly. We were worked hard and played hard, for games were by no means neglected. We had an excellent cricket ground and a very good cricket coach, Bentley, the Yorkshire professional, a racquet court, a pack of foot beagles, and boats to sail and row.*

Since their father was the Prince of W(h)ales the royal cadets were promptly christened by their fellows 'Sprat' and 'Herring' respectively. The usual catechism undergone by less exalted new entries took the form of such embarrassingly personal queries as, 'How do you like being a prince?' 'What do you do when you're at home?' And 'Do you ever get licked?' In later life King George V said of these *Britannia* days:

> It never did me any good to be a prince, I can tell you, and many was the time I wished I hadn't been. It was a pretty tough place, and so far from making any allowances for our disadvantages the other boys made a point of taking it out of us on the grounds that they'd never be able to do it later on. There was a lot of fighting among the cadets and the rule was that if challenged you had to accept. So they used to make me go up and challenge the bigger boys — I was awfully small then — and I'd get a hiding time and again. But one day I was landed a blow on the nose which made it bleed badly. It was

* From *King George V — A Personal Memoir* by J. Gore.

the best blow I ever took for the doctor forbade me fighting any more.*

This was only one of the indignities the unfortunate 'Herring' had to endure. The other cadets thought that he and his brother were allowed unlimited pocket money, whereas in fact they received no more than the regulation shilling a week. Because of this erroneous belief and also because he was the smallest boy (at 15 he measured only four feet ten inches and weighed a mere 88 lb.) Prince George was made to bring goods back from the tuckshop which other cadets had ordered. These were frequently confiscated, but the unlucky prince was never paid back for what he had spent on their behalf!

It was known to the higher-ups that Prince Eddy, being in direct line for the throne, would not be making the Navy his career. With youthful precocity Prince George himself told his instructors not to bother about his brother who was not going to sea but to devote their attention to him.

Asked on one occasion how he would like to be the heir presumptive, he replied, 'I'm jolly glad I'm not. My brother has to take all the kowtowing and gets a rotten time while I lark about and enjoy myself.'

He had no inkling that fate would decree his brother's death at the early age of 28, and that he himself would have to make the great sacrifice of his life and reshape his ambitions along a path leading to the throne. He would dearly have liked to become a serving admiral, but circumstances were to force him into being a king.

Prince Eddy was a somewhat lethargic youth, but the younger boy was much more lively and eagerly lapped up instruction, distinguishing himself at mathematics and boat handling. Naval life suited him; his interests and his sense of humour belonged to the sea. Living up to his childhood nickname of 'Right Royal Pickle', he one night tucked a couple of marlinespikes into the bed of the First Lieutenant, following that august officer's discovery of which 'there was a great row'. When he owned up to the crime his leave was stopped for a week.

* From *George V*, by Sir Harold Nicolson.

In July 1879, the two princes passed out of the *Britannia* fairly creditably along with the other 48 cadets in their term. Of these, two were to reach the rank of Admiral of the Fleet, one of them being George himself; and thirteen others became flag officers. At the Admiralty the following notations pertaining to his time in the *Britannia* were entered on Prince George's official record: *General Conduct:* 'Very good indeed.' *Ability:* 'Good.' *Professional knowledge:* 'Good.' *Temperate:* 'Yes.' *Remarks:* 'Knows French and a little German.' Then, on July 25th, 1879, the princes were appointed to H.M.S. *Bacchante* which was to be their seagoing home for the next three years.

When the Prince of Wales informed the First Lord of the Admiralty, then Mr. W.H. Smith — 'Old Morality' — of this arrangement the latter was shocked at the idea of both princes sailing in the same ship, and brought the matter before the Cabinet. Disraeli, the Prime Minister, wrote to the Queen pointing out that the proposal would disquiet the public mind and that should any accident happen the Government would justly be called to account.

He was tartly told to mind his own business by Her Majesty, who replied, 'I entirely approve the plans for my grandsons, which should never have been put before the Cabinet. The Prince of Wales only mentioned it to Mr. Smith and was, with right, extremely annoyed at his doing such a thing. It was not done when the Prince of Wales and Prince Alfred went on long journeys together.'

Disraeli apologised, and on August 6th the princes joined their new ship off Cowes where she had been acting as guardship for regatta week. Before she sailed to join the Channel Squadron the Prince and Princess of Wales, the Duke and Duchess of Edinburgh and the Duke and Duchess of Connaught all went on board to be shown round privately.

The *Bacchante* was a two-funnelled screw corvette of 4,430 tons, built of iron cased with wood, and a comparatively new ship, having been launched in October, 1876. She was 307 feet long with a beam of 45½ feet, and was armed with two 4½-ton muzzle-loading guns on the upper deck, twelve more on the main deck, and two 64-pounders aft; also a secondary armament of Nordenfelt machine guns, and half a dozen Whitehead torpedoes which could be fired from underwater tubes. Her engines developed 5,250 i.h.p., and in her bunkers she carried 400 tons of coal. But, like all screw ships of her day, she was fully rigged for sail. In command was Captain Lord Charles Scott, whose own son was one of the 16 midshipmen and cadets who messed in the usual cramped gunroom.

This compartment was some 14 feet long, eight feet wide and seven feet high. The customary large mess table took up most of the available deck space, and the occupants found it a close fit when they sat down to meals. Wooden lockers topped with leather cushions to provide seats ran round three sides of the mess, and a curtained doorway cut into the fourth gave access to the half deck.

Overhead was a deep shelf crammed with books and nautical instruments, dirks, telescopes, backgammon and chess boards, writing materials, photo albums and other personal belongings. There were two ports to admit daylight and fresh air, and a sliding window separated the mess from the steward's pantry, from which 'the lady of the gunroom' dispensed tea or cocoa, biscuits, sherry and bitters and, on special occasions, even brandies and sodas. Hanging on two of the white-painted bulkheads were portraits of the Prince and Princess of Wales.

The daily routine for the 'young gentlemen' was not vastly different from that in the *Britannia*. Thus they were roused from their hammocks at 6.15 a.m., for drill, breakfasted half an hour later, and mustered with the rest of the ship's company for evolutions at 8 o'clock. At 9 there were Divisions and Prayers, followed by drills and routine ship duties. Dinner was at noon, and work resumed at 1.30 p.m. At four o'clock there were more evolutions, followed by supper at 4.30. Hammocks were got up at 7.30, and at 8.30 the gunroom officers were turned in for the night. In harbour, however, lights out was at 10 p.m. In addition to sea duties special instruction was given, which included cutlass and rifle drill, gun drill, company drill, seamanship, and a two-hour daily school period.

The princes were treated the same as the other midshipmen and cadets, which included going aloft for sail drill, but they were excused from standing night watches at sea. Instead they took extra lessons under the tutelage of Canon Dalton, who also made the boys keep a meticulous daily diary. When the *Bacchante* finally paid off these youthful accounts of life at sea, duly expanded and edited by the indefatigable Dalton, were eventually published in two thick volumes. But even the most sycophantic reviewer had to confess they made anything but lively reading!

A fellow cadet in the *Bacchante,* recalled that:

the companionship in one of Her Majesty's gunrooms in those days was of necessity a very close and intimate one. Weeks and weeks at sea living on food that was more than monotonous and also exceedingly nasty. Mostly salt pork and ship's biscuits. Remember, there were no comforts in those days – no such things as electrical freezing plant, so fresh vegetables,.fruit and fresh provisions lasted a very very short time after leaving harbour. Also one got rather bored at always seeing the same old faces round the same old table, and tempers at times were apt to get frayed and irritable. Yet I never remember Prince George losing his temper.*

But being high-spirited youngsters there was plenty of skylarking to enliven things, into which the 'Royal Pickle' entered with gusto. One night he wrote in his journal:

After dinner much amusement trying to sit on an empty corked bottle on the deck, at the same time holding a candle in each hand, one of which was lighted, the other to be lighted from it without rolling over.†

After a spell in home waters cruising with the Reserve and Channel Squadrons, the former under the command of Prince Alfred, the *Bacchante* then sailed for a cruise in the West Indies. At Bermuda Prince George performed his first ceremonial duty as a member of the royal family when he laid the foundation stone of the Sailors' Home. In his less exalted naval capacity he was required to take charge of the funeral firing party at a burial on shore.

Deaths on board were not unusual in those days, for many

* From *King George V – A Personal Memoir* by J. Gore.
† From *A Century of British Monarchy* by H. Bolitho.

sailors were killed by falling from aloft, but in this case it was the schoolmaster who had died.

Not unnaturally, local pressmen took a keen interest in the doings of the young royal sailors. One eager journalist, trailing them after a visit to the Botanical Gardens where their faces had become smeared with yellow pollen through sniffing some outsize tropical lilies, excitedly telegraphed home that the princes had had their noses tattooed! This extraordinary report seems to have gained some credence, for in her next letter to Prince George, his mother, Queen Alexandra, asked her son, 'How can you have your impudent snout tattooed?'

On January 8th, 1880, they were rated midshipmen and, after the *Bacchante's* return to England and a month's leave, rejoined the ship for her world tour with the Flying Squadron. While the ships were delayed at the Cape during the Transvaal negotiations the princes were taken by the High Commissioner to visit Cetewayo, the famous Zulu chief, who was kept on a farm near Capetown. Prince George, who described him as a 'bloodthirsty old chap who wanted to wash his spears in the blood of the Boers', was later involved in a carriage accident caused, he said, by a 'boozy coachman.'

On another occasion he narrowly escaped having his legs broken while the *Bacchante* was exercising with her Whitehead torpedoes at a spar towed astern of the ship's whaler of which he was coxswain. One of the torpedoes went off course, rammed the boat and got stuck in her planking. Later he won 'a nice little cup' in the squadron regatta.

Queen Victoria was scared that the princes might have to form part of a naval brigade if hostilities should be resumed, but the Prince of Wales rather hoped that they would see some fighting! Instead, however, they were to experience another kind of hazard.

At the height of the gale the squadron encountered after leaving the Cape, the worst ever experienced in those waters, the *Bacchante's* rudder head cracked due to a flaw in the forging, thus rendering her almost helpless and in imminent danger of capsizing. There was no other ship nearby, for the rest of the squadron had become widely scattered.

It was now that Captain Scott brought off a brilliant feat of seamanship. In order to prevent the ship, which was practically out of control, from broaching to and bring her before the wind while temporary repairs could be effected, he ordered the entire watch on deck to climb into the fore weather rigging and to spread out from top to bottom of the shrouds. The pressure of the wind on their bodies gradually forced the ship's head to leeward. If at any time she had got into a trough of the waves she would have been swamped. After five anxious days a jury rudder was eventually rigged, and the *Bacchante* was finally able to reach the port of Albany, in western Australia, under steam.

Although the visit to Australia was in no sense a royal tour, the Flying Squadron called at all the principal ports, which included Melbourne, Sydney and Brisbane, during which the royal midshipmen were able to accept invitations to visit copper and gold mines, go horse riding and make trips to places of interest. Prince George turned out to play cricket for the *Bacchante's* second eleven against an Australian team, and sampled the thick, heady Australian beer which he thought too expensive at two shillings a bottle.

When the *Bacchante* went into dock at Melbourne for her rudder to be repaired, the princes transferred to the *Inconstant,* in which their cousin, Prince Louis of Battenberg, was serving, for their scheduled visit to Fiji. En route to Port Jackson before the start of the trip the *Inconstant* had an ominous encounter which to the superstitious boded ill for the rest of the voyage.

One night during the middle watch a 'brig rigged ship enveloped in a mysterious red glow' was sighted by the masthead lookout. She was none other than the legendary 'Flying Dutchman'. In all, 13 persons on board the *Inconstant* beheld the apparition, among them the officer of the watch and the duty midshipman.

Whether an illusion or not, the traditional ill luck followed, for next morning the smart young sailor who had first sighted the famous ghost ship fell from the foretopmast crosstrees and was killed. Later on the admiral himself became seriously ill, although he stubbornly refused to relinquish command to the next senior officer.

After leaving Australian waters the squadron visited Japan, where Prince George did in fact have himself tattooed – with a dragon on the arm – Hongkong, Singapore, Ceylon, Egypt, Palestine, Greece, Crete, Corfu, Sicily, Spain, and so back to

Portsmouth, having covered in all a distance of 45,000 miles. Before finally leaving the *Bacchante* both princes were confirmed by the Archbishop of Canterbury at Osborne House with some of their shipmates looking on.

For Prince Eddy this was the end of the line so far as the sea was concerned (he was later to join the army), but for Prince George his naval career was just beginning. He had already proved himself to be a fine seaman, active and daring, and full of enthusiasm for naval life.

'The sight of England's oaken and iron walls tearing through the black water,' he wrote in his journal, 'fills one with a strength and joy such as nothing else can give.' The Navy imbued him with a sense of duty which remained with him all his life. More prosaically, his official report on discharge from the *Bacchante* testified that his general conduct, ability and professional knowledge were all 'Very Good'.

Now came a brief hiatus in his naval career when he was sent to Switzerland to learn foreign languages, being borne for the period on the books of the Portsmouth depot ship *Duke of Wellington*, so that his naval service showed no significant break in continuity.

Following this, on May 1st, 1883, he was appointed to H.M.S. *Canada* for service on the North America station. The *Canada* was a 2,380-ton corvette fitted for sail and steam, built of steel and iron cased with wood, and commanded by Captain Francis Durrant.

Among Prince George's messmates in her gunroom were three young men, Rosslyn Wemyss, Hugh Campbell and Sydney Fremantle, who were all destined to become famous admirals. Commander-in-Chief of the station was Vice-Admiral Sir John Commerell, one of the first naval officers to win the Victoria Cross in the Crimean war.

Captain Durrant had been appointed to be the prince's 'Governor', and was told that his charge was to be treated the same as other officers, to be given no special honours when visiting ports and no State receptions. Even so, the press continued to take an inquisitive interest in the doings of the royal midshipman, but their reports were frequently more imaginative than factual. One article declared that he was covered with tattooings of mermaids and dolphins.

'How the devil do they know?' he commented disgustedly.

On June 3rd, 1884, he was promoted Acting Sub-Lieutenant, having gained six months time towards promotion in the *Britannia*. His official reports continued to be uniformly 'Very Good', with the added remarks, 'Zealous and thoroughly reliable. Very sociable, popular and a good messmate'. In the autumn of that year he returned home to undergo courses for confirmation in rank. Two of these were held at the Royal Naval College, Greenwich, where a Captain Currey was appointed to be his 'Deputy Governor'.

A letter to Currey from Durrant detailing the former's duties in this respect reveal a somewhat surprising circumscription of the prince's life by his normally liberal-minded father. 'My dear Currey,' wrote Durrant:

During your stay at the Royal Naval College, Greenwich, with H.R.H. Prince George, it is the wish of the Prince of Wales that you should consider yourself as Prince George's companion and friend to whom he may always come for advice and assistance, and also that you will kindly give that advice unasked if you see any occasion for so doing. It is H.R.H's wish that Prince George should not leave the neighbourhood of the College except to join in such sports as are undertaken by the members of the College as a body, or on the occasions when he will go from Saturday till Sunday evening to visit at such places as will be specially approved by the Prince of Wales (of which you will be notified), and H.R.H. hopes that you will accompany Prince George at these times – unless some well known friend is accompanying him. All expenses of every description that you may incur for Prince George, or whilst going anywhere with him, will be defrayed, and I shall be obliged if you will let me have the account of them monthly. Any letters addressed to the Governor of Prince George you will be so good as to open and forward to me with your opinion if they concern any local matters, so that I may reply to them; the same will apply to any letters addressed to Prince George (after he has seen them) which may require answering, as it will not be desirable that H.R.H. should answer them himself. It will not be advisable that Prince George should accept any invitations to balls, dinners, etc., while studying at the College without the sanction of H.R.H. the Prince of Wales.*

Queen Victoria also took this opportunity to warn her grandson against 'the evil temptations which beset all young men, and especially princes. Beware of flattery, too great love of amusement, races, betting and playing high,' she wrote, adding, 'I hear what a good steady boy you are.'

In fact, since he was kept painfully short of cash — even in the *Canada* he was forced to confess to a fellow midshipman that he never had much pocket money — he could hardly have created much of a splash on his meagre allowance. On one occasion when he and Currey were on their way up to London for an evening out, Prince George asked to be allowed to pay the cabman himself as he had never yet done so. Currey gave him the fare plus a shilling tip!

At Greenwich, therefore, he kept his nose to the grindstone, playing billiards, bowls and racquets in his off-study moments, and earned the commendation of his instructors for his 'sound and honest work'. On passing out he obtained 931 marks out of 1,000 for seamanship and a first-class pass in torpedo work.

He was then appointed to H.M.S. *Excellent,* the naval gunnery school at Portsmouth, to undergo courses in gunnery and pilotage. A cabin had been built for him and he was required to live in the establishment while under instruction. Captain of the school was the redoubtable 'Jacky' Fisher, and Prince George's personal instructor was Lieutenant Percy Scott, who had served on board the *Inconstant* and was to become a famous gunnery expert.

At that time an inter-establishment field-gun competition was held annually at the gunnery school, which was open to sub-lieutenants attending technical courses at Portsmouth and ratings between the ages of 17 and 22. The competition was a simplified version of the famous Royal Tournament display, and in 1885 Prince George took part in the competition as a member of the sub-lieutenants' team. At the end of his courses he passed out with first-class marks in gunnery, but obtained only second-class in pilotage. This result, however, was not the fault of the

* From *King George V — A Personal Memoir* by J. Gore.

pupil. In a letter to the Queen's secretary, Captain Fisher wrote that:

> Prince George only lost his first class at pilotage by 20 marks. The yarn is that one of his examiners — and old salt horse sailor — didn't think it would do to let him fancy he knew all about it!

On October 8th, 1885 the prince was promoted lieutenant.

When the question of a new appointment for him came to be considered the Prince of Wales informed the Admiralty that he would prefer his son to be sent to H.M.S. *Thunderer* in the Mediterranean, whose captain, H.F. Stephenson (later Admiral Sir Henry Stephenson), was an extra naval equerry and lifelong friend of the family. Stephenson had recently returned from a successful expedition to the Arctic and formerly commanded the royal yacht. He had also commanded the *Carysfort* during the world cruise of the Flying Squadron with the two princes. The Admiralty agreed, and the Prince of Wales accordingly wrote to his old friend:

> I feel that in entrusting my son to your care I cannot place him in safer hands, only don't spoil him, please! Let him be treated like any other officer in the ship and I hope he will become one of your smartest and most efficient lieutenants. He is sharp and quick and I think likes the Service, but he must be kept up to his work as all young men of the present day are inclined to be lazy.

'I hope,' he added, 'that he don't smoke too much or eat too much meat.'

Although he would not have approved of this letter in its entirety, Prince George was pleased with the arrangement, and wrote to his new commanding officer:

> I cannot tell you how delighted I am that Papa and Mama have chosen you to be my next captain. I am certain I shall like the *Thunderer*. I would sooner serve under you than with any other captain because I have known you now ever since I

King George V as a naval cadet in 1879

The young Prince Albert Victor and Prince George (later King George V) wearing sailor suits

King George V and Prince Edward (now Duke of Windsor) leading the procession at the funeral of King Edward VII

can remember anybody and we have always been such good friends. And I am quite sure I shall be happy all the time I am in the *Thunderer*.*

But in fact Stephenson's command was a rather poor choice. Not only was she one of the oldest vessels on the Mediterranean station, she had an unenviable reputation as a 'hoodoo' ship. Of a class similar to the *Devastation*, the Navy's first sail-less turret battleship, with a main armament of four 38-ton muzzle-loading turret guns, she had been launched at Pembroke Dock in 1871.

Four years later, while undergoing steam trials in Stokes Bay, near Portsmouth, a boiler exploded, resulting in 45 deaths and many injured. In 1879 while carrying out gunnery exercises in the Sea of Marmora one of her big guns, which had accidentally been loaded with two charges because of a misfire, burst, killing two officers and 8 ratings. This disaster, however, brought about an Admiralty inquiry into the advantages of breech-loading guns, and eventually resulted in the abolition of muzzle-loaders in the British Navy.

Soon after the prince joined her as fifth lieutenant her increasing defects, which required constant patching up, finally came to public notice. Press reports alleged that she was worn out and considered it little short of a scandal that she should be kept in service. But the Prince of Wales wanted his son to stay with Stephenson, and asked the Admiralty if this could be arranged. The First Lord replied:

Until we receive the report on the *Thunderer* from the Admiral-Superintendent at Malta we cannot decide what course to take with her, but no time will be lost in coming to a decision when the whole state of the case is put before us. If the *Thunderer* was to come home and be put out of commission I will not fail to bear your Royal Highness's wishes in mind and will endeavour to meet them as far as I may be able.*

But in fact lengthy repairs to the ship were required and, due to

* From *A Royal Correspondence* by Sir F. Stephenson.

I

the Prince of Wales's expressed fears that his son might contract fever and sunstroke while the *Thunderer* was in dockyard hands at Malta, the latter was temporarily transferred to the *Dreadnought,* whose executive officer was Prince Louis of Battenberg, Captain Stephenson exchanging commands with Captain Bedford of the *Dreadnought*. During a visit paid by the fleet to Egypt history again repeated itself.

One day while the *Dreadnought* was engaged in the unpleasant evolution of coaling ship at Alexandria the Khedive himself made an unexpected ceremonial call. Introduced to an overalled Prince George, sweating and reeking of coal dust, he, like the Spanish Admiral de Langara in 1779, expressed astonishment at finding a grandson of the Queen of England so humbly employed. Royalty, however, had its compensations, and during a visit to Greece Prince George was able to stay at the royal palace with that country's king and queen. In Malta he played polo at the Marsa, went on picnics with his uncle the Commander-in-Chief and his family, and played billiards in the Union Club. In Spain he visited a bullfight, about which he afterwards wrote, 'I never saw a more disgusting sight and I never wish to see another one.'

It was during his Mediterranean service that he first grew his beard. When she learned of it his mother disapproved. 'I can't understand why you have so much hair about you,' she wrote.

In May 1887 he was granted leave to attend the Jubilee celebrations of Queen Victoria. As stated earlier, the Queen had at last allowed the Prince of Wales to be made an honorary Admiral of the Fleet, and during the Jubilee review at Spithead, where 135 warships were assembled for inspection by their Sovereign, Prince George acted as his father's flag lieutenant.

On his return to the Mediterranean he continued to serve in the *Dreadnought* until April, 1888, when he was transferred at the Duke of Edinburgh's request to the fleet flagship *Alexandra*. He left her in the autumn, and in February of the following year was appointed to H.M.S. *Northumberland,* flagship of Vice-Admiral John Kennedy Baird, commanding the Channel Squadron. Captain Sachaverell Darwin, a seaman of the old school, was her flag captain and he ran a 'taut' ship. Prince George, who corresponded regularly with Stephenson throughout his naval career, wrote, 'I like old Darwin, but he is a bit tough!'

The Channel Squadron spent most of its time cruising between Gibraltar, Tangier, Vigo and Corunna, carrying out manoeuvres, drills and gunnery exercises. But now as a welcome break from this rather monotonous routine Prince George was to receive his first command.

The occasion was the grand autumn manoeuvres of 1889 when a fleet of more than one hundred British warships, including twenty battleships, assembled at Spithead to be ceremonially inspected by the Emperor Wilhelm II of Germany, who had recently succeeded as Kaiser, the Prince of Wales and members of both Houses of Parliament, and later by the Queen herself. Included in this impressive array of naval might were 38 first-class torpedo boats. All were captained either by young lieutenants or Warrant Officers, and in command of T.B.No.79 was Lieutenant Prince George of Wales.

First introduced in 1876 as a natural corollary to the invention of the torpedo, the early torpedo-boats were small craft of less than 30 tons displacement. As time went on they increased in size, speed and seakeeping qualities, but service in them was always uncomfortable and occasionally hazardous. T.B.79 had been built by Yarrow's at Poplar in 1886. She was of 75 tons displacement, 125 feet long, with a beam of 13 feet and draught of four feet six inches, and could steam at 22½ knots. She carried a crew of 16 officers and men, and was armed with five torpedo tubes. Living quarters were sparse and uncomfortable. in the extreme and there was only one small cabin to be shared by captain and officers.

Although she was of improved design, 'we always felt sorry for 79 in any weather,' said another officer of her flotilla. 'She shipped an unusual amount of water since her torpedo tubes were in her peak.'

The review, which had to be postponed because of a gale, was followed by a mock war exercise scheduled to last 14 days. Ireland – 'a strong maritime power' – was to be the enemy, and the fleet was divided into two individual squadrons. 'A' Squadron, commanded by Rear-Admiral Sir George Tryon, fated to lose his life in the tragic *Victoria/Camperdown* collision in the Mediterranean four years later, was the defending force; and 'B' Squadron, commanded by Admiral Baird, the 'enemy', but with a strength little more than one-third that of the defenders. Headquarters of 'A' Squadron were at Milford Haven, and of 'B' Force at Queenstown and Berehaven. The exercises were bedevilled throughout by the vilest of weather, and many of the ships sustained damage. 8 torpedo boats were attached to 'B' fleet, among them T.B.79.

Before the exercises began Admiral Baird wrote to the Queen's secretary:

Her Majesty is anxious to know how Prince George gets on in the torpedo boat. It is a bit trying for him, or anyone, at first, and I am afraid his first experience was not very encouraging. Coming across to Ireland they met a head wind and nasty sea which shook them all up a good deal, H.R.H. among the number and from what I can hear they were nearly all troubled with mal de mer. I have coupled Prince George with Colin Keppel (son of Admiral Sir Henry Keppel and a great friend of the Royal Family) who has another torpedo boat and they will work in pairs. This will answer very well for they are old friends and Keppel is well up in torpedo boat work. They have just returned from a 24-hour cruise and none of them are the worse. We are expecting hourly that war will be declared and then we become enemies of England – a queer position for a Royal Prince to find himself in. Hoping Her Majesty will not feel anxious concerning him, you may depend on my doing all in my power for his welfare.' But the Queen noted on this letter, 'The Queen cannot help feeling anxious about her dear son, for torpedo boats are dangerous. Remember how many the French lost not five months ago, and Alfred always said he was very anxious about them.*

But in fact the prince was to distinguish himself in command. When 'war' was declared the torpedo boats of 'B' fleet were sent up the west coast of Ireland to make a defended base at Lough Swilly. Press representatives were on board ships of both fleets, and the doings of the royal participant in the exercises were invariably headlined, often embarrassingly giving away the movements of units to both sides.

*From *King George V – A Personal Memoir* by J. Gore.

Soon after 'hostilities' commenced a correspondent telegraphed from Haulbowline Island:

Six of our first-class torpedo boats came in from Berehaven whither they had been despatched yesterday. The little flotilla included the senior officer's vessel, No.80, and Prince George's craft No.79. Soon afterwards Admiral Erskine, the Port Admiral, visited H.R.H., whose boat was at the time engaged in the disagreeable occupation of coaling against the wharf. Prince George had distinguished his boat by expending a little gilt upon her bows, and he appeared on the whole to take considerable pride in his small and not too comfortable craft. But the torpedo boat at sea in half a gale of wind would be found a trying habitat even by the veriest enthusiast, and I dare say that ere the manoeuvres are ended Prince George, like all the other torpedo boat captains, will have had enough of his command.

A few days later another correspondent reported that:

Prince George with T.B.79 and T.B.42 (Lieutenant Keppel) steamed into Greenore harbour and requisitioned water and coal. Prince George and other officers dined at the Greenore hotel. There was great excitement and large crowds visited the boats. Later they left under secret orders.

Then, on August 24th, it was reported from Londonderry that:

T.B.41 was towed into Lough Swilly today by T.B.79 commanded by Prince George. The former broke down while cruising outside, and the night being very stormy she was at the mercy of the waves until picked up by Prince George's boat. She had a narrow escape of being wrecked and her crew suffered terribly.

What had happened was that three of the torpedo boats had been sent to sea on patrol one night with orders to return to harbour at daylight. It was a very rough night, and while returning to harbour one of the three, commanded by a Warrant Officer named Ahearne, broke down and had to anchor close to a lee shore with heavy seas running. No.79 at once went to her assistance, but the tow rope broke. Prince George promptly returned to harbour to pick up a new hawser, then went back again and this time successfully towed his stricken consort out of danger. 'The service,' wrote the captain of the *Inflexible,* under whose orders the vessels were operating, to the Prince of Wales, 'was not unattended by danger and required both nerve and judgment, and would have reflected credit on an officer of far wider experience than H.R.H.'

Prince George's own comment on the affair was, 'It has been a most damnable day — very tired.' Later he wrote to Stephenson, 'I saw the Queen and she was very pleased with what I did in my boat.'

Unfortunately, but perhaps predictably, 'B' Fleet was soundly defeated, and at the end of the exercises the ships dispersed, many of them to enter dockyard hands for badly needed repairs after the battering they had taken from the weather. In addition some of the torpedo boats had suffered fatal casualties, two of them seamen who were suffocated by sulphur fumes from coal when they battened themselves down to keep out the wind and rain. When T.B.79 hauled down her commissioning pennant at Portsmouth her royal captain thanked his crew for the hard work they had done, shook hands with each man and presented him with a picture of himself and a golden sovereign.

After a trip to Berlin with his father to return the Kaiser's State visit, and a small-calibre gunnery course in H.M.S. *Excellent,* Prince George was next appointed as Lieutenant and Commander of H.M.S. *Thrush.* Destined for the North America and West Indies station, the *Thrush* was a brand new first-class composite screw gunboat of 805 tons, built by the Greenock Foundry Company. Barquentine rigged, but carrying 105 tons of coal, her engines could drive her at a top speed of 13 knots under forced draught. She was armed with six 4-inch guns, two 3-pounders and two Nordenfelt machine guns. Her complement was 7 officers and 57 men, who included 2 boys and 9 marines.

Older and more experienced than many commanders, the prince would have been promoted to that rank in Jubilee year, but the Duke of Edinburgh advised against this as he felt that his own reputation had suffered through preferential treatment. Nevertheless Prince George was thrilled with his new appointment, and anxiously consulted Stephenson, now flag captain to the Admiral Superintendent at Chatham, about his choice of officers. They included one lieutenant as executive officer, a navigating sub-Lieutenant, surgeon, engineer and assistant paymaster.

The ship formally commissioned at Chatham on May 6th, 1890, and the prince's father signified his intention of coming down to see her before she sailed. But an unexpected *contretemps* intervened. On May 9th the Prince of Wales wrote to Stephenson:

> I am glad the 17th will suit for us to go to Chatham and inspect *Thrush*. Our son tells us that there is a case of scarlet fever on board, now sent to hospital. The danger is that the disease may spread all over the ship, and it would never do our son going to sea with this disease prevalent. The Princess is very nervous about it, also that he may give it to all of us which would necessitate our being in quarantine for the whole Season! Please consult *Thrush's* doctor and advise what had best be done.*

In the event Prince George's parents decided that the risk of infection was too great, and Stephenson himself saw the gunboat off on her way down to Sheerness. There the Commander-in-Chief, Admiral Thomas Lethbridge, impervious to germs, put the little warship through her paces.

'He made us do every possible thing and I think was pleased,' noted her captain. This was probably just as well, for when the *Thrush* reached Devonport she was ordered to tow Torpedo Boat No.70 to Gibraltar before sailing to join her station.

In those days machinery was still unreliable, and when halfway across the Bay of Biscay the new gunboat ran into trouble. From Gibraltar, dated June 15th, Stephenson received the following account from Prince George.

> I must write you two lines to tell you how the *Thrush* has got on since we left Plymouth. Well, we sailed from there on the 1st towing the T.B., that was Sunday. We went on gaily till

* From *A Royal Correspondence* by Sir F. Stephenson.

Monday night. At 9.30 we were in the middle of the Bay when suddenly without warning our engines brought up all standing. We then discovered that the slide and eccentric rods were both bent nearly double; lucky to say it was a dead calm at the time, and I made the T.B. get up steam and remain by us all night. We were quite helpless. We proceeded at once to put the spare rods in and with the whole engine room staff working all night we were ready in exactly 12 hours when we went on again. It then came on to blow hard from the south-west with a heavy sea and the poor boat was having a very bad time of it, so I decided to go into Ferrol where we arrived the following day at noon. We knocked about a good deal all night and needless to say I was seasick, but this ship is an excellent sea boat and we took very little water in. We stopped at Ferrol two days and had lovely weather there, arriving here on the afternoon of the 9th. We towed the T.B. all the way. The dockyard are making new rods in place of those that were bent and we shall be ready by next Saturday, the 21st and shall probably sail on 22nd.*

Following this somewhat alarming experience the *Thrush* sailed to join her proper station on June 25th. After calling at Las Palmas for coal, she completed the 2,750-mile voyage to Bermuda in 17 days. Her captain endeavoured to eke out his fuel by the use of sail but to no avail. 'Steamed the whole way,' he told Stephenson, 'and had lovely weather with strongish north-east trade and had sail set all the time. But she won't sail a bit.' In fact, despite the 'lovely' weather, the voyage was something of an ordeal, with the gunboat rolling incessantly and the heat in the engine room standing at around 140 degrees.

From Bermuda she went on to Halifax to join the flag of Vice-Admiral George Watson, the Commander-in-Chief, who noted that Prince George 'brought in a happy ship, efficiently manned and commanded.' The station had been much reduced from earlier times, and now comprised only one second-class battleship, the flagship *Bellerophon* herself, four third-class cruisers, two sloops, a gun-vessel and the gunboats *Partridge* and *Thrush*. During the latter's 15 months on the station the squadron visited most of the

* From *A Royal Correspondence* by Sir F. Stephenson.

eastern ports of Canada, and the West Indian islands of St. Lucia, Jamaica, Trinidad, Barbados, and Havana, in Cuba. In between visits there was plenty of sea time, 37 days out of 70 being spent under way. Like Prince William a century earlier, the *Thrush's* royal captain ran his ship efficiently and was always on board for Sunday Divisions even when in harbour.

At home his elder brother was about to become engaged to Princess May of Teck, and Queen Victoria now began to look round for a suitable bride for her sailor grandson. But at 25 Prince George felt himself married to the sea and, since a royal tragedy had hit the world's headlines a few months previously, used this as ammunition in his opposition to the idea of marriage. In 1889 the Archduke Rudolph, heir to the throne of Austria, who had been married off to the Princess Stephanie of Belgium at the age of 22, murdered his mistress and committed suicide at a hunting lodge at Mayerling. This, said Prince George, was an example of the folly of marrying too young. Little did he dream that he himself was destined to wed his brother's fiancée.

On July 13th, 1891, the *Thrush* sailed for England on the completion of her commission. She arrived at Chatham early in August and was duly inspected by the flag captain to the Commander-in-Chief. This was no mere formality.

'Captain Leicester Keppel came on board to inspect us,' recorded Prince George.

> Mustered by the open list, Divisions, General and Fire Quarters, man and arm boats, collision stations, out collision mat, drilled small arms men, made plain sail and furled, mustered bags and hammocks, and inspected books.

These requirements having been met to Captain Keppel's satisfaction, the ship then paid off, and on August 24th the prince was promoted to Commander. Although he did not know it, his active sea career was nearing its end.

That year the Prince of Wales and his family gathered at Sandringham to spent Christmas together. It was a time of special happiness. In November the Prince's fiftieth birthday had been marked by the presentation to him of a handsome gold cigar box by a representative group of actors and managers in recognition of

H.R.H's patronage of the theatre; Prince George had recovered from a sharp attack of typhoid fever and was looking forward to a new naval appointment; and public announcement had been made to a chorus of popular approval of the engagement of Prince Eddy, now the Duke of Clarence, to Princess Mary.

But in the short space of three weeks rejoicing turned to grief. An epidemic of influenza was sweeping Europe, bringing many deaths in its wake. The Duke of Clarence caught the germ and, despite all that the royal doctors could do, he died on January 14th, 1892.

Prince George, who had calculated that the children of his brother's marriage would place him even farther away from the line of succession, now to his dismay found himself in the position of heir presumptive. His whole life was about to undergo a drastic change.

In May he was created Duke of York, given a personal staff and a suïte in St. James's Palace. More to his taste, however, in June 1892, he was appointed acting captain of the second-class screw cruiser *Melampus* to take part in the summer manoeuvres. A steel-protected vessel of 3,400 tons, the *Melampus* had been launched at Barrow in 1890 and this was her first commission. Along with the recently built *Andromache, Tribune, Latona, Thetis, Indefatigable* and *Apollo,* she was a unit of one of the new 'homogeneous' cruiser squadrons.

After commissioning at Portsmouth on June 29th, the *Melampus* spent several weeks working up with the squadron in Lough Swilly, carrying out torpedo and gunnery firings and other exercises, followed by steam tactics in Torbay. The squadron then rejoined the fleet in readiness for the manoeuvres.

The main purpose of these was to discover the best way of coping with torpedo boat attacks and to institute effective counter-measures. The opposing sides were known as the 'Red' and 'Blue' Powers. Blue, the 'enemy', occupied the eastern coast of Ireland; the remainder of the Irish coast and the whole of the western coastline of England, from the Clyde to the Tamar, was 'Red' territory. Each side had its own fleet, that of the Red, or defending Power, being divided into three squadrons under Vice-Admiral Fairfax, the Commander-in-Chief. Red fleet comprised more than 50 warships, including 14 battleships and 16 cruisers, as well as gunboats, coast defence ships manned by Reservists, and torpedo boats. *Melampus* was attached to the Second Division of this fleet. The Blue fleet under Rear-Admiral Henry St. John consisted of six battleships, six cruisers, four torpedo-gunboats and more than a score of torpedo boats, and they were free to attack Red ports and merchant shipping where they could.

As had happened three years previously, the manoeuvres were beset by unseasonably bad weather, particularly in the Irish Sea, as a result of which there were many accidents and mishaps. The cruiser *Andromache* went aground, several ships had engine breakdowns, and the commander of one of the 'enemy' battleships died suddenly thus delaying the opening of 'hostilities' until after his burial. Press representatives sailed with the fleets, and once again the Admiralty and the official umpires complained that their reports gave away secrets to the opposing sides.

The *Melampus* was attached to a 'flying division' scouring ports and harbours for enemy ships, necessitating much sea time with her royal captain frequently seasick. Night after night he was forced to remain on the bridge, and for six days never took his clothes off. Even his enthusiasm for naval life began to wear thin.

In his diary he wrote:

> The flagship made any number of mistakes and we all got anyhow. I hope I shall never be in any other manoeuvres . . . hate the whole thing. I am overtired and feel quite done up.

His temper was not improved by various scurrilous press accounts which had been written about him.

The Times correspondent with the Red Fleet reported that:

> The officers of the *Melampus* from the captain downwards were very annoyed at reports current a few weeks ago that the ship was not really intended to take her full share in the labours and anxieties of the manoeuvres. These have been refuted by the zeal, assiduity and professional devotion of the Duke of York and his officers. *Melampus* has borne her full share, and for nearly a week the Duke never spent a night in bed. Everyone who knows the anxieties and re-

sponsibilities which beset every captain of a man of war in such circumstances will acknowledge that this is no inconsiderable feat of endurance, and I believe that H.R.H. has himself acknowledged that he had begun to feel the strain. He looks much stronger than when the manoeuvres began, and this result has been attained without relaxing in any way the rigid requirements of the Service.

Once again the Red fleet won, the manoeuvres proving the value of mobile defences against torpedo boat attack. The real answer, however, lay in the torpedo-boat destroyer, the first of this new and handy class of vessel making its appearance in the following year. At the end of the manoeuvres when the fleet dispersed the *Melampus* returned to Portsmouth to pay off, and the Duke of York sadly turned his back on the sea to take up the life of a country gentleman. But a complete break had still to come.

On January 2nd, 1893, under special Order in Council he was promoted captain, albeit in excess of establishment. Four months later his engagement to Princess Mary was announced, and in July they were married.

He was still, however, a naval officer on the active list and kingship lay in the distant future. On June 8th, 1898, he was appointed in command of the twin-screw, first-class cruiser *Crescent*. It is possible that he owed this appointment to his old friend Stephenson, who had now become Vice Admiral Commanding the Channel Squadron. Reported the *Naval & Military Gazette:*

> This week the Duke of York resumes his active service afloat by hoisting his pennant on boatd the *Crescent*. He thus returns to sea duty after a lapse of 6 years when as acting captain he commanded the *Melampus* during the manoeuvres of 1892. The Navy will welcome this and the country will be pleased. None has so thoroughly and completely tasted naval life.

Due to a strike in the south Wales coalfields the annual manoeuvres that year had been cancelled, and the *Crescent* was exployed on 'particular service' with twelve other vessels cruising and exercising for several weeks around Ireland and the north of

Scotland. In July she joined the Channel Squadron at Kirkwall in the Orkneys. Eight battleships were present as well as cruisers and a host of small craft, and the highlight of the drills and evolutions in which they were exercised was the landing of all the Marines of the Fleet in full war kit.

Prince Louis of Battenberg, Stephenson's flag captain, was in command of the brigade, assisted by his brother captains, all mounted on horseback.

Following this the *Crescent* was detached to act as guardship for Cowes week, after which she returned to Portsmouth. The Commander-in-Chief, Admiral Sir Michael Culme-Seymour, formally inspected her and reported to the Admiralty, 'Crew good, ship creditable'. The *Crescent* then paid off and the Duke was piped ashore, this time for good.

On January 1st, 1901, he was promoted to rear-admiral supernumerary to establishment; on June 26th, 1903, to vice-admiral, and on March 1st, 1907, to full admiral. Power had been obtained by the Admiralty in May, 1905, under Order in Council to retain the Duke on the active list after becoming liable to retirement for non-service. Thus a way was left open for him to return to sea. But this was not to be, and in August, 1908, he flew his flag for the first and last time on an occasion which made world headlines.

Two years earlier the first of a new type of warship, the battle cruiser *Indomitable,* had been laid down at Messrs Fairfield's yard at Govan. Nearly as heavily armed as Fisher's famous *Dreadnought,* and in fact another of his brainchildren, she displaced 17,250 tons and boasted the then incredible speed for her size of 25 knots. The Duke, now Prince of Wales, had gone to Canada to attend the tercentenary celebrations of the founding of Quebec, and the new battle cruiser went over to bring him back. Despite having to contend with fog and icebergs, she made the 2,880-mile return voyage from Quebec to Cowes in 5 days 18 hours, at times putting on bursts of speed in excess of 26 knots.

Said the *Naval & Military Record* of her feat:

The arrival of the *Indomitable* at Cowes from Quebec marks the completion of the swiftest long distance voyage ever made by a battleship in the history of the world. The achievement of propelling a vessel of nearly 20,000 tons displacement at a speed equal and even superior to that of the *Lusitania* is one of which the whole nation might be proud. The greatest interest has been taken in the trial because the cruiser is also fitted with wireless and maintained communications with Canada or this country throughout the voyage.

Thus the *Indomitable's* record-breaking run was also a triumph for Senator Marconi, the inventor of this new marvel of the age, who declared that this didn't limit the range of wireless! Not only did the battle cruiser fly an admiral's flag throughout the trip, the royal flag officer himself took a turn in her stokehold, tossing in an extra half dozen shovelfuls of coal for luck.

On May 6th, 1910, King Edward died, and next day the new Sovereign, now King George V, became an Admiral of the Fleet. Although no longer able to take an active role at sea, he continued to concern himself closely with naval affairs about which he held decided views, and never forgot that he was titular Lord High Admiral. In 1920 the Admiralty issued revised uniform regulations for naval officers which reduced the width of their sleeve lace from 5/8-in to 1/2-in, without going through the formality of obtaining their Sovereign's covering approval. The King was extremely annoyed and announced that he would not follow the new regulations, instructing his sons to retain their $\frac{5}{8}$-inch lace. Although a few years later the width was increased to nine-sixteenths of an inch he still refused to make any alteration, and even today when in naval uniform the royal Admirals of the Fleet continue to wear $\frac{5}{8}$-inch gold lace on their sleeves!

When Battenberg became First Sea Lord he revived the suggestion of the former Duke of Edinburgh's uniform committee that Admirals of the Fleet should receive a baton like Field Marshals.

But King George declared that as he always carried a telescope he would only find a baton an encumbrance, and anyway he disliked having to carry a baton even when wearing his Field Marshal's uniform.

On the occasion of his Jubilee in 1935 an article in an American magazine recalled that:

King George's entire experience from 12 on had been of the sea. His career was as definitely the Navy as was the career of any braided admiral twice his age. And his retirement was just as galling in itself and infinitely more galling in its circumstances.

He had spent something over 15 years on active service in the Royal Navy, and thoroughly deserved the appellation of 'Sailor King'.

CHAPTER VI

SARDINE

On the evening of June 23rd, 1894, an anxious husband sat in the drawing room of the White Lodge at Richmond trying to read *Pilgrim's Progress*. But his attention kept wandering from the printed page, for upstairs, attended by doctors and nurses, his wife was expecting a baby. At last, at 10 p.m., the lusty cries of a new-born infant broke the tension, and soon afterwards the proud father was informed that his wife had given birth to a son. The news was at once conveyed to Queen Victoria, and Mr. Asquith, the Home Secretary, hastened to inform Parliament that a prince had been born to the Duke and Duchess of Cornwall and York.

In direct line to the throne, the child was christened Edward Albert Christian George Andrew Patrick David, the last four names being those of the patron saints of England, Scotland, Ireland and Wales. Officially he was known as Prince Edward, but at home he was always called David.

The latter half of the nineteenth century was a good time to be born, especially for those in the upper crust of society. Britain was mighty and prosperous, possessing an Empire upon which the sun never set, and a Queen apparently gifted with immortality who was related by marriage or other ties to most of the ruling houses of Europe. Income Tax was 8d in the pound, electricity was replacing gas and oil lighting, the motor car was starting to appear, the gramophone, wireless telegraphy, animated pictures, and flying machines were just around the corner. Conditions for the lower classes were improving, with higher wages and shorter working hours, and holidays by the sea. Beer was 2½d a pint and tobacco equally cheap. The Royal Navy was supreme on the seas and the country secure.

In December of 1895 the Duchess of York gave birth to a

Prince George, Duke of York (later King George V), as a captain on board H.M.S.
Crescent: Torbay, June 1898
From a photograph by J. C. Dinham, Torquay

Prince Albert (left), later King George VI, and the Duke of Cornwall (now Duke of Windsor) as naval cadets

second son, rather to her husband's dismay and disappointment. For not only would he have preferred a girl, but unhappily the date of the birth coincided with the anniversary of the deaths of the Prince Consort in 1861 and Princess Alice in 1878, always an occasion of sorrow to Queen Victoria. But fortunately the Queen did not seem to mind. The latest arrival was duly christened Albert Frederick Arthur George, but his family knew him simply as Bertie.

The father of the two boys early decided that both should enter the Navy as soon as they were old enough, a view concurred in by their grandfather, the Prince of Wales. Meanwhile, once they had passed out of the nursery stage, they were to be taught by a private tutor and their boyhood strictly supervised. He dismissed the question of a public school for the elder on the grounds that contact with other boys would surround him with flattery and sycophancy and give him a wrong idea of values. Simply expressed, the ultimate objective of the scheme of training he had worked out for Prince Edward was the moulding of a State servant on whom would rest the integrity of the Empire.

Accordingly, in 1902, when the youngsters were aged seven and six respectively, the Duke brought along to them a bewhiskered and rather forbidding looking individual whom he introduced as their new tutor. Prior to this they had been in the charge of a governess, to whom they had often proved something of a trial. But from now on things were to be very different.

The new arrival was 39-year old Henry Peter Hansell, a product of Malvern College and Magdalen, Oxford, one-time master at a public school and formerly private tutor to their cousin Prince Arthur of Connaught. Frederick Finch, a stalwart footman, was put in charge of their daily domestic routine, and Sergeant-Major Wright of the Coldstream Guards appointed to teach them drill, including the use of small arms, albeit these were mini-sized models. A methodical time-table was introduced at York Cottage, Sandringham, which was their home, and Hansell fitted out one of the rooms as a schoolroom. This was furnished with standard type desks, hard wooden seats, a blackboard, and the necessary primers and exercise books.

At 7 a.m., daily the princes were hauled from their beds by Finch, and, half an hour later, washed and dressed, they were

K

seated in the schoolroom ready for prep work. Breakfast was at 8.15, and by 9 they were back in school for instruction until lunch time, with a short play break.

In the afternoon they went for a walk, or played games, which included football and cricket with the village boys, almost their only contacts with other human beings outside the Royal circle. They were also taught swimming, squash, riding and shooting. More lessons followed this recreational period until teatime, which was the last meal of the day. Afterwards they had a brief session with their parents, if the latter were not away on official duties, and were then whisked off to bed.

They stood in considerable awe of their father, who ran his home on warship lines, with his study as the captain's cabin. He continually impressed upon his offspring that they must never get the idea that they were different from, or better than, other (well born) people, that they were not to be prigs or snobs, and always to be courteous to others.

'Papa believed in God, the invincibility of the Royal Navy, and the essential rightness of whatever was British,' wrote H.R.H. the Duke of Windsor in *A King's Story*.

Despite his educational qualifications, Hansell was not a very competent teacher nor much of a disciplinarian. The two princes, soon to be joined by a younger brother, Prince Henry, were high-spirited and mischievous, and Hansell often complained about their disobedience. 'But,' said Prince Edward, 'it is no use me being Prince of Wales some day unless I can do what I like.'

Their father knew that mathematics was one of the most important subjects in the naval entry examination, and kept a close eye on their progress in this respect. On one occasion he tested their knowledge by setting them the problem of finding the average weight of stags shot in the previous season from the particulars which were meticulously entered in his game book. The task took the boys a whole day, but they were unable to arrive at an answer which agreed with his. Accordingly the Duke engaged a special mathematics teacher to instruct them in algebra and geometry. Hansell had recommended a preparatory school for his pupils, but his advice was brusquely rejected.

'My brother and I never went to a prep school,' said the Duke; 'the Navy will teach them all they need to know.'

Early in 1907, when David was 12½, he was called before the Naval Interview Board for oral examination as to his fitness for entry into the Service. At this intimidating ordeal he had to face an admiral, a naval captain, a headmaster, and a senior Civil Servant from the office of the First Lord. One of the questions asked him was whether he was afraid of the dark. A few days later he learned that he had been selected to compete in the written examination.

His proud father had been informed by the Board that David was the best boy they had examined and that he had done remarkably well in the test. Two weeks later, after a great deal of hard cramming, David sat the 3-day written examination along with 100 other boys, some of them from overseas.

Only 67 places were available, and the royal candidate prayed devoutly that he would not fail. All was well, however, and after days of nail-biting suspense he was at last called into that fearsome study to be informed by a smiling parent that he had passed, and would shortly be going to the cadet training establishment.

More changes had been made in the entry arrangements for naval cadets as a result of Fisher's reforms in the Navy's educational system. All officers, whether destined for the executive or engineering branches, now underwent a common entrance examination and programme of training before going to sea, in a college which had been built on shore to replace the old warship *Britannia*.

In March, 1902, King Edward had visited Dartmouth to lay the foundation stone of the new establishment, and soon the graceful pile of buildings designed by architect Sir Aston Webb arose on the grassy slopes of the Dart.

But the old ships were still retained for use as instructional classrooms, the name *Britannia* being transferred to the newly built college. But as the revised entry regulations included lowering the age of candidates, additional accommodation was needed in the meantime.

After his mother's death at Osborne House, in the Isle of Wight, which had been her favourite residence but one he had never liked, King Edward ordered the State apartments to be closed, and gave the place to the nation to be used as a convalescent home for officers of the fighting forces. At Fisher's suggestion part of the building was converted into a new college for naval cadets in which they would undergo the first two years of their four-year training period before moving on to Dartmouth for the last two.

Accordingly, in July 1903, a collection of single-storey buildings to provide dormitories, officers' quarters, mess halls, classrooms and engineering workshops, constructed of timber and a hard plaster known as uralite, was hastily erected around the old stables. The new establishment was ready for occupation in little over a month, and the King, accompanied by the Prince of Wales, went down to Cowes to open it. The latter noted in his diary:

> Papa and I went to see the new college for cadets at Osborne, which is quite charming. I should like to be a cadet again and go and live there.

But since by the time he went there the boys could kick holes in the walls, and the structure was steadily deteriorating, this was not an opinion to be shared by his elder son.

In command of the college, whose motto was *Disciplinâ, Fide, Labore,* and responsible for administration, discipline and the teaching of naval history, was Captain Edwin Alexander-Sinclair with a staff of 27 officers. Known as 'Term Officers', these were mostly executive lieutenants in their middle twenties. The educational side of the establishment was presided over by Headmaster Charles Godfrey, who, with a staff of 32 masters, conducted this along tutorial lines. There were twelve dormitories, all named after famous admirals, each of the six 'terms' being allotted two. These 'terms' or classes, were divided into two 'watches', port and starboard, as on shipboard, the juniors joining the port watch and graduating in the passage of time and improvement in ability to the starboard watch.

Individual dormitories were in charge of senior boys known as cadet captains, who were responsible for the cleanliness and discipline of their dormitory and could award punishments to the 'warts' under their charge. The cadets slept in narrow iron cots, with a wooden chest at the foot in which to keep their clothes and personal possessions.

The daily routine was equally as spartan as it had been in the old *Britannia,* with life being made even more difficult at the whim of individual cadet captains. Thus the boys were routed from their beds by these tyrants at 6 a.m., daily in summer and 6.30 in winter, to gabble their prayers, clean their teeth and jump into a cold bath before rushing off to assembly in the large central hall, known simply as 'Nelson', upon an oaken crossbeam of which was spelt out in large brass letters that great sailor's motto, 'There is nothing the Navy cannot do.'

Everything had to be done at the double, and the new cadet soon learned that there was only one right way to do anything – the Navy way.

Wrote a contemporary chronicler, slightly inaccurately, of the life of a naval cadet at that time:

> He dresses at a chest and sleeps in a hammock, getting to know himself and his associates with that deadly stark intimacy that only flourishes in the Navy. There are no excuses in his Service. He must not answer back; he must do as he is told – not immediately but sooner, much sooner. These are the years that weed out those who have mistaken their calling. The incompetents go home and curse the Navy evermore. The virtuous stay on and learn to steal brass boiler tubes from their boats, learn to smoke – secretly in the fighting tops (they are forbidden tobacco till they are 18) fall into and out of all manner of tight places that require dexterity and a cheek of cold drawn brass, pick up more than they learn under the instructor from the talk of Warrant Officers and men and the carefully watched mistakes of their elders – and when they reach commissioned rank impart their lore to their successors with a dirk scabbard.

New batches of cadets – 'frightened 13-year olds', someone had called them – entered Osborne every January, May and September; and in May 1907 the slight, fair-haired and somewhat tearful Cadet Edward of Wales, properly uniformed by Messrs Gieves under the expert eye of his father, set out with this parent in the Admiralty yacht *Enchantress* for Cowes and his new life.

It was the custom for new boys to join Osborne two days before the commencement of a fresh term while the rest of the college was still on leave, in order to give these tyros an opportunity to become acclimatised. David was therefore turned over to Captain Sinclair with the admonition that he was to be shown no favours and, doubtless mindful of his own experiences while undergoing courses at Greenwich and Whale Island, the Prince of Wales also gave instructions that his son was not to leave the college except in the company of an officer or master or his own parents. The new cadet was duly entered in the port watch of Exmouth Term and, after his father had bade him farewell, settled down to await with some apprehension the arrival back from leave of the rest of his college mates.

His fears as to the nature of his reception by them were well founded. Every new entry was normally subjected to a merciless inquisition as to the status in life of his father and the sort of home he had, while at the same time being closely scrutinised for any peculiarities in physical appearance or personal mannerisms which could be seized upon in order that their unfortunate possessor might be dubbed with an appropriate nickname.

As he has ruefully recalled in his autobiography *A King's Story*, Prince Edward's replies to these questions marked him out for special attention; but as the only personal 'defect' which could be fastened on was his slightness of figure, and because his father had now become the Prince of W(h)ales, he was christened 'Sardine'.

Some of the senior cadets took a dislike to the colour of his hair and emptied a bottle of red ink over his head. Being unable to clean the stuff off in time to attend 'Evening Quarters', he decided that it would be politic to duck this assembly rather than be compelled to give away his tormentors, and was duly punished by the award of three days extra drill. This consisted of doubling round the parade ground with a rod held across the back of the shoulders.

On another occasion his head was forced through a classroom window by his fellows, and the sash brought down hard on his neck to remind him of the fate of Charles I! Once when he inadvertently referred to 'my grandfather, the King' in conversation he was promptly beaten for violating the code of honour connected with his presence at Osborne.

It is not to be wondered at that he did not go out of his way to make any special friends, remaining, however, always courteous and outwardly imperturbable. Among his college mates were several budding admirals, and one other youngster destined to achieve a different kind of fame. He was George Archer-Shee, subject of a famous lawsuit against the Admiralty, and later the inspiration of a play by Terence Rattigan.

In 1806 the daily meals for the 'young gentlemen' under training at the Naval College in Portsmouth dockyard consisted of one pint of milk 'straight from the cow' and a half pound loaf for breakfast; roast beef and plum pudding, or roast mutton and fruit pies, for dinner; and for supper tea and as much bread and butter as they could eat. But a century later the food at Osborne was meagre and unappetising. On Saturdays the cadets lined up to receive their shilling a week pocket money, which was promptly spent on fruit, sweets and ice cream at the college canteen. But the money soon ran out and the cadets were hungry again. Although he found the life at Osborne hard and, like his father in the latter's *Britannia* days, had to endure additional hazing because of his royal status, the 'Sardine' never complained and his letters home were always cheerful.

The college curriculum comprised mathematics, physics, electricity and engineering, navigation and seamanship, which included knots and splices, the compass, signals, and boat-pulling and sailing. The 5,600-ton twin-screw, second-class cruiser *Eclipse* was attached to the college to take the cadets on short Channel cruises, and the barque-rigged sloop *Racer* for training them in practical seamanship. On the educational side the cadets were taught French, English composition and literature, geography and general naval history. Each boy had a tutor, but it was his Term Officer who set the standard and moulded the characters of the youngsters in his charge. In addition to gymnastics and general athletics, there were plenty of outdoor sports, which included paper-chases, cross-country running, and, later, the college was presented with a pack of Basset hounds. Team games included Rugby and Association football, cricket and hockey, the cadets being classified according to their proficiency. While not particularly outstanding, Prince Edward took part in all these activities and enjoyed them. The college also put on amateur theatrical shows, such as *A Midsummer Night's Dream*, with cadets acting the part of fairies, and a Christmas pantomime was staged every year. Prince Edward sang treble in the college chapel choir.

Examinations were held at the end of each term and the results posted up on the college notice boards. But in addition each cadet was given a progress report in a sealed envelope to hand to his parents. Since Prince Edward found himself near the bottom of the class, this constituted something of an ordeal for him. The first report, however, brought forth no complaint from his father, but when the second revealed no improvement he was compelled to spent part of his leave swotting up under a special tutor.

When he handed over the third report he was so convinced that it was as bad as the others that he dissolved into tears before even the seal of the envelope had been broken.* Happily, this time his progress had at last begun to move in an upward direction.

The two years at Osborne were divided into six terms, and in Prince Edward's final term his younger brother, Bertie, joined that establishment. But because of the gulf which separated seniors from juniors they were able to spend very little time in each other's company and, as will be seen, the new royal sailor had to endure his own trials and tribulations bereft of all but the moral support of the elder initiate. In May 1909 the 'Sardine' moved on to Dartmouth for the start of the summer term at that establishment.

Although he had to become a 'wart' all over again, he found the change a decided improvement. Dartmouth was, after all, the senior training college and boasted real traditions. Also the cadets there sported the regulation full-length overcoat instead of the short reefer jackets worn at Osborne. The food was better, studies more advanced, and the cadets were given more liberty. They could actually enjoy the company of members of the opposite sex at the Saturday night dances, even if the few females available were mostly the wives and daughters of the staff officers.

A medal had been introduced in 1897 as part of Queen Victoria's Jubilee celebrations, to be awarded to the cadet who, in the opinion of his fellows, was foremost in good conduct and gentlemanly bearing. Today the medal no longer exists, but it has been replaced by various other awards for the best results in leadership and work. The college boasted first-class sports grounds, including tennis courts — even the great W.G. Grace turned up to play cricket there; and there was also the pack of beagles which

* *A King's Story*

had been introduced in 1878 by a former First Lieutenant. Prince Edward became one of the Whips and proved himself to be a good runner. He pulled a useful oar in the college regattas, and appeared as one of the 'First Lord's sisters' in a college production of *H.M.S. Pinafore.*

As at Osborne, everything was required to be done at the run, life being made even more breathless by the sadistic definitions of speed decided on by various individual cadet captains. One evening the captain of Prince Edward's dormitory rang his bell for silence, then announced to his assembled juniors that they were a bunch of lazy good-for-nothings and needed a good shake-up. Accordingly the time allowed for undressing, donning their pyjamas and running down to the bath-house before turning in would be reduced from one minute to thirty seconds, laggards being given a beating.

Since this evolution was well nigh impossible of accomplishment, even by the most fleet, in so short a time, many of the unfortunate cadets attended evening prayers practically naked beneath their outer uniforms.* But no one dared complain, although in a letter to his mother the 'Sardine' obliquely mentioned that 'there is an awful rush here'! Nevertheless, he liked Dartmouth and made a number of friends. But by 1910 the sands of his naval life were already beginning to run out.

Early in May of that year when both the princes, who had been on leave from their respective establishments, were packing their bags in readiness to face the start of a new term, the arrangements for their departure were abruptly cancelled. King Edward, whose health had for some time been giving rise to anxiety, suddenly went down with what at first was publicly announced as a chill, and later bronchitis. His condition rapidly worsened, and shortly before midnight on May 6th he died. From a window in Marlborough House next morning the awed cadets observed that the Royal Standard over Buckingham Palace was flying at half mast. When they told their father about this, he muttered, 'That's all wrong. The King is dead, long live the King', and ordered the Standard to be run up on the flagstaff on the roof of Marlborough House.

The nation was at once plunged into mourning, and the

* *A King's Story*

departure of the two princes was further delayed until after the funeral of their grandfather. It was on that solemn occasion that Prince Edward realised that he, too, would become King in his turn. When he finally returned to Dartmouth his college mates began to address him as Prince Edward instead of 'Sardine'.

In June, 1911, he was told by his father that he was to be created Prince of Wales on his birthday. After that terrifying ordeal when, robed and coroneted and clutching his father's hand, he had been publicly presented at Carnarvon Castle as their prince to the people of Wales, he went back to Dartmouth to complete his final term. But in place of engineering he now had to learn politics, and was accordingly permitted to read all the daily newspapers instead of one specially approved journal.

The 9,800-ton armoured cruisers *Cornwall* and *Cumberland* were attached to the college as seagoing training ships, and the prince had looked forward to joining one or other for the customary cruise with the rest of his term-mates. But this, too, had to be forfeited. Instead he was required to attend on his father at the latter's coronation in Westminister Abbey. On that day, however, he was rated midshipman.

After the ceremonial and festivities were over, the King arranged with the Admiralty for the royal midshipman to join his first seagoing ship. She was H.M.S. *Hindustan,* a coal-burning, twin-screw battleship of the *King Edward* class, later to be known because of their cranky steering as 'the Wobbly Eight'. Completed between 1905 and 1906, and the largest ships to be added to the Navy, they were of 16,350 tons displacement, and were armed with four 12-inch guns mounted in pairs in two fore and aft turrets, four 9.2's and ten 6-inch. 18 000 horsepower engines gave them a speed of 19 knots. The *Hindustan* also enjoyed the distinction of being the first British battleship to be built, engined and armed by a private firm.

Commanded by Captain Henry Campbell, an old friend and former shipmate of King George, she was a unit of the Second Division of the Home Fleet under the flag of Vice-Admiral Sir George Callaghan. At that time the First and Second Divisions of the Home Fleet, whose Commander-in-Chief was Admiral Sir Francis Bridgeman, later to become First Sea Lord, comprised 15 battleships, 10 cruisers and 50 torpedo-boat destroyers.

The prince joined his ship at Cowes in early August as her junior midshipman, and was started off almost on the wrong foot by no less a person than Captain Campbell himself.

When a lieutenant-commander happened to enter the wardroom of the *Hindustan's* he discovered a small midshipman seated in one of the armchairs smoking a cigarette. The officer purpled at such temerity.

'What's your name, and what the deuce are you doing in the wardroom?' he asked furiously.

The midshipman rose shakily, stubbing out his cigarette. 'Wales, sir,' he replied. 'The captain brought me in here. I hope you won't mind frightfully.'

'What, you cheeky young devil,' exclaimed his senior. 'Get out of this before I kick — dammit, I believe you *are* Wales!'

'Sorry, sir,' muttered the blushing prince, 'I believe I am, too — but I can't help it.'

That was the first and last time he would appear in the sacred wardroom uninvited by his seniors, for the gunroom was the proper home for midshipmen, however exalted in status, and it had been impressed upon Captain Campbell that the Royal Sailor was to be given no favours.

Although by no means reaching anything like present-day standards of messing afloat, the gunroom of H.M.S. *Hindustan* was a considerable improvement on those of the past whose cramped and ill-ventilated conditions had had to be endured by former royal sailors.

But the old and traditional customs were still carried on. Thus, whenever the cries 'Fork in the beam', 'Breadcrumbs,' 'Fishbones,' or 'Matchboxes' were uttered by the Mess President, all 'warts', or 'crabs', had to obey with alacrity or suffer a beating, albeit the junior 'crab' was none other than H.R.H. the Prince of Wales, K.G., Duke of Cornwall and Baron Rothesay.

'Fork in the beam' was a term dating back to the days of sailing warships when the members of the midshipmen's berth included men over forty years of age down to youngsters of eleven and twelve. After the grog had circulated in the evening and the talk was becoming neither prudish nor refined, the youngsters had to scuttle out as fast as they could when the mess president reached up and literally stuck a fork into one of the overhead deck beams.

'Breadcrumbs' meant that the junior members were to stop their ears; 'Fishbones' that they must close their eyes: and 'Matchboxes' to shut their mouths. But on the whole the gunroom mess of the *Hindustan* treated their junior member kindly. Although not allowed to smoke or drink until he was 18, he was permitted to partake of a glass of port on guest nights and to smoke while coaling ship.

He was worked hard, being required to learn as much about his job in three months as the average midshipman learned in three years. He ran a picket boat when in harbour on duty trips between ship and shore and ship and ship in all weathers, and served as junior control officer in one of the 12-inch gun turrets. In those days admirals were paid £5 a day, lieutenants between ten and sixteen shillings, and midshipmen one shilling and ninepence. The prince certainly earned his. One of the *Hindustan's* senior officers remarked of him that, 'Throughout the whole period of his training on board he was an extremely hard worker, and struck all those about him, high and low, as what we call a "live wire". It was obvious that he liked the life, and earnestly endeavoured to do credit to himself and to those entrusted with his tuition in various departments.'

During his service in the *Hindustan* the Home Fleet spent its time cruising between Portland and various south coast resorts, Berehaven, in Ireland, and around the north of Scotland, exercising and carrying out evolutions and gunnery practices. Admiral Bridgeman's command had now been increased to four divisions, comprising in all some 135 warships, which included three of the new battle-cruisers.

When it became known that the fleet was to pay a visit to the Clyde, the loyal citizens of Dunoon and Rothesay sought permission to entertain the prince since he was Baron Rothesay. But, unlike William IV, who was required to wear two hats during his service as a junior naval officer, there were to be no special junketings for the Prince of Wales. The civic authorities were therefore informed that it was impossible for the Prince of Wales to make any exceptions while visiting ports in the *Hindustan*.

'His Royal Highness', they were told, 'will on all occasions be considered an officer of the Navy. This means that the Prince will only accept general invitations to officers.'

Then came a fateful day in the late autumn of 1911 when the Home Fleet was at Portland, coaled and ready to sail again, the prince was summoned to Sandringham. There his father broke the news to him that he must give up all idea of a sea career, take educational trips abroad, and finally go up to Oxford.

'You must remember,' the King remarked sadly, 'that I, too, loved the Navy.'

When war broke out in 1914 the Prince joined the Grenadier Guards, but in France he found himself attached to the headquarters staff of the Commander-in-Chief of the British Expeditionary Force and, to his disgust, was not allowed anywhere near the firing line. But he was still a naval officer and, after the war, was promoted to captain, supernumerary to establishment. It was in that rank and travelling in a warship that he began a series of world tours as Britain's ambassador of goodwill extraordinary. On September 1st, 1930, he was stepped up direct to vice-admiral, and to full admiral on January 1st, 1935. In the following January King George V died, and when next day he succeeded his father as Edward VIII the new monarch became an Admiral of the Fleet.

His last appearance afloat, both as Sovereign and naval officer on the active list, took place on November 12th, 1936, when he paid a visit to the Home Fleet at Portland. At a smoking concert held in the hangar of the aircraft-carrier *Courageous* that evening, the sailors were treated to a spectacle that had never been seen before and almost certainly will never be seen again. It was their royal Admiral of the Fleet in full gold-laced mess dress playing the 'bones' in a stokers' mouth-organ band – an impromptu turn which delighted officers and men, and gave them an opportunity to demonstrate vocally the enormous personal affection in which he was held by the Navy. It brought the house down!

As Duke of Windsor he is now the Navy's senior Admiral of the Fleet.

CHAPTER VII

MR. JOHNSTON

Eighteen months after David's departure for Osborne, Bertie himself was called before the Naval Interview Board. The constitution of this body had been enlarged and, in addition to the admiral chairman, his junior naval colleague, and a headmaster, there were also a colonel of Royal Marines and two other civilians to quiz the trembling applicants. The new royal candidate was very shy and diffident, but as his nervousness wore off slightly his answers grew more confident.

The Board, however, were favourably impressed – 'if he had been a costermonger's son we would have passed him' – and a month later Prince Albert took the written examination. He did 'extremely well' in this, obtaining good marks even in mathematics, a subject he had always found maddeningly difficult to master.

Hansell's final report on him to the Prince of Wales stated that:

He has reached a good standard all round, but one must remember that he is at present a scatterbrain and it is perfectly impossible to say how he will fare at Osborne under the influence of all the excitement attendant on the new life. Like his brother he cannot get on without a bit of a shove, and after our experience of Prince Edward's first two terms I do hope that he will not be left too much to himself. At present they must have a certain amount of independent help and encouragement, especially encouragement; a too literal interpretation of the direction that they are to be treated exactly the same as other boys who have had three or four years at a private school must lead to disaster. However, I think that the experience has been bought and that Prince

Albert will profit by it. At the same time he requires a firm hand, but in that respect the excellent discipline of Osborne will be just what he requires. I have always found him a very straight and honourable boy, kind-hearted and generous; he is sure to be popular with other boys.*

And so, in the early summer of 1909, with the injunction to his new instructors that he was to be treated as a cadet and made to realise his responsibilities, Prince Albert, along with seventy other apprehensive youngsters, was enrolled in the Grenville Term at Osborne Naval College.

The hazing to which he was subjected was very similar to that which had been endured by Prince Edward. But as well as being nervous, shy and homesick, Bertie suffered from a stammer, which became aggravated whenever he was called upon to answer questions in class. This speech defect, like his later gastric ailments, may well have been due to mistreatment in his infant days by the royal children's nurse who made no secret of the fact that David was her favourite. The more sadistic of his college mates made this a further excuse for kicking him around. But, like his elder brother, he did not complain. Although timid and diffident and slow to make friends, he remained cheerful and easy-going with no trace of side, and managed to retain a surprising sense of fun and mischief.

The college was now commanded by Captain Arthur Christian, who had taken over from Alexander-Sinclair in July 1908. He proved to be rather less of a disciplinarian than his predecessor, and often took parties of cadets with him on shooting expeditions. The Grenville's Term Officer was Lieutenant William Phipps, a noted athlete, and Prince Albert had for his tutor Mr. James Watt, the Second Master, who, appropriately enough in view of his name, also headed the Science Department.

But although the new royal sailor tried hard, his performance both at studies and games failed to match up to the grit and perseverance with which he tackled them. Because of his more lively personality Prince Edward easily outshone his younger brother, yet a senior staff officer who knew them both remarked that, 'the younger will outstrip the elder.' Another officer,

* From *George VI* by Sir J. Wheeler-Bennett.

commenting on Prince Albert's continual war against ill-health and shyness, testified that 'his courage during this time was amazing.'

Nevertheless, his term reports remained little short of calamitous; he was invariably in the last half-dozen or even nearer the tail end. His masters were disconcerted and his father annoyed. Cadets who aspired to continue on to Dartmouth were required to obtain a minimum aggregate of marks in the final examination or be put back. But as time went on and his last term approached it seemed unlikely that Prince Albert would make the grade. Accordingly his father enjoined him to pull up his socks.

'My dearest Bertie,' he wrote:

> I am sorry to have to say that the last reports from Mr. Watt with regard to your work are not at all satisfactory. He says you don't seem to take your work at all seriously, nor do you appear to be very keen about it. My dear boy, this will not do; if you go on like this you will be at the bottom of your term. You are now 71st and you won't pass your examination and will very probably be warned this time if you don't take care. You know it is Mama's and my great wish that you should go into the Navy and I believe you are anxious to do so, but unless you now put your shoulder to the wheel and really try and do your best to work hard you will have no chance of passing any of your examinations. It will be a great bore, but if I find that you have not worked well at the end of this term I shall have to get a master for you to work with all the holidays and you will have no fun at all. Now remember, everything rests with you, and you are quite intelligent and can do very well if you like. I trust you will take to heart what I have written and that the next report will be a good one.*

Thus exhorted — and threatened — Bertie did indeed put his shoulder to the wheel, but when the next examination results were posted they showed that once again he was practically at the bottom. 'There is,' says his biographer, 'no record of his reception at Sandringham.'

Nevertheless, he duly passed into Dartmouth, although his entry

* From *George VI* by Sir J. Wheeler-Bennett.

in the spring of 1911 had been delayed due to an epidemic of measles, which caught both princes along with many of the other boys. Prince Albert had already been laid low once before with a bad attack of whooping cough while at Osborne. This and other minor ailments brought him in contact with one of the college doctors, Surgeon Lieutenant Greig, who eventually became not only his friend and medical adviser, but in later life as Group Captain Sir Louis Greig, Comptroller of his household when he was created Duke of York.

The captain of Dartmouth was Hugh Evan-Thomas who, as a rear-admiral was later to command the Fifth Battle Squadron attached to Beatty's battle-cruiser force at the battle of Jutland; and the headmaster Cyril Ashford, who had formerly taught at Harrow. Prince Albert's Term Officer was Lieutenant Henry Spencer-Cooper, a navigation specialist, Engineer Lieutenant Start enlarged his knowledge of science and engineering, and his tutor was the Reverend Henry Arkwright.

Besides illness, there were other and more interesting interruptions to the prince's studies at Dartmouth, such as the coronation of his father in June 1911, the investiture of his brother as Prince of Wales, and the Coronation Naval Review at Spithead, at which he was allowed to be present with his parents in the royal yacht.

In May 1912, the King held another naval review, this time at Weymouth, and once again Cadet Prince Albert accompanied his father. Although marred by heavy rain followed by fog, this last was a less ceremonial and more business-like display of naval strength. Under the command of Admiral Sir George Callaghan, six lines of warships were drawn up for inspection by his Majesty, which included 28 battleships and 3 battle-cruisers, eleven heavy cruisers, several flotillas of 33-knot destroyers, and nearly 50 submarines, then an untried weapon of war.

Impressive as this great concourse of warships appeared to the onlookers, Mr. Churchill, the First Lord who, with the Prime Minister Mr. Asquith, and the Second Sea Lord, Admiral Prince Louis of Battenberg, were on board the royal yacht, was at pains to point out that the British Navy was by no means as strong as it should be, and that within the next twenty months no fewer than 65 battleships would be required for his new fleet organisation.

L

For naval rivalry with Germany was hotting up, fanned by the Kaiser's recent declaration at the launch of yet another new warship at Hamburg that the German Navy was being strengthened 'so that no one can dispute with us the place in the sun that is our due.' There could be only one effective disputant.

Another new arm of the sea service made its appearance at this review when two pioneers of naval flying, Lieutenant (later Air Commodore) Samson in a 'hydro-aeroplane', and Lieutenant (afterwards Air Chief Marshal Sir Arthur) Longmore in a mono-plane, flew out to greet the royal yacht on its arrival in Weymouth Bay. The King and Prince Albert, accompanied by the First Lord, also went for a trip in one of the latest 'D' class submarines, which submerged to periscope depth and did a short cruise lasting about twenty minutes, surfacing in thick fog. Only a few months earlier the submarine *A.3,* once honoured by a visit from Queen Alexandra and the Princess Victoria, had been lost with all hands in a collision with her parent ship.

Dinner guests in the royal yacht that evening included, in addition to Churchill and Battenberg, Admirals Jellicoe, Beatty, Sturdee and Cradock — the latter fated to meet his death at the battle of Coronel three years later. When he got back to Dartmouth again the prince for once had the edge over his contemporaries, the most senior of whom had never experienced a more exciting naval occasion than a picnic run to Stokes Bay in an elderly torpedo boat.

Although anxious to work, and good at boat handling and practical seamanship, Prince Albert continued to maintain his lowly position in the term examinations, and was accordingly compelled to sacrifice part of his holiday time at Balmoral in order to receive extra tuition in mathematics and physics. In his final term he was placed 61st out of 67, which brought forth from Captain Evan-Thomas the comment, 'I think he will do.' A quiet and unassuming personality, the royal sailor had gained steadily in popularity.

'He had a tremendous lot of guts,' was said of him, and, 'he never asked for a favour all the time he was at Dartmouth.'

In January 1913 the Grenvilles joined H.M.S. *Cumberland* for the greatly anticipated training cruise. By no means a holiday trip, since the cadets were required to put their theoretical seamanship into practice by running the ship themselves, this lasted for several months, during which the ship visited Teneriffe, St. Lucia, Trinidad, Barbados, Martinique, Dominica, Puerto Rica, Jamaica, Havana, Bermuda and a number of ports in eastern Canada and Newfoundland. Captain Aubrey Smith, another old friend of the King, was in command, and Spencer-Cooper, known as 'Scoops', went along as the prince's 'governor'. Much to his disgust Prince Albert was required to officiate at a number of minor functions in his royal capacity during the cruise, at which he was petrified with nervousness.

One such occasion was the opening of a new wing of the Yacht Club at Kingston, Jamaica. A number of the local girls had managed to get places close to the dais on which the blushing prince had to stand. Their giggles and attempts to touch him caused him the greatest embarrassment and confusion. Thereafter he got a friend to stand in for him so long as no actual speechmaking was called for. He disliked the attentions of the press, and wrote in his diary:

> I was hunted all the time by photographers, and also by the Americans who had no manners at all and tried to take photographs all the time.*

His unofficial stand-in gleefully informed the eager pressmen that the prince was treated the same as the other cadets, ate the same food, slept in a hammock like them, and had to perform the same duties. The only difference was that he wore a bowler hat on Sundays! The *Cumberland* returned home in July, but before the cadets dispersed for summer leave the King went on board to greet his son, thanking Spencer-Cooper for all he had done, and adding, 'I am pleased with my boy.'

Prince Albert was rated midshipman on September 15th, 1913, and early in October was appointed to H.M.S. *Collingwood*. Built in 1910, she was a Dreadnought battleship of 19,250 tons, armed with ten 12-inch and eighteen 4-inch guns, and carried a complement of 724 officers and men. Her 27,000 horsepower engines gave her a top speed of 21 knots, and in her bunkers she stowed 2,700 tons of coal, for oil fuel had yet to come.

* From *George VI* by Sir J. Wheeler-Bennett.

Commanded by Captain James Ley, a former shipmate of King George V in H.M.S. *Canada,* the *Collingwood* was also the flagship of Vice-Admiral Sir Stanley Colville, commanding the First Battle Squadron of the Home Fleet.

Along with seven of his newly promoted term-mates, the royal midshipman, henceforth to be known simply as 'Mr. Johnston', joined his new ship at South Queensferry. Once again the injunction to the prince's commanding officer had been to treat him the same as other midshipmen. In fact, the royal sailor insisted on this in his everyday contacts with his shipmates, and was quick to resent any attempt to wait on him by older ratings 'I am a midshipman,' he would remind them sharply.

Thus he slept in a hammock in the gunroom flat, which was forward in the *Collingwood* class of ship, the lower deck accommodation being aft, and kept his clothes and personal belongings in a wooden sea chest. Daily he and the other fourteen midshipmen were turned out at 6 a.m., and after gulping a mug of cocoa, fell in on the upper deck for physical drill before breakfast. Working hours were spent on routine ship duties, interspersed with periods of school study, seamanship instruction and drills. The prince had been allocated to the Forecastle Division, and his action station was in the control cabinet of 'A' (the foremost) 12-inch gun turret, where he operated a fire control instrument known as a Dumaresq, by means of which – having been provided with such data as speeds and courses of own ship and enemy and rate of opening or closing – a rough read-off of the range could be obtained. He ran a duty boat when the fleet was in harbour, participated in the back-breaking task of coaling ship, and played football for his Division. His divisional officer, said of him:

He always put his back into whatever was going on, rushing through the intense effort of the day and then finishing up with the traditional bread and cheese, onions and beer before turning in. All his work was done cheerfully and well, but perhaps best of all was the way he handled the picket boat when he was in charge of her, while he was more than a good hand at the sailing races.*

* From *George VI* by Sir J. Wheeler-Bennett.

His own messmates testified that, 'he was never one to push himself forward, but he would fight to the last ditch for a pal.'

Towards the end of October the First Battle Squadron left Portland to carry out manoeuvres and exercises in the Mediterranean, during which the ships visited Malta, Alexandria, the Piraeus, Salamis Bay, Naples and Barcelona, arriving back at Devonport on December 29th. In one of his letters home telling of his experiences the prince mentioned that, 'I fell out of my hammock with the help of someone else and hit my left eye on my chest. It swelled up and yesterday it was bandaged up. I did not cut it, but it was very sore all round'.

In his reply the King suggested that he should do the same to the other fellow if he got the chance! Christmas Day was spent at Gibraltar, for much of which it was the unlucky 'Mr. Johnston's' turn to take charge of the duty picket boat, ferrying passengers, ranging from the Marine postman going ashore with the mail to alcoholically overripe libertymen returning from leave.

The year 1914 began with little hint of the shattering events which were to come. There was trouble in Mexico, and gun-running in Ulster. In May the liner *Empress of Ireland* sank after a collision in the St. Lawrence river with great loss of life, and at home the suffragettes, whose militant activities ranged from bomb-throwing to horsewhipping politicians, staged a march on Buckingham Palace.

In June a division of four battleships of the Second Battle Squadron, accompanied by the First Light Cruiser Squadron, went to Kiel at the invitation of the Kaiser for the opening of a yachting week he hoped would outshine Cowes, being joined later by Rear-Admiral Beatty, who with the First Battle-Cruiser Squadron had been visiting Russia and entertaining the Tsar on board his flagship. Other ships of the Home Fleet were dispersed around various British seaside resorts, the *Collingwood* being anchored off Brighton where her midshipmen were having an enjoyable time showing girls from Roedean round the ship.

Then came news of the assassination at Sarajevo, and the overture to the colossal drama of the first world war began. At the review which followed the test mobilisation of the fleet at Spithead, the King visited a number of ships, including the

Collingwood, where Midshipman 'Johnston' duly marched past him at the salute along with the rest of her officers. But father and son had no opportunity to get any closer than that, for all leave was cancelled. On July 29th the fleet sailed for Scapa Flow to take up its war station, and three days later the order went out to mobilise the Naval Reserves.

At midnight on August 4th, 1914, the battleship *Collingwood*, now a unit of the newly titled Grand Fleet and no longer a flagship, lay at anchor in one of the long menacing lines of warships drawn up in the Flow. Among the officers and men who came on duty to stand the middle, or 'graveyard' watch, was Midshipman 'Johnston', who was to record an historic occasion in his journal.

> I got up at 11.45 and kept the middle watch till 4. War was declared between us and Germany at 2 a.m. I turned in again at 4 till 7.15. Sir John Jellicoe took over the command from Sir George Callaghan. After divisions we went to control. I kept the afternoon watch till 4 p.m. Two German trawlers were captured by our destroyers. Papa sent a most interesting telegram to the fleet. I put it down in words. 'At this grave moment in our national history I send to you and through you to the officers and men of the fleets of which you have assumed command the assurance of my confidence that under your direction they will revive and renew the old glories of the Royal Navy and prove once again the sure shield of Britain and of her Empire in her hour of trial.'*

Once again, after nearly 140 years, a son of Britain's reigning monarch was serving with her fleet in war time.

Jellicoe at once put to sea and carried out a massive sweep of northern waters, while elsewhere our blockading squadrons moved to their patrol areas. Advanced elements of the British Expeditionary Force were safely transported to France, covered by the Grand Fleet which sortied almost as far south as Heligoland. Had the High Sea Fleet ventured out of harbour at that time a clash between the two forces would have been inevitable. The Germans began to lay mines in the North Sea, and their U-boats

* From *George VI* by Sir J. Wheeler-Bennett.

left port to begin operations against our warships and merchant-men. Until the inadequate defences of Scapa Flow against submarine attack could be strengthened, Admiral Jellicoe took his ships round to Loch Ewe.

And it was now, to his intense disgust, that Prince Albert fell ill. Appendicitis was diagnosed, and he was transferred first to a hospital ship, then to a shore hospital in Aberdeen. There he was operated on, but for weeks afterwards continued to suffer considerable pain and discomfort. Although he worried the naval medical board to pass him as fit, they merely prolonged his sick leave. In December, however, the board relented to the extent of permitting him to take up a temporary appointment in the Operations Division of the Admiralty. But he chafed at being an armchair sailor and longed to get back to the *Collingwood*. Finally, in February, 1915, he managed to persuade the doctors and the Second Sea Lord to allow him to rejoin his ship.

But life in the Grand Fleet had become monotonous and unexciting. Periodically the ships went out on North Sea sweeps and gunnery exercises, which usually lasted for three days and were followed by ten days in harbour. Once when they were returning from an abortive sortie a prowling U-boat was rammed and sunk by the battleship *Dreadnought*. It was later learned that she was *U.29*, commanded by Otto Weddigen who, in *U.9*, had torpedoed the *Aboukir, Hogue* and *Cressy* in September, 1914. Because of the enemy submarine threat the Admiralty was reluctant to approve of these activities outside the now defended Flow, requiring the fleet to be maintained at the fullest strength and the highest state of readiness.

Although 'Mr. Johnston' was allowed to resume his normal duties as a midshipman, which included keeping night watches, he was far from being fit, and after three months had a relapse and was again transferred to a hospital ship. A careful medical examination revealed that he was still suffering from intestinal trouble which had not cleared up. The most effective treatment, said the doctors, was a quiet regular life and careful dieting.

Passing on their report to the King, Captain Ley added that he doubted whether the prince could ever rejoin his ship. But, knowing what this would mean to his son, his Majesty replied that if the only alternative was invaliding it was better that the prince's

health should suffer rather than that he should experience the
bitterness of disappointment at not being with his ship in battle.

After a lengthy spell of sick leave, during which he again
performed light duties in the Admiralty, and passed his examination for sub-lieutenant, he was promoted to that rank in
September, 1915. Then, in the spring of the following year, he was
allowed to rejoin the *Collingwood.* He had arrived back in time to
take part in the greatest sea clash since Trafalgar.

Towards the end of May 1916, the Admiralty learned of enemy
naval activity which indicated that the German fleet might be
coming out, and alerted Admiral Jellicoe. Accordingly, in the late
afternoon of Tuesday, May 30th, the Grand Fleet made ready to
leave harbour. When the signal to raise steam was received in the
Collingwood, Prince Albert was again a patient in her sick bay. But
this time he was suffering from only a minor stomach upset caused
by eating something that disagreed with him. News that the enemy
might really be coming out acted as a miraculous cure. The prince
promptly leaped from his bed, dressed hurriedly and went to his
action station in the foremost turret.

By midnight the Grand Fleet was at sea, steaming southwards to
rendezvous with the battle-cruiser fleet which had earlier sailed
from Rosyth. In the afternoon of the 31st Beatty's scouting forces
encountered, first, German advance units, then the whole of the
High Sea Fleet. After a brief but hard-hitting exchange of fire, he
turned northwards to lead the unsuspecting enemy on to the
approaching British battle fleet. Action was joined between the
two main forces soon after 6 p.m. H.M.S. *Collingwood* was with
the First Battle Squadron, which was commanded by Vice-
Admiral Sir Cecil Burney in the flagship *Marlborough.*

At one stage the squadron came within nine miles of the leading
enemy ships and was frequently straddled by heavy shells. In an
attack by enemy destroyers more than a score of torpedoes were
fired at the British battleships, one of which struck Burney's
flagship, and another was narrowly avoided by the *Collingwood.*

In his journal Prince Albert afterwards wrote:

I was in A turret and watched most of the action through one
of the trainer's telescopes as we were firing by director when
the turret is trained in the working chamber and not in the

gunhouse. At the commencement I was sitting on the top of A turret and had a very good view of the proceedings. I was up there during a lull when a German ship started firing at us and one salvo straddled us. We at once returned the fire. I was distinctly startled and jumped down the hole in the top of the turret like a shot rabbit. I didn't try the experience again. The ship was in a fine state on the main deck, inches of water sluicing about to prevent fires from getting a hold on the deck. Most of the cabins were also flooded. The hands behaved splendidly, and all of them in the best of spirits as their heart's desire had at last been granted, which was to be in action with the Germans. Some of the turret's crew actually took on bets with one another that we should not fire a shot. A good deal of money must have changed hands I should think by now. My impressions were different to what I expected. I saw visions of the masts going over the side and funnels hurtling through the air etc. In reality none of these things happened and we are still quite sound as before. No one would know to look at the ship that we had been in action. It was certainly a great experience to have been through. When I was on top of the turret I never felt any fear of shells or anything else.*

In fact, although her part in the action was brief, the *Collingwood* got off 84 rounds of 12-inch at the enemy and 35 rounds from her secondary batteries. From his perilous perch on the roof of the turret the prince witnessed the blowing up of the battle-cruiser *Invincible,* flagship of Rear-Admiral Sir Horace Hood, a former captain of Osborne, and the destruction of the armoured cruisers *Defence* and *Warrior.* It was no wonder that he had visions of masts going over the side and funnels hurtling through the air. When he finally left the ship he was presented with the White Ensign which had been worn by the *Collingwood* throughout the battle, of which he was enormously proud.

Although German material losses at Jutland had been lighter than the British, the morale of the High Sea Fleet began to deteriorate and, except for minor sorties later in the year, it did not again emerge to seek another encounter for the rest of the

* From *George VI* by Sir J. Wheeler-Bennett.

war. Thus it was back to Scapa and boredom for the frustrated Grand Fleet. But less than three months after he had written to his father to say that he had really got over his gastric ailments than the prince was again laid low, this time with a duodenal ulcer. A long rest was prescribed, and more months of sick leave followed. Restless and unhappy at having nothing to do, he applied for some form of active duty, and was appointed to the staff of the Commander-in-Chief, Portsmouth.

One day he accompanied the admiral for a trial run in the new fleet submarine *K.3*. The 'K' class were large, steam-driven vessels with retractable funnels, designed to work with the battle fleet. Twenty-eight were originally ordered, but fewer than 20 were actually built. They were unlucky craft, their flush decks giving them a tendency to dive too steeply, and several of them came to grief in one way or another. Since commissioning a few weeks earlier *K.3* had already run into trouble, which included being accidentally fired on by a British patrol craft.

While preparing to carry out a submerged run in Stokes Bay with her distinguished visitors the vessel suddenly dived at a steep angle. Officers and men were thrown from their feet, but the prince and a sub-lieutenant who were aft at the time managed to hang on to a projection. The submarine hit the bottom at 150 feet and remained with her bows firmly stuck in the sea bed and her stern and revolving screws showing above water. Fortunately after twenty minutes the captain managed to shake her free and she surfaced safely. In those days submarine rescue methods were in their infancy, and there was no escape apparatus for the crew. Far from being scared, the prince considered the incident to be a great experience!

He was promoted to lieutenant in June 1916, and twelve months later was appointed to the battleship H.M.S. *Malaya*, Captain the Hon. Algernon Boyle. An oil-burning super-Dreadnought of the *Queen Elizabeth* class, armed with 15-inch guns, the *Malaya* belonged to the Fifth Battle Squadron, and while temporarily attached to Beatty's Battle-Cruiser Force had come under heavy fire at Jutland. She had been built at the charge of the then Federated Malay States, and was thus permitted to fly in battle and on ceremonial occasions the multi-striped silk flag of the Federation. The squadron had rejoined the Grand Fleet after

Jutland, itself now commanded by Admiral Beatty, and it was while she was at Scapa that on the night of July 9th, 1917, the battleship *Vanguard,* anchored only a short distance away, blew up. There were only three survivors of the disaster, one of whom died shortly after being picked up.

Describing the tragedy in a letter to his father, Prince Albert wrote:

> She blew up at 11.15 last Monday. The explosion was not very loud as a certain amount of people did not hear it. I was asleep at the time, having gone to bed early. Most ships sent boats away to the scene of the accident at once to pick up bodies, etc. The sea all around was covered in wreckage and oil fuel. The next morning nothing was to be seen of the ship at all above the water. The north shore of Flotta [an island upon which an 18-hole golf course had been laid out by officers of the Grand Fleet] was covered with wreckage which had been washed ashore and several bodies amongst it. Working parties ashore were hard at work clearing it all away for two days. The *Vanguard* was lying in the billet which we had left only two days before. We had gone to a buoy next to the *Queen Elizabeth* for our regatta. It gave us a great shock at the time, but now things have settled down again normally.*

The cause of the disaster remained a mystery, although there were rumours that a dockyard saboteur was responsible. The court of inquiry decided that the explosion could have been caused by unstable cordite, but they were unable to attribute blame to any person. The fleet moved down to Rosyth soon afterwards, and the prince told his father that, 'Scapa Flow is now in an awful state, it appears, as all the bodies from the *Vanguard* have been coming to the surface. I expect that is the reason why we are here now. This isn't official, but I met somebody who had heard from one of the ships left up there.'

In June the King himself had paid a four-day visit to the fleet in its northern anchorage, staying with Admiral Beatty on board the flagship *Queen Elizabeth.* He inspected a number of ships and

* From *George VI* by Sir J. Wheeler-Bennett.

establishments, which did not include the *Malaya* – although father and son did meet – the golf course, and the arrangements for recreation ashore. On the conclusion of his stay the King sent a signal to Admiral Beatty thanking officers and men for 'their patient endurance'. Although they did not know it, a serious crack had begun to develop in the enemy's morale, and outbursts of insubordination and rioting were taking place in the High Sea Fleet. By the following winter the mutinous crews would steam their ships across the North Sea to surrender.

But 'Mr. Johnston' was not fated to be on the spot when that happened. He became ill yet again, and this time even his seemingly unquenchable spirit sank to its lowest ebb. 'I feel that I am not fit for service at sea even when I recover from this little attack,' he told the King. After another period of hospitalisation, he was finally operated on for the duodenal ulcer, a measure, said the surgeon, which should have been taken much earlier. But he could not go back to sea.

In January 1918, at his own wish and that of the King, who thought that one of his sons should belong to the Navy's new arm, he joined the Royal Naval Air Service, and was appointed to H.M.S. *Daedalus,* a 'stone frigate' located at Cranwell, near Grantham. Little more than a collection of hangars and hutments for the training of naval pilots and air gunners, the station was commanded by a rear-admiral. Here the prince was put in charge of some 2,500 boys. He was made Flight Lieutenant on April 1st, when the R.A.F. was formed, and went up in an aeroplane for the first time.

'It was a curious sensation,' he told his mother, 'and one which takes a lot of getting used to. I would much sooner be on the ground – it feels safer!'*Later, however, after serving in France on the staff of Lord Trenchard and in the Air Ministry, he duly qualified as a pilot.

But he was still a naval officer and wanted to return to sea. Since, however, most of the young men of his generation were going back to civil life, it was felt that this would be incongruous. Instead he went up to Trinity College, Cambridge, with his brother Henry. Although unlikely to be required again for active naval service, he was promoted to commander on December 31st, 1920,

* From *George VI* by Sir J. Wheeler-Bennett.

to captain on June 30th, 1925, rear-admiral on June 3rd, 1932, and vice-admiral on January 1st, 1936. In December of that same year, when he succeeded his brother as King George VI, he, too, became an Admiral of the Fleet.

His commanding officers had said of him that he was at all times 'zealous and hardworking, an agreeable shipmate, and would have made a good senior officer'. Cheated by ill-health of his naval career and, like his father, called by Fate to the throne, that was what he had at all times striven to be.

CHAPTER VIII

FLYING SAILOR

In the early afternoon of August 25th, 1942, a Sunderland flying boat of Coastal Command lifted off the darkly amber waters of Cromarty Firth, turned northwards at the mouth of the estuary, and climbed to 1,500 feet. The aircraft was heavily laden, for in addition to the usual crew of ten, sufficient fuel for a 1,200-mile ocean flight, and a load of depth charges in case a prowling U-boat should be sighted en route, the Sunderland carried four extra passengers, one of them a lean handsome man wearing the uniform of an Air Commodore. His official title was Chief Welfare Officer, R.A.F. Home Command, and he was setting forth on a routine inspection of Air Force establishments in Iceland.

But the Sunderland was fated never to reach its destination. Because of the hilly terrain in the far north of Scotland, the flying boat was ordered to follow the coastline as far as Duncansby Head before setting course north-westwards over the open sea for Iceland. But it was a poor day for flying, and about half an hour after take-off the aircraft flew into heavy cloud. In the hope of obtaining a visual sighting of the coast the pilot began gradually to descend. Tragically, he was unaware that the Sunderland had been steadily drifting inland.

Near the little village of Dunbeath a farmer named Morrison and his son Hugh were working outdoors on their homestead when they heard the roar of aircraft engines almost overhead, but were unable to see the machine in the low overhang. Less than a minute later there came a tremendous crash, to be followed by a deathly silence. The Morrisons at once guessed what had happened. While Hugh got out his motor cycle and sped off to inform the police in Dunbeath and get help, his father organised a search party.

After an hour they came upon the burning wreckage of a crashed aircraft close to a heather-dotted crag known as Eagle's Rock. It was obvious that the Sunderland had flown straight into this hill and exploded. Bodies were strewn all round, and it seemed that everyone on board must have been killed instantly. Not until next day when a trouserless and badly burned airman collapsed outside the door of a small cottage several miles away were the authorities aware that there had been a solitary survivor. He was Flight Sergeant Andrew Jack, rear gunner of the crashed Sunderland, who had been thrown clear when the tail assembly broke off at the moment of impact.

But by then the identity of the dead Air Commodore was known, and his charred body had been conveyed to Dunrobin Castle before being taken south to Windsor for burial in St. George's Chapel. He was Rear-Admiral H.R.H. the Duke of Kent, another royal sailor, first to have flown the Atlantic and the first to die in an air disaster.

Prince George Edward Alexander Edmund, fourth son of King George V, was born on December 20th, 1902, at York Cottage, Sandringham. By the time he was out of the nursery stage the little school conducted by Mr. Hansell had closed down, and the prince and his brother Henry were packed off to St. Peter's Court, Broadstairs, a fashionable preparatory school. He, too, was intended for the Navy, and accordingly when he reached the age of 14 he took the qualifying examination and was duly entered in the R.N. College Osborne, in the Starboard Watch of Hawke Term.

The first world war was now in progress, and command of the college was held by Captain E.S.H. Boyle, a retired officer, with a number of over-age lieutenants as Term Officers. But Mr. Watt was still the Second Master, and in turn he became the tutor of another prince. The new royal cadet's experiences followed the now familiar pattern, and his performance at his studies were equally unimpressive; in one term examination he came 76th out of a class of 92.

He managed to improve on this as time went on, but only fractionally, passing out from Dartmouth in May 1920, almost at the bottom of his class. Thus, as Prince Albert remarked when he heard, 'he has kept up the best traditions of the family!' But he was a cheerful and amusing young man, popular with his classmates, fond of sport, and no mean pianist.

By now the war had ended, and training cruises for senior cadets had been reinstituted. They were now required to spend eight months at sea in H.M.S. *Temeraire,* an old Dreadnought battleship of 18,600 tons, completed in 1909. Armed with ten 12-inch guns and sixteen 4-inch, and consuming a mixture of solidified oil fuel and coal to drive her engines, she carried some 2,600 tons of the latter commodity in her bunkers.

Considered to be ideally suitable as a seagoing training ship for the new post-war breed of 'young gentlemen', she possessed an added interest for them in the fact that as a unit of the Fourth Battle Squadron of the Grand Fleet she had taken part in the battle of Jutland. The 1920 cruise took the cadets first to Bergen and Oslo, in Norway, and subsequently farther afield to Vigo, Gibraltar, Algiers, Malta, Palma and Lisbon, before returning to Portsmouth in December to pack them off on Christmas leave preparatory to joining the various ships of the fleet to which the Admiralty might direct them.

On January 15th, 1921, the prince was rated midshipman, and in company with 16 other newly promoted 'warts' appointed to H.M.S. *Iron Duke,* flagship of Admiral Sir John de Robeck, in command of the Mediterranean Fleet. In August of the following year, when the admiral was switched to command of the Atlantic Fleet, Prince George was transferred to the new flagship *Queen Elizabeth* as her senior midshipman.

At that time the Atlantic Fleet was still the Navy's largest seagoing command, with nine battleships and two battle-cruisers, two cruiser squadrons, an aircraft-carrier, seven flotillas of destroyers and two flotillas of submarines. But the Washington Disarmament Conference had been held in February and retrench-ment was in the air, for not only were ships to be scrapped but naval personnel drastically reduced. Thus when action was taken on the Geddes Committee's report a few weeks later, hundreds of whole-time professional naval officers found themselves stranded high and dry 'on the beach'.

During his period of service as midshipman in the *Queen Elizabeth* Prince George was loaned to the destroyer *Mackay* to undergo the necessary spell of small ship training, but towards the end of the year he fell ill and had to be operated on for

King George VI

From the painting by Denis Fildes

Prince George, Duke of Kent, brother of King George VI, as a lieutenant, R.N.

appendicitis. The operation left him unusually weak and he had to take several months of sick leave, at the conclusion of which he was able to undergo the usual technical courses at Portsmouth and Greenwich for sub-lieutenant, being promoted to that rank in February 1924.

In January of the following year he was appointed to H.M.S. *Hawkins,* flagship of Vice-Admiral Sir Allan Everett, commanding the China Squadron. Soon afterwards Everett was relieved by Admiral Sir Edwyn Alexander-Sinclair, who had captained Osborne College during Prince Edward's stay there as a cadet.

At that time the China Squadron comprised five cruisers: the *Hawkins* herself, of 9,750 tons, armed with seven 7.5-inch guns; *Carlisle, Diomede, Despatch* and *Durban*, all under 5,000 tons, armed with 6-inch guns, and built as part of the emergency war programme; four sloops, and 12 submarines. Patrolling the Yangtse and West Rivers were 18 shallow-draught gunboats. The station was a busy and interesting one, and there were many tricky diplomatic and other problems cropping up to keep the Navy occupied, for China was in a state of flux. For more than a decade after the death of President Yuan Sheh Kai there had been no authoritative central government in the country. The provincial governors who had seized power in the north wished for the return of the deposed Emperor; but the Nationalists in the south, originally headed by Sun Yat Sen, desired to establish a Chinese Republic and to expel all foreigners from the country.

Although bedevilled by the depredations of troops of the warring factions and by bandits and pirates, foreign trade continued to function under the protection of the Royal Navy. Dubbed 'running dogs of the Imperialists', the imperturbable sailors nevertheless paid scrupulous regard to the susceptibilities of the Chinese in their difficult and delicate task. In 1925 Sun Yat Sen died and his mantle descended upon Chiang Kai Shek, who began to lead a crusade against the divided northern war lords.

The British cruisers were able to navigate as far up the Yangtse river as Hankow, where they could defend the British Concession against attack and lend support, if required to the gunboats of the Yangtse Flotilla. A good deal of their time, however, was spent lying in the muddy Whangpoo acting as guardship off Shanghai, then a teeming international *entrepot,* alternating this duty with

M

recreational spells at Wei-hai-wei, where the annual regatta was held, or occasional cruises as far afield as Hong Kong, and Penang and Port Swettenham, in Malaya.

The gunboat base was at Hankow, but the rear-admiral commanding the Yangtse Flotilla flew his flag in the 600-ton gunboat *Bee,* and was thus able to move about the river from Shanghai to Ichang, some 900 miles up country, in order to oversee his 'parish'. Piracy and banditry were rife along the whole length of the river, and in addition to these hazards there was always the likelihood of the gunboats being fired upon without warning by troops of the various war lords, or being required to land their men in the defence of foreign concessions against howling mobs. Prince George was lent for several months to H.M.S. *Bee,* and was thus able to experience at first hand this uniquely adventurous side of the Navy's work, reminiscent of Victorian times, in which the youthful gunboat captains could be called upon to cope at the drop of a hat with battle, murder and sudden death.

A typical example of the imbroglios in which the Navy became involved during the prince's service in China was the 'Wanhsien Incident' which occurred in 1926. An intransigent Chinese general forcibly detained some British merchant ships at the riverside town of Wahnsien, several hundred miles above Ichang. Two British gunboats went to their rescue, but were themselves cut off and threatened with a full scale attack by Chinese troops and shore batteries. All attempts at diplomatic intervention having failed, the Commander-in-Chief approved of the mounting of a cutting-out expedition to get the vessels away by despatching an armed river steamer filled with officers and men from the cruisers at Hankow. Prince George was one of those who volunteered to take part in the expedition, but, not unnaturally, permission was refused and he had to remain in the flagship. Watched with tense anxiety from the operations room of H.M.S. *Hawkins,* this Nelsonic manoeuvre unfortunately failed of its purpose. Because of the excellence of the Chinese grapevine, information regarding the Navy's preparations for the rescue attempt reached Wahnsien and surprise was lost.

In a short sharp action with the entrenched Chinese forces, a score of naval officers and men were killed and wounded, but the gunboats were able to make their getaway. The merchantmen were later released by more peaceful means, but to add insult to injury the Chinese formally complained to the League of Nations about British brutality!

A popular and competent officer, and at his own wish rarely called upon to officiate at functions ashore wearing his other hat, Prince George was in due course promoted to lieutenant in February 1926, and at the end of his period of service on the station returned home to undergo four months' study in France in order to qualify as an official interpreter in French, which would thus add a few shillings to his daily rate of pay of 13/6d.

In October of the following year he was appointed in that capacity on the staff of Vice-Admiral Sir Hubert Brand, now commanding the Atlantic Fleet in the battleship *Nelson*. Together with her sister ship, *Rodney,* these were the only two modern capital ships in the Atlantic Fleet. Their four consorts were of the ageing *Iron Duke* class, now nearing the end of their useful lives. To back up this 'battle squadron' there were but four cruisers, two flotillas of destroyers and no submarines at all. Routine exercises were restricted and gunnery firings limited because of stringent economies which were imposed upon naval expenditure.

But the prince, never a very robust individual, was now compelled to take several spells of sick leave, which boded ill for his continuance in the Service. In 1927 he accompanied the Prince of Wales on an official visit to Canada, and in July of the following year was appointed to the cruiser *Durban,* now home from China in readiness to be switched to the America and West Indies station. Based on Bermuda, the warships stationed in these historic waters in which all the other royal sailors had served in the past, had dwindled to a mere handful of cruisers and two sloops.

Apart from brief routine exercises, they spent most of their time in carrying out show-the-flag cruises, which, however, made a useful contribution to Britain's image in the western hemisphere. Thus when the *Durban* arrived on the station, with her royal sailor junior of the three lieutenants in her complement, she found herself scheduled to set forth on an extensive tour of South American ports. The cruise lasted for several months, during which she visited Montevideo, Buenos Aires, Callao and Valparaiso, at all of which the prince, like William IV before him, was required to officiate at exhausting functions in a dual capacity.

It became increasingly apparent that, much as he would have liked to continue serving in the Navy, shipboard life did not suit the prince's constitution, and when he returned to this country early in 1929 his father decided that he should be withdrawn from active service. Altogether he had served for nearly ten years.

He was promoted to commander in February 1934, and to captain on January 1st, 1937. On June 8th, 1939, he was made rear-admiral, and when war broke out three months later, appointed in that rank as Staff Officer (Intelligence) to the Commander-in-Chief, Rosyth. Only too well aware, however, that he would be unable to take a more active part in the naval war, he turned over to the Royal Air Force in 1940 in the rank of Group Captain. Since he had also been made Air Vice-Marshal in June 1939, he could have assumed that more exalted status, but preferred to serve in the junior grade, and earned promotion in due course to Air Commodore. His work as supervisor of welfare on the staff of the Inspector General of the Royal Air Force took him to air stations up and down the country, and in 1941 he flew the Atlantic to inspect Air Force establishments in Canada and the United States. Then came that fatal crash in 1942.

Today a Celtic cross on a lonely hill-top in the far north of the Scottish Highlands marks the site where the royal sailor met his death in an element which, from the early days of heavier-than-air flight, the Navy had adopted and made its own.

CHAPTER IX

SUPREMO

The year 1922 was a fairly eventful one, both in Britain and abroad, but not all the happenings which occurred could be said to qualify for history's description of that fevered post-war era as 'the Gay Twenties'. The first International Disarmament Conference was held in Washington, and there was wrangling in the debate over the annual Naval Estimates in Britain's Parliament as to whether the money should be spent on battleships or aeroplanes.

Fighting had broken out in the Near East between Greece and Turkey, and in Italy a young patriot named Benito Mussolini led his blackshirted followers in a march on Rome. Grave trouble again erupted in Ireland, which overflowed into a shocked London when Field Marshal Sir Henry Wilson was assassinated on the steps of his own house by two Sinn Feiners. Marie Lloyd died at the early age of 52, and the P & O liner *Egypt* sank after a collision off Ushant, taking with her to the bottom more than £1 million in gold bullion. Pogo sticks became all the rage in Britain, and entertainment for the million was born with the advent of sound broadcasting.

In February the Princess Royal was married to the Earl of Harewood, but undoubtedly the wedding of the year took place five months later at St. Margaret's, Westminister. It was a truly glittering occasion. King George V and Queen Mary were present with other European royalty, and the Prince of Wales was best man. The happy couple were Lieutenant Lord Louis Mountbatten, R.N., son of the late Marquess of Milford Haven, and the beautiful Edwina Ashley, daughter of Lord Mount Temple and granddaughter of millionaire Sir Ernest Cassel.

Eight years earlier the bridegroom, then a small and woebegone 'wart' of 14 at Osborne Naval College, had stood by himself choking back tears as he strove to digest the stunning and almost unbelievable news that his dashing and beloved father had resigned the post of First Sea Lord — some even said that he had been forced to take this step. It was then that the young cadet vowed to himself that he, too, would some day hold the highest professional post in the Royal Navy despite the accident of his royal birth.

His Serene Highness Prince Louis Francis Albert Victor Nicholas of Battenberg, second son of Admiral Prince Louis of Battenberg, was born on June 25th, 1900, at Frogmore House, Windsor, and distinguished himself at his christening a month later by swiping the spectacles from the nose of his august great-grandmother, Queen Victoria, as she bent over him. Although the name Richard was not one of those bestowed upon him at that ceremony, he was always to be known to his friends and intimates as 'Dickie'.

Since his father was a distinguished naval officer there was no doubt that his career, too, would be in the Royal Navy. As a small boy he led a somewhat irregular home life due to the travels of his parents occasioned by the exigencies of the naval service and visits to royal relatives. At an early age he was taken to Malta by his mother, where his father was flying his vice-admiral's flag in the battleship *Venerable* as second in command of the Mediterranean Fleet.

But when he reached the age of 10 these wanderings ceased, and he was sent to Locker's Park preparatory school to be groomed for the Navy. Three years later, having passed the necessary qualifying examination with flying colours, he was entered at Osborne in the Starboard Watch of Exmouth Term.

But before his first two years of training at this establishment were up the world was at war. Until that unhappy day in 1914 when he learned of his father's resignation, young Louis had taken life fairly easily and was not particularly outstanding either at studies or games. But by the end of his final term at Osborne his new-found resolution had begun to show results, and his passing-out position was better than it might have been.

When he moved on to Dartmouth his sights were set considerably higher. Because of wartime conditions the training period had been shortened, so that instead of rounding off their naval education with the usual eight months training cruise, senior cadets were now sent direct to the fleet. Indeed, some had already lost their lives in the sinking of the cruisers *Aboukir, Hogue* and *Cressy.*

In place of the normal parochial details of college doings which formerly filled the pages of the *Britannia* magazine, that journal was now largely given over to stories by former cadets of exciting actions at sea in which they had taken part. But among the few domestic jottings for which space could be found it was recorded that Cadet Battenberg of Exmouth Term played the drums in the college band, and wielded the sabre in the annual skill-at-arms tournament. He was now working hard at his studies, became in due course a popular cadet captain, and in 1916 finally passed out a creditable eighteenth in a class of 80. On July 15th he was rated midshipman, and soon afterwards, along with other newly fledged 'crabs', was appointed to H.M.S. *Lion,* flagship of Admiral Beatty's Battle Cruiser Squadron.

But after Jutland the remainder of the war at sea entailed mere outpost actions away from home waters. The main British and German fleets became almost hemmed in by growing barriers and counter-barriers of mines, while the necessity of combating the deadly menace of the U-boat deprived the Grand Fleet of increasing numbers of its screening light craft, without which it could not put to sea.

In November 1916 Admiral Jellicoe became First Sea Lord, and Beatty replaced him in command of the Grand Fleet, transferring his flag to the battleship *Queen Elizabeth.* In February 1917, Midshipman Battenberg was himself appointed to the fleet flagship. Five months later, when King George V changed the family name from Guelph to Windsor, the head of the Battenberg clan in England, now living practically in retirement on the Isle of Wight, followed suit by switching their name to the Anglicised Mountbatten. 'Dickie' thus lost his princely title and became simply Lord Louis Mountbatten — but he was still a royal sailor.

Beatty now moved the Grand Fleet down from Scapa Flow to Rosyth where, as 'a fleet in being', it continued to pose a powerful and ever watchful surface threat to German naval aspirations. The enemy, however, was now pinning his hopes on the success of an all-out U-boat campaign, which had the effect, in April 1917, of bringing America into the war.

Enduring the busy tedium of life in the battlefleet, Mountbatten concentrated on the business of learning his job, and towards the end of the year was lent to the submarine *K.6* to undergo the customary spell of small ship training. As already mentioned, the 'K' class, of which 14 were serving with the Grand Fleet, were 2,000-ton turbine-driven submarines, capable of high surface speeds to enable them to keep up with the battlefleet.

Shortly after Mountbatten joined *K.6*, nine of them became involved in a disastrous series of collisons, an affair which was afterwards sardonically referred to by the sailors as 'the battle of May Island'.

It happened on the evening of February 1st, 1918, when the Grand Fleet sailed from Rosyth for exercises in the North Sea. Proceeding slightly ahead of the surface ships, four submarines of the 12th Flotilla, to which *K.6* belonged, and five from the 13th Flotilla, were steaming along in two parallel lines. Off May Island, in the Firth of Forth, they unexpectedly encountered a number of local minesweepers returning to base, whose commanding officers had not been informed of the fleet's movements. In order to avoid running into the minesweepers the submarines were forced to make emergency alterations of course, and in the darkness and confusion they began ramming one another. Unaware of what was happening ahead of them, the approaching surface units ploughed at high speed through the centre of the melee. At least five of the submarines were in collision, either with each other or with larger vessels, and it was miraculous that only two were actually sunk. One of these had been rammed by *K.6*, which was herself near-missed by *K.7*.

A few months after Mountbatten had returned to the gunroom of the *Queen Elizabeth* from his experiences as an honorary member of 'the Trade', as service in submarines was known, he was promoted to sub-lieutenant and appointed to be second in command of the patrol vessel *P.31*.

The 'P-boats' were small fast ships which had been specially built for submarine hunting. Displacing some 600 tons, they were fitted with depth charge throwers in addition to conventional guns and torpedoes. Shallow draught vessels, they had low upperworks to reduce their outline, and a specially strengthened steel stem for ramming U-boats. They could steam at 20 knots, and were able to turn almost in their own length. More than 40 were built for the purpose of relieving the hard-pressed destroyers of patrol and escort work.

When Dickie joined *P.31* at Portsmouth she was engaged on troopship escort duties and continued on this chore to the end of the war, which by then had barely three months to run. After the end of hostilities *P.31* and half a dozen of her sisters were formed into an anti-submarine training flotilla at Portland, instructing officers and men in the techniques of the new submarine detecting device known then as Asdic and today as Sonar, and Dickie remained as her First Lieutenant until August 1919. In the period of retrenchment and reorganisation which followed the signing of the peace treaties a large number of ships were paid off, which meant that many young naval officers found themselves temporarily unemployed.

The Admiralty therefore decided to give these young men the opportunity to undergo a short university course. Dickie was one of those selected, and he duly attended Christ's College, Cambridge, for two terms, creating a precedent while there by becoming the first naval officer to·lead the Union debate against Oxford.

In 1919 the Prince of Wales had started out on the first of his series of Empire tours, travelling to Canada in the battle cruiser *Renown*. In the following year he was scheduled to make an extensive tour of Australasia, visiting some of the West Indian islands en route and continuing on through the Panama Canal to the Pacific, and invited Mountbatten to accompany him. In 1921 the prince set out on a third official tour, this time of India, and again Mountbatten, now promoted to lieutenant, went with him as his aide-de-camp.

Thus once more history repeated itself, for as a young sub-lieutenant Prince Louis of Battenberg had also toured India with a former Prince of Wales. Another interesting echo of the past lay in the fact that Captain Meade who commanded the *Renown* was a son of Lord Clanwilliam, who had commanded the Flying Squadron to which the *Bacchante* with Prince George and Prince Albert on board had been attached for their world cruise in 1880. It was after his return to England from the Indian tour that Dickie married the girl whom he had first met at a ball twelve months previously, and then went off with her to enjoy an extended period of leave.

But although some of his detractors dubbed him a playboy because of his fast cars and racing motor-boat, his professional career was in fact all-important to him, and he had planned his way of life with mathematical precision. After serving for a spell as a 'salt horse' lieutenant in the battleship *Revenge,* flagship of the Second Division of the Atlantic Fleet, he decided to specialise in Communications, a rapidly developing science in the dawning age of electronics, and in 1924 underwent a long course at the Signal School in Portsmouth. Passing out top of the class, he continued on to the R.N. College, Greenwich, to take an advanced course in wireless telegraphy.

In April, 1926, as a fully fledged specialist, he became Flag Lieutenant to the Vice-Admiral Commanding the Reserve Fleet, at that time totalling more than 150 ships of all classes. Twelve months later he was promoted to lieutenant-commander and appointed to the Mediterranean Fleet flagship as Assistant Fleet Wireless Officer on the staff of the Commander-in-Chief. In March of the following year he was transferred to the destroyer leader *Stuart,* with his own 'parish' as Staff Signals Officer to the Captain (D) Second Destroyer Flotilla.

In 1928 the Mediterranean Fleet, under the command of Admiral Sir Roger Keyes, wartime hero of Zeebrugge, was once more Britain's largest, comprising six battleships, two cruiser squadrons, the aircraft-carrier *Eagle,* four flotillas of destroyers, two sloops for Red Sea patrol duty, and a flotilla of submarines, which included the 3,000-ton *X.1,* up to then the largest submarine ever built. Keyes had introduced a station routine which was not disimilar, except for ships and weapons, from that which had been operated towards the close of the 19th century, but on nothing like the lavish scale of those days. For one important result of the efforts of the League of Nations to outlaw war had been to bring about a general reduction in armaments, which progressively limited in size the navies of the principal maritime powers.

Because of Britain's post-war economic difficulties, even more severe cuts had had to be made in her Naval Estimates, and ammunition expenditure and fuel consumption were limited in the fleet. Nevertheless, by extracting the maximum training value from available resources, efficiency was maintained, technical advances made in ships and weapons, night fighting methods improved, and anti-aircraft defences developed.

The Mediterranean Fleet programmes followed an established pattern. In the spring the ships exercised at combined manoeuvres with the Atlantic Fleet, after which they dispersed to make a round of visits to French, Italian, Adriatic and Greek ports which lasted for most of the summer months. Whenever the ships returned to Malta from these seagoing excursions, officers and men could indulge themselves in their off-duty time in such pursuits as polo and racing on the Marsa, football and cricket on the sports grounds at Corradino, Tombola, dances, opera-going and amateur dramatics in the evenings, and picnic parties at the week ends. Admiral Keyes was a keen polo player and kept his own string of ponies on the island. Although an indifferent performer at first, Mountbatten set himself to improve, even wrote a beginner's guide to the game, and eventually captained the Commander-in-Chief's side, known as the 'Centurions'.

In April 1928 the even tenor of life in the Mediterranean Fleet was rudely disturbed when the *Royal Oak* affair suddenly hit the headlines. Flagship of Rear-Admiral Bernard Collard, commanding the First Battle Squadron, the *Royal Oak's* captain and commander laid an official complaint against their admiral just as the fleet was about to sail from Malta for its scheduled exercises with the Atlantic Fleet.

These important manoeuvres had to be cancelled so that an investigation could be held, and this was followed by the formal court-martialling of both complainants on charges of contravening regulations. Amid the unwelcome glare of world press attention, the Navy's dirty linen was publicly washed. Captain Legge, Mountbatten's commanding officer, was one of those called to sit in judgment on the *Royal Oak's* commander in the first of the courts-martial, which were held at Gibraltar.

The affair had repercussions beyond the comparatively light sentences passed upon the two officers at the storm centre, for Admiral Collard was compulsorily retired soon afterwards, and because he was considered to have mishandled the situation Admiral Keyes subsequently failed to achieve elevation to the post of First Sea Lord, to which he had been led to believe that he would be translated. Years later Mountbatten himself would be appointed to supersede Keyes in an important post, much to the latter's loudly proclaimed dissatisfaction.

In 1929 Mountbatten returned home to take on the job of Chief Wireless Instructor at the Portsmouth Signal School, and after two years in the post received a fresh appointment to the Mediterranean, this time as Fleet Wireless Officer on the staff of the Commander-in-Chief, now Admiral Sir Ernle Chatfield, Beatty's former flag captain. Among the innovations the new staff officer introduced was a Combined Communications Centre ashore in Malta, and improved methods of wireless communication and coding in the fleet.

Although, like his father, Mountbatten had his sourer critics who ascribed his success mainly to influence because of his royal birth, there was no doubt as to Dickie's powers of intellect, imagination and ingenuity. Experts in his own specialist field, both officers and men, considered him an exceptional wireless officer, and he was the author of two handbooks on the subject. He worked hard and played hard, and in his spare time invented a number of time-saving gadgets, which ranged from zip-fronted trousers to a navigational distance corrector.

He had always been interested in films and filming, and, while on holiday in the United States, had visited Hollywood, met many of the top movie stars, and actually appeared in a short film with Charlie Chaplin. As a result of his efforts and his pull with the moguls of the film industry the Royal Naval Film Corporation came into being, through the agency of which the latest films are made available for showing in the fleet at comparatively low cost.

In 1930 another disarmament conference was held, at which Britain agreed not to replace any of her ageing capital ships, and to reduce still further her battleship strength in return for permission to build a number of large cruisers.

But scarcely had the ink had time to dry on the London Naval Agreement than a new era of aggression began. Japan attacked China and annexed Manchuria, and when disapproval of her action was expressed at Geneva, the Japanese delegates walked out of the League of Nations, never to return.

The spell-binding oratory of an Austrian ex-corporal named

Adolf Hitler was attracting a large following in Germany, which country had now begun to build warships of a new type, ingeniously designed to circumvent treaty limitations, known as 'pocket battleships'; there was revolution in Spain, and Mussolini's air force was bombing Arabs in Libya. Its authority continually flouted, the League of Nations gradually became a dead letter, and in view of the worsening world situation Britain began at last to modernise her fleet, and finally to re-arm in earnest.

The Navy had become short of most classes of warships, and especially destroyers and escort vessels. New and larger destroyers were accordingly put in hand to replace the famous 'V' and 'W' classes which had rendered yeoman service from 1917 onwards, and were in fact to continue to do so well into the second world war. Among the new destroyers coming into commission were the 'D' class, launched in 1932. Displacing 1,375-tons, they were armed with four 4.7-inch guns and eight torpedo tubes, and could steam at more than 35 knots.

In April, 1934, Mountbatten, now promoted to commander, was appointed to H.M.S. *Daring* which, with her eight sister ships, were intended to replace the earlier 'V' and 'W' boats comprising the First Destroyer Flotilla of the Mediterranean Fleet.

Just as his father had done in his day, Dickie set to work to make his new command the crack ship of the fleet. But after only a few months on the station, he and his fellow captains were forced to give up their smart new vessels. The 'D' class destroyers were first ordered home to undergo a special refit to make them habitable for service in tropic waters, then sailed for Singapore to be turned over to the China Station in exchange for a number of old 'V' and 'W' boats which were due for replacement.

Mountbatten now found himself in command of H.M.S. *Wishart,* a slower and more lightly armed vessel and a distinct come-down from the larger and more powerful *Daring*. But Dickie still had his same crew, and under his inspiring leadership the *Wishart* quickly climbed to eminence in smartness and general performance, and in the fleet regatta managed to win most of the cups from her consorts.

At this stage in its history the Mediterranean Fleet had dwindled considerably in size due to the bite of former economies and the slowness of replacement of ageing ships; but in 1935 it was called upon to face a menacing situation which pointed up the need for more urgent re-arming. Encouraged by the success of Japan over the occupation of Manchuria, Mussolini proceeded to invade Abyssinia.

Britain rallied the members of the League of Nations to impose sanctions against the aggressor, and the Mediterranean Fleet, hastily reinforced by a brace of capital ships and a handful of cruisers loaned from the Home Fleet, was ordered to Alexandria in case the Italian dictator should be tempted to retaliate with force.

For a time the two countries teetered on the edge of war, but fortunately shrank from taking the ultimate step. Sanctions crippled Italy's trade, but they did not check her army's advance. Within a year, although guerillas continued to fight on, Abyssinia's main resistance collapsed, the Emperor fled to England, and the country was annexed by Italy.

In the following year Hitler, who had come to power in 1934 and cancelled Germany's membership of the League, occupied the Rhineland. The aggressive Powers were on the march. Civil war broke out in Spain, and as well as helping to enforce the provisions of the Non-Intervention Agreement, under which other Powers pledged themselves to remain aloof, the Royal Navy engaged in its customary humanitarian task of evacuating refugees from that strife-torn country. At the end of a busy two-year commission Mountbatten came home to take up a new appointment in the Naval Air Division.

This was then a comparatively small Admiralty department, headed by a naval captain, and with only two naval airmen on the staff. The Division was engaged in an uphill fight to put the Navy's flying arm firmly on the map. Originally created in 1912, the Royal Naval Air Service had numbered some 55,000 officers and men operating 3,000 aircraft by 1918 when it was merged with the Royal Flying Corps to become the unified Royal Air Force.

Six years later a separate Fleet Air Arm was formed, but its administration had to be shared with the Air Ministry, which was also responsible for the maintenance of its aircraft and the training of its crews, and the provision of new aircraft as required by the Admiralty.

But, due to the limited funds available, naval aircraft lagged behind the R.A.F. in design and quantity. Five aircraft-carriers were in service, but only the smallest of these had actually been designed and built for the job, the rest were converted from other types of ship. Besides· suffering from divided control and economies, the Fleet Air Arm was also up against conservatism within the Navy itself, many of whose senior officers believed that naval aircraft could have no more important use than as spotters for naval gunnery.

In 1936, however, re-armament was beginning to move faster, and the Naval Estimates for that year almost doubled those of 1934. Among the new warships scheduled to be built were three aircraft-carriers.

Naval defence against air attack was being improved by the development of multi-barrelled short-range weapons. During his service in the Naval Air Division, Mountbatten, who had flown in an aircraft for the first time at Eastchurch back in 1911 when his father was Second Sea Lord, was directly responsible for the adoption by the Admiralty of a new and potent weapon for the defence of ships against dive-bombers.

Brainchild of an Austrian refugee named Gazada, who had peddled his invention in vain to the United States, this was the Oerlikon gun, which could fire 20 mm. projectiles at a rate of upwards of 500 rounds a minute. Thousands of these excellent little weapons were eventually manufactured for fitting in warships and merchantmen, both British and American, in the second world war.

On June 30th, 1937, Mountbatten was promoted to captain, and left the Admiralty in the following year to undergo the usual senior officer's technical, tactical and staff courses. By the time he had completed these the war clouds were piling up over Europe, and a fresh command was awaiting him. A new flotilla of destroyers, designated the 'K' class since their names all began with this initial letter, were nearing completion in the building yards. Displacing nearly 1,700-tons, they were faster and more heavily armed than the earlier 'D' class, and Mountbatten was appointed to H.M.S. *Kelly* and to command of the newly formed Fifth Destroyer Flotilla of the Home Fleet.

When the ship was commissioned at Chatham in August 1939, war was already very near, but by working his willing crew flat out, Mountbatten shortened the normal commissioning period from three weeks to three days. Having seized Czecho-Slovakia, Hitler turned his attention to Poland, next on his list for conquest. At Munich in 1938 France and Britain had guaranteed Polish independence, and although they had failed to support the Czechs, it was now clear that the Nazi dictator had no intention of honouring agreements. Both countries therefore prepared to stand by the threatened Poles. But Hitler was not to be checked. Staking everything on a lightning throw, he attacked Poland on September 1st, 1939. Two days later the British and French ultimatums to Germany expired, and the second world conflict had begun.

From the outset the Royal Navy was hard at work on its traditional tasks: transporting troops to France and the Middle East, organising convoys, instituting a contraband control system, hunting U-boats, and disposing its ships to guard the ocean trade routes. The Germans laid mines round our coasts and at the entrances to ports and estuaries. Most were of the moored contact variety, but some, dropped by the Luftwaffe, were of a new magnetic type. Until an antidote was found many merchantmen and a number of warships fell victim to these mines. German aircraft attacked British shipping in the Channel and North Sea, and farther afield.

The Fifth Destroyer Flotilla was busily employed on patrol and escort work. While searching for a U-boat thought to have attacked a coastal convoy, which had actually run into a minefield off the Tyne, the *Kelly* herself struck a mine and was badly damaged, but managed to get back to port. Later she was to suffer more severely when she was torpedoed during the evacuation from Norway. Although ordered to abandon his crippled ship, Mountbatten had her taken in tow, and after surviving four days of continuous enemy dive-bombing attacks, she eventually reached her original building yard at Hebburn. During the months that the *Kelly* was under repair, Mountbatten shifted his headquarters on shore but continued to exercise command by embarking in any vessel of his flotilla which happened to be available.

The war was continuing to go badly for Britain. In April 1940 the Germans occupied Denmark and invaded Norway, and the allied expeditionary force sent to aid the Norwegians failed of its purpose due to lack of adequate air cover, and had to be withdrawn with heavy naval losses. In May the Germans launched

Admiral the Earl Mountbatten of Burma

Prince Philip, Duke of Edinburgh, as First Lieutenant of the destroyer *Whelp*

an onslaught against Holland and Belgium, and drove through the French defences in the north. Cut off by the enemy advance, the British Expeditionary Force fought its way back to the Channel coast and had to be evacuated by sea. In June the French sought an armistice, and Mussolini chose that moment to enter the war on the side of Hitler.

The British Mediterranean Fleet, based at Alexandria because of the vulnerability of Malta to air attack, now faced a hostile Italy, whose land forces in Libya moved forward to attack Egypt. But the Italian Fleet was reluctant to face Admiral Cunningham at sea, and in a daring night torpedo attack the Fleet Air Arm almost crippled it in its base at Taranto.

By the early part of 1941 the Italian land forces had been driven out of Cyrenaica, but now Hitler came to the aid of his battered ally. The Germans invaded Yugo-Slavia and Greece, and British units were withdrawn from North Africa to aid the hard-pressed Greeks. German troops landed in Libya and drove our depleted forces back into Egypt. Yugo-Slavia capitulated and the Greeks were speedily overcome. The British troops which had been sent to their assistance were evacuated by the Navy, and some were landed in Crete whose defences were being strengthened. But before this work could be completed, the Germans launched an airborne assault on the island.

By now the *Kelly* and her consorts had arrived in Malta to operate against enemy convoys to Tripoli. But in order to prevent the Germans from reinforcing their paratroops in Crete by seaborne landings, Admiral Cunningham now called in all his available ships to patrol round the embattled island. Enemy troop convoys en route from the mainland were annihilated, but under the unremitting enemy air attacks a number of British warships were sunk or severely damaged.

When their ammunition and fuel began to run out and Admiral Cunningham ordered them back to Alexandria to replenish, the Luftwaffe stepped up its efforts against the retiring ships. Among the naval units which had been operating to the north-westward of Crete were several destroyers of the Fifth Flotilla. As they withdrew from the area at high speed the *Kelly* and *Kashmir* were attacked by more than a score of enemy dive-bombers. Hit by half a dozen bombs as she swerved and twisted, the *Kashmir* heeled

N

over and sank, and soon afterwards the *Kelly* was struck squarely by a 1000 lb. bomb. She capsized with her guns still firing and after floating bottom upwards for half an hour, she, too sank. Along with 278 other oil-covered and machine-gunned survivors, Mountbatten was eventually hauled from the water by H.M.S. *Kipling* which, after successfully dodging further bombing attacks, managed to reach Alexandria safely. Since there was no other available ship for him, Dickie had to bid farewell to the remnants of his devoted crew and return to England.

His next command was to have been the aircraft-carrier *Illustrious* which, after having been severely damaged in air attacks off Malta, had been sailed across to the United States to be repaired in the Norfolk Navy Yard. But before her refit was completed, however, Mountbatten was recalled by Churchill to take over the post of Chief of Combined Operations from Admiral Sir Roger Keyes, his old Commander-in-Chief in the Mediterranean in 1928.

This inter-Service organisation had been formed soon after the Dunkirk evacuation at the direction of the Prime Minister, who ordered that raids upon the coasts of Nazi-occupied Europe were to commence as soon as men and assault craft became available. At first such forays were limited to small tip-and-run raids by special service troops, later given the name of Commandos, but in an attack on the Lofoten Islands, off Norway, nearly 1,000 troops, supported by destroyers, took part.

When Mountbatten assumed command of this *ad hoc* organisation he speedily put it on a proper footing, with its own headquarters, planning and training centres, and an allocation of assault ships and landing craft. He encouraged ideas and suggestions from all and sundry, drew on scientific resources and technological inventions for new kinds of weapons and equipment, and devised unorthodox methods and tactics for use by his Commandos.

'This is the only lunatic asylum in the world run by its own inmates,' he proclaimed.

As Combined Operations Command grew in size and importance it became necessary for Mountbatten, then only a mere naval captain, to discuss and finalise his plans with the Chiefs of Staff Committee and pass on orders to Force Commanders for approved operations. He was accordingly promoted to the acting rank of Vice-Admiral and, with the honorary ranks of Lieutenant-General and Air Marshal, given the right to wear two other hats besides. Under his energetic leadership no less than ten combined operations were mounted during the first six months of 1942. These included raids on Vaagso, Bruneval, St. Nazaire, and the full scale defence-testing assault on Dieppe. Although the latter was a military failure, the lessons learned were of vital importance in ensuring the success of the first long-range amphibious operation of the war, the Anglo-American landings in North Africa, which took place in November of that year.

In 1943 when the allied advance into Europe had successfully begun, Mountbatten, who had helped to plan the various invasion operations, including Overlord which was yet to come, was appointed Supreme Commander of the newly created South-East Asia Command, with the acting rank of full admiral.

Here, 'Supremo' as he came to be called, directed and finally brought to a triumphant conclusion the Burma campaigns in operations which have become military history and are outside the scope of this book. But statistics can help in the assessment of achievement and when, in September, 1945, he received the formal surrender in Singapore of the Japanese, this triple-hatted Royal Sailor, still only a naval captain in substantive rank, was commanding some 600,000 British, American, Chinese, Indian and African troops, 98 air squadrons, and more than 150 allied warships, ranging from battleships to midget submarines. With the enemy surrender he had also become responsible for the administration of a million square miles of territory inhabited by 130 million people. Not even his father had achieved such distinction.

The tasks of disarming three quarters of a million Japanese troops, rescuing and repatriating hundreds of thousands of allied prisoners of war and internees, and arranging for the handing back of ex-enemy occupied territories were completed by June, 1946, when South-East Asia Command was wound up and Mountbatten returned to England.

For his services he was made a Knight of the Garter and created Viscount Mountbatten of Burma; in 1947 this was raised to an earldom. He was also promoted in the ordinary course to

Rear-Admiral and earmarked for command of the First Cruiser Squadron in the Mediterranean.

But before taking up this new appointment he was asked to carry out an important diplomatic mission. India was about to be granted full independence, and because of the cordial relations he had established with the country's political leaders during his service in South-East Asia he was considered to be uniquely qualified to supervise the arrangements for the smooth transfer of power. Mountbatten agreed to undertake the task, and was duly appointed to be Viceroy of India. He was thus the last holder of the office, and when the troubles due to partition had been finally resolved, became the Dominion's first Governor-General.

He returned to England again in 1948, and soon afterwards took over the First Cruiser Squadron, the Commander-in-Chief, Mediterranean, being Admiral Sir Arthur Power who had commanded the East Indies Fleet under the former 'Supremo's' own orders! The composition of the station had changed radically since the war. The aircraft-carrier had become the new capital ship, and in place of the majestic battle squadrons which for so many years had ridden at anchor in Malta's Grand Harbour, there were now only cruisers, destroyers and frigates.

Under the post-war Naval Estimates a modest programme of naval construction, conversion and modernisation was in progress. Warships of the future were to be smaller and armed with more sophisticated weapons. Britain was no longer mistress of the seas, but was to share this role with other Powers as a partner in the newly formed North Atlantic Treaty Organisation.

In June 1949 Mountbatten was promoted to the rank of Vice-Admiral, and a few months later appointed to the post of Fourth Sea Lord and Chief of Supplies and Transport. After two busy years at the Admiralty he returned once more to the Mediterranean, this time as Commander-in-Chief.

The 'Cold War' was in progress, and in the Far East bitter fighting was being waged between Communists and United Nations forces in Korea. Under the provisions of the N.A.T.O. agreement a common defence force was finally set up, with its headquarters in Europe, and in December 1952 Mountbatten was chosen to be the first allied naval Commander-in-Chief, Mediterranean, with heavy responsibilities if war should break out.

He set to work to plan the first N.A.T.O. exercises, in which the warships of six nations were to take part, and in the following year personally conducted these at sea. His professional ability, personal charm and persuasive powers helped considerably to iron out the initial difficulties involved in welding into a coherent force warships of different navies with widely varied technical and tactical practices.

When he finally hauled down his flag in April, 1955, to take up the appointment of First Sea Lord, his popularity had grown to such an extent that admirals of six nations, British, American, French, Italian, Greek and Turkish, manned the oars of his galley to row him out to the ship which was to bring him home. He was now about to attain the peak of his professional career, and thus to redeem in full measure the vow he had taken as a young cadet at Osborne more than forty years earlier.

But the Service over which he presided was vastly different in structure, weapons and equipment from the Navy his father had helped to fashion in 1914. New and devastating weapons were emerging, along with various forms of high speed attack against which effective counter-measures had to be developed. Aircraft-carriers formed the hard core of the fleet; cruisers were equipped with radar-controlled, rapid-firing guns, and fitted with auto-mated, remote-controlled propulsive machinery giving higher speeds; a new class of super destroyers was coming into service, equipped with ship-to-air and close-range guided weapons, and gas turbines to boost their powerful engines; conventional destroyers were being ousted by small but powerfully armed frigates; and the nuclear submarine was about to emerge as the capital ship of the future. Other technical innovations were crowding on to the naval scene.

In 1958 the new post of Chief of the Defence Staff was created. Its first holder was Marshal of the Royal Air Force Sir William Dickson, but in July 1959 Mountbatten was chosen to succeed him. Four years later a profound change was brought about in the control and direction of the Navy, which had remained almost unaltered since the days of Pepys.

In order to centralise the administration of Britain's armed forces and improve control of defence policy, an integrated Ministry of Defence was set up. The Sea Lords retained their traditional titles and functions, but moved to a new unified headquarters away from the famous old Admiralty building in which they had for so long been housed. Mountbatten still had his detractors, and some of these even averred that he had suggested the dissolution of the old Board of Admiralty in requital for what had happened to his father. But the formation of an integrated Defence Ministry was entirely a Governmental decision.

Finally, after completing six crowded years as head of this complicated inter-Service organisation, having been persuaded to stay on for twelve months over the normal period, Dickie Mountbatten, now Admiral of the Fleet the Earl Mountbatten of Burma and Baron Romsey, K.G., P.C., G.C.B., O.M., G.S.I.E., G.C.I.E., G.C.V.O., D.S.O., was placed on half pay, and thus brought to an end what few can deny to have been the most distinguished active naval career of any royal sailor.

CHAPTER X

DUKIE

Pinned to the notice board of the Operations Room in the shore headquarters in Malta of the British naval Commander-in-Chief, Mediterranean Fleet, in September 1950, was a list of all the warships on the station, together with their commanding officers. Well down the list in order of seniority and class of ship was the name of a young frigate captain who, on occasions, the Commander-in-Chief, Admiral Sir John Edelsten, was himself obliged to salute.

He was Lieutenant-Commander His Royal Highness the Duke of Edinburgh, K.G., commanding the frigate *Magpie,* and a dual personality. On board his ship as a unit of the fleet the Duke was just another naval officer, entitled only to the minor courtesies appropriate to his rank. But wearing his 'other hat' as husband of the Heir to the Throne and a Royal Sailor, special honours were accorded him, when even the admiral would bow his head and call him 'sir'.

As captain of the *Magpie,* however, the Duke was ruler only of a tiny self-contained community numbering fewer than 200 officers and men, by whom in accordance with tradition he was referred to — outside his hearing — as 'the owner', 'the Old Man', or, more irreverently, 'Dukie'. Fifty closely printed pages of that section of the Navy's 'Bible', the King's Regulations & Admiralty Instructions, headed 'Instructions to Captains', and ranging from the use of safety matches on board to whether or not a sailor may be given permission to sport a beard, plus some ten years' seagoing experience in war and peace, helped to guide him in the efficient conduct of his naval duties.

The 1,375-ton *Magpie,* built in 1943 under Britain's emergency war programme, belonged to the Second Frigate Flotilla, whose senior officer, tall, bluff Captain Christopher Bonham-Carter, was the Duke's immediate superior. In signalled messages at sea or in harbour the Duke was unceremoniously addressed by his chief merely as 'Magpie', for in naval communication procedure the name of the ship means in fact her commanding officer. Packing a more powerful punch than that formerly carried by conventional destroyers of pre-war days, the *Magpie* was armed with six 4-inch guns and a battery of automatic weapons, and had a speed of 20 knots. During the second world war she had earned distinction as a unit of the legendary Captain Walker's famous Second Escort Group of submarine killers which, during one sortie in the Atlantic, sent a total of six U-boats to the bottom.

The Duke's normal shipboard day began around 5.30 a.m., at the same time as his ship's company were being routed out of their hammocks. But even before they had rigged the hoses for scrub decks, 'Dukie', a trained early riser from his bleak schooldays, clad in mufflered monkey jacket and a pair of old flannel bags, was up and about to oversee the domestic workings of his domain. At sea the day's work might include gunnery firings, flotilla exercises or manoeuvres with the rest of the fleet, now a sadly diminished force from the great days of the past, with a light fleet carrier as the largest unit, backed up by three or four cruisers and no more than a dozen frigates and destroyers.

In port there were harbour drills, ship cleaning or self maintenance, and other routine duties. At 9 o'clock the hands trooped aft to the small quarterdeck for Divisions and Prayers, where the Duke conducted the brief religious service in accordance with the centuries old Naval Discipline Act, whose first provision has always covered public worship on shipboard. Another of his 'ecclesiastical' duties as ship's captain was the publication of the banns of marriage of any member of his ship's company contemplating wedlock. Less pleasant was the daily mid-morning session of 'Defaulters', when offenders were brought up before him for judgement, commanding officers of H.M. Ships being required to act as magistrate, or judge and jury.

When he took command of the *Magpie* the Duke had warned his crew that he would be tough but just. He aimed to make her the crack ship of the station, but he was well aware that wherever libertymen congregated on shore with the liquor flowing there would inevitably be jibes aimed at the crew of 'the Duke of Edinburgh's yacht'.

'Don't you take it,' he told them. 'Anyone who comes up before me on a charge with two black eyes can be sure I'll be on his side.'

Although 'Dukie' earned the respect and confidence of his men he did not, however, manage to win their whole-hearted affection in quite the same way as in the past his maternal great-grandfather, the legendary Prince Louis of Battenberg, had effortlessly succeeded in doing with his crews. But *autre temps autre moeurs,* and sailors as well as ships change over the years.

Nevertheless, the *Magpies* took a particular pride in their special ship, and were quite ready to go into action without waiting for the customary drop of a hat if anyone should utter a derogatory word about her or her captain. When they played football or cricket on the sports ground at Corradino their royal skipper turned out for their teams as often as he was able; reciprocally, if he happened to be playing polo for the officers on the Marsa they loyally thronged the sidelines to give him rather more than the traditional 'chucking up'.

Since the *Magpie* was a small vessel, her captain's quarters were almost as narrow and cramped as those of Prince William in the *Pegasus* more than 160 years earlier. His cabin boasted little in the way of furniture beyond a bunk, cupboard and chest of drawers, a small armchair of standard pattern, and a desk for the transaction of official and private correspondence. A steel chest secured to one of the bulkheads contained the ship's confidential books and a small supply of cash for contingencies. Here the Duke took breakfast and tea in solitude, but for lunch and dinner shared the wardroom mess with his officers.

In larger units of the fleet a secretary is appointed to deal with the captain's correspondence. But in a small 'private ship' such as the *Magpie* no secretarial staff is allowed in complement, and the Duke had to add this, rather more voluminous task than in the normal run of frigates, to his daily chores. A junior lieutenant acted as accountant officer to look after the victualling and the periodical disbursement of ship's company pay, and a seaman typist tapped out official letters for the royal captain to sign. At sea he was rarely off the bridge, for the safe and efficient handling of a warship is her captain's first and most important duty, and there are no excuses for its neglect.

Considering the heavy responsibility involved in the charge of a modern warship packed with thousands of pounds worth of sophisticated weapons and equipment, the Duke was by no means overpaid, for at that time, the pay of a lieutenant-commander was only slightly more than £700 a year. Like other married officers he received an additional £1 a day Marriage Allowance, and three shillings daily 'Command Money', all subject to the deduction of Income Tax on the PAYE system.

When his wife, then the Princess Elizabeth, came out to Malta to be with him, the royal captain, like other married men whose wives were able to stay in the island, went ashore to join her at the end of the day's duties in the villa which had been placed at their disposal. But each morning he was back on board by 9 o'clock, or earlier if his ship was due to take part in exercises.

Whenever the *Magpie* was sent to pay official visits to various countries bordering the Mediterranean command, the Duke was required to wear his 'royal hat'. But he disliked the ceremonial involved, and preferred to consider himself simply a naval officer like any other.

By July 1951, when he had served ten months in command, and could reasonably look forward to completing the commission and to further and more interesting appointments in the developing post-war fleet, fate took a hand in his naval career. In June it was announced that Princess Elizabeth, accompanied by the Duke, would pay an official visit to Canada and the United States. On completion of this visit the King and Queen would then leave England to make a tour of Australia. The Duke therefore would not be taking up another naval appointment until after Their Majesties' return. But in a few short months all had been changed. The 57-year old King George VI suddenly died, and Princess Elizabeth became Queen.

Just as had former royal sailors, the Duke wished to make his way in the Navy entirely by his own efforts. He was, therefore, considerably gratified when, in the half-yearly list of naval promotions published on June 30th, 1952, he found that he had gained his third stripe.

'The Duke', stated the Admiralty, 'has been selected for

promotion by the Board solely on his merits as a naval officer, as shown by his record of service in war and peace, and in competition with all the other lieutenant-commanders due for promotion.'

When he visited Dartmouth naval college in the following year to present prizes to the cadets, 'Dukie' told them that, 'Service in the Navy is a privilege enjoyed by those who prove themselves capable of discharging satisfactorily the duties imposed on them. Promotion,' he added with justifiable pride, 'is not a question of jobs for the boys.'

* * * * *

The story of this latest in the list of British Royal Sailors began on June 10th, 1921, when a son was born to the Princess Andrew of Greece in a rather shabby villa called 'Mon Repos' on the island of Corfu. It was an oddly staged and difficult birth, for the local doctor was no expert gynaecologist, and the baby was delivered on an old dining room table.

'Mon Repos' was almost a hundred years old and in a very primitive condition, for it lacked electricity, gas, running hot water, or any proper heating. The servants were recruited from the local peasantry, except for the housekeeper who was Scottish, and the 'Nannie' who was English, and there was very little money about to run the household. Prince Andrew himself was away at the time fighting the Turks in Asia Minor.

Fifth child to be born to the royal parents, the new arrival was the grandson of King George I of the Hellenes who, as a naval cadet, had been chosen to take over the throne of Greece in 1863 after 'Affie' had been declared ineligible for the honour. Christened Philippos, later anglicised to Philip, the baby's full and sonorous titles was Prince of Schleswig-Holstein-Sonderburg-Glucksburg.

On his mother's side he was a great-great-grandson of Queen Victoria, and he had many other royal relations scattered throughout Europe. Later he would follow his father's lead, who called himself Prince of Greece and Denmark, until, in 1947, he finally renounced his Greek claims and became a British subject as Lieutenant Philip Mountbatten, R.N.

While still an infant he came within an ace of being rendered fatherless in an episode which was a hangover from the days of the old Turkish Empire, and brought him his first contact with the Royal Navy.

When at the end of the first world war the politicans were re-shaping the map of Europe, they drew up the treaty of Sêvres which mandated the city of Smyrna and part of the pre-dominantly Hellenic populated hinterland of western Anatolia to Greece. But in order to curb the growing power of Mustafa Kemal, victor of the Dardanelles, and to support the tottering Sultan, the allies delayed ratifying the treaty. Hostilities broke out between Greeks and Turks, which at first favoured the Greeks.

Then followed a series of disastrous defeats, until, in 1922, the Greek forces were finally forced to abandon Smyrna itself, which was thereupon burned by the vengeful Turks. Ships of the British Mediterranean Fleet stood by to evacuate refugees from the stricken city. In the revulsion of feeling against the Greek monarchy which followed this debacle, King Constantine abdicated and a group of dissident officers seized power.

Three former prime ministers and Prince Andrew, who had commanded an army corps in the recent fighting, were put on trial and sentenced to death. The unfortunate politicians were executed, but Princess Andrew's appeals to various European Heads of State to intervene on behalf of her husband were successful, and his sentence was reduced to banishment. The British cruiser *Calypso* thereupon collected the family and took them to Rome, the young Prince Philip making the voyage in an orange box which had been converted into a makeshift cradle as being less hazardous for a vigorous baby than a full-sized naval bunk.

For the next few years the family lived in a Paris suburb where, when he was old enough, Philip attended a boarding school run for the children of wealthy American expatriates. Among his numerous relatives were two uncles in England: George, second Marquess of Milford Haven, who had himself been a naval officer, and Lord Louis Mountbatten. At George's invitation Philip came to stay with the Milford Havens, and for three years went to school in Cheam with their son David.

When he eventually rejoined his family it was decided, at his married sister, Theodora's, suggestion to enter him in a new kind of public school which had been founded by the German-Jewish educationist Dr. Kurt Hahn under the patronage of her father-in-law, Prince Max of Baden, at the latter's castle of Salem. But soon after Hitler came to power Hahn was arrested on a charge of corrupting German youth. Influential friends managed to obtain his release, however, and he came to England where he was helped to open a new school at Gordonstoun, on the Moray Firth. With the rise of Nazism, Salem eventually closed down, and it was considered politic to get Philip out of Germany. Accordingly he was sent back to this country where he could continue his education at Gordonstoun.

Although he did not care for the tough monastic regime which was a special feature of the school, he accepted it, and eventually became head boy, or Guardian. He was good at mathematics and geography, a fine athlete, and fond of sailing, which formed part of the curriculum.

Of his royal pupil Dr. Hahn wrote:

He is a born leader but will need the exacting demands of a great service to do justice to himself. Prince Philip will make his mark in any profession where he will have to prove himself in a full trial of strength.

During the holidays he stayed with one or other of his uncles, and when the question of his future came up for discussion both thought that he should join the Navy. Philip later confessed that of his own free will he might well have chosen the R.A.F. His father suggested that he should join the Greek Navy where he would obtain early promotion, but the majority decision came down in favour of the Royal Navy.

Accordingly, after having spent some months with a naval crammer, Philip took the examination for special entry cadet early in 1939. At that time candidates were required to be between the ages of 17 and 18 and, in addition to an oral test, had to take a written examination, which included mathematics, English, general knowledge and history. Philip came sixteenth of the 34 who were successful. Normally special entry cadets were given only twelve months training, the first term being undergone at

H.M.S. *Excellent,* followed by two terms in the training cruiser, at the end of which they were rated midshipmen. But the clouds of war were gathering and, since it seemed that hostilities were inevitable, the technical training establishments were already making arrangements to cope with the huge inflow of reservists and other new entries which would follow mobilisation, and thus needed all their available space. The latest batch of special entry cadets was therefore sent down to Dartmouth to be accommodated at the naval college. Designated the Frobisher Term, they were given their own specially appointed Term Officers, but in all other respects integrated with the rest of the cadets.

Because of their age and special status as 'Pubs', or public school entries, they were spared the hazing and other minor indignities which fell to the lot of the general run of junior 'warts'. But they were required to work harder, for their training period had been cut to a bare eight months.

Prince Philip, as the Admiralty directed he should be called, took heed of the advice of his uncle Louis, who had impressed upon him the necessity of obtaining good marks if he wished to gain a commission. He did so well, in fact, that when he passed out at the end of the year he gained the King's Dirk as the finest all-round cadet of his term, and also carried off the Eardley Howard-Crockett Prize, which was awarded to the best special entry cadet.

In July 1939, the King and Queen paid a visit to Dartmouth, and with them came their 14-year old daughter 'Lilibet'. When he first set eyes on her the young royal cadet little thought that eight years later they would be married. But at this first encounter he found being invited on board the royal yacht and meeting them no more for him than 'an amusing experience'.

When, in January 1940, he emerged from Dartmouth proudly sporting his midshipman's white patches, Britain was at war with Nazi Germany. Thus the question of a seagoing appointment for him presented something of a problem to the Admiralty for, strictly speaking, this Prince of Greece and Denmark was a neutral citizen. The Foreign Office could only suggest that, as he must not be taken prisoner, he should be sent to a ship not employed on warlike duties. Clearly, however, it would be difficult to find any seagoing unit of the Navy coming within such a category. Even conscientious objectors who volunteered nevertheless to serve in minesweepers, supposing these to be unarmed vessels employed on humanitarian work, had to be informed that they were as likely to be engaged in battle with the enemy as any other naval unit.

However, there were British warships operating outside home waters, which constituted the immediate combat area. Because of the shortage of proper escort vessels, certain of the older British battleships were being detached to work as convoy escorts. One of these, H.M.S. *Ramillies,* originally a unit of the Second Battle Squadron of the Home Fleet, was about to proceed to the Indian Ocean where she would be employed escorting troopships from India and Australia to the Middle East. Accordingly Prince Philip became one of the twenty frustrated midshipmen who crowded her gunroom.

During his absence from Britain on this innocuous service the 'phoney war' in the west abruptly burst into savage eruption. Almost in a single night Norway was invaded and Denmark overrun by the enemy. Then at the beginning of May the Germans launched their blitzkrieg against the allies in Europe. In less than three weeks they had smashed through to the Channel coast, and the epic of Dunkirk followed.

In this same month Prince Philip, now at least partially a combatant since Denmark had been occupied, was transferred to the 10,000-ton cruiser H.M.S. *Kent,* patrolling between Bombay and Mombasa. Loaned from the China station, she was chiefly on the lookout for enemy surface raiders, of which at least four were at large in the Indian Ocean. But these powerfully armed vessels which, disguised as innocent merchantmen, accounted for the destruction of many thousands of tons of allied shipping and at least one unwary Australian cruiser, were far too elusive, and the *Kent* never spotted so much as a glimpse of one of them.

After three uneventful months of patrolling she was ordered to a new operational area, but before departing called in at Colombo to land the disconsolate prince to await a fresh appointment. In September 1940, he embarked in his new ship, which was the cruiser *Shropshire.* Based on Simonstown, she had earlier joined in the hunt for the German pocket battleship *Graf Spee,* and managed to capture an enemy supply ship. But during the weary weeks that the royal midshipman served on board she had no further luck, and he began to chafe under the monotony of days of fruitless steaming over seemingly empty seas. He decided to apply for more active naval duty.

There was now no question of him being a neutral. For when Mussolini brought Italy into the war after the fall of France, one of his early moves had been to attack Greece. The small Greek Navy fought courageously to the end against impossible odds, and the Greek Government appealed to Britain for aid. In response troops and supplies were sent to establish a forward base in Crete, but the British already had their hands full elsewhere. The Italian army in Libya was advancing upon Egypt in strength, and in the Sudan and East Africa Italian forces outnumbered our own. The Mediterranean Fleet was reinforced and the Army of the Nile strengthened.

In a brilliantly fought campaign General Wavell hurled the Italians back in Cyrenaica, and Admiral Cunningham's ships proved more than a match for their fleet. But with the intervention of Hitler British land and sea forces in the Mediterranean were soon to be stretched to the limit. As a result of his application for a more active appointment, Midshipman Prince Philip was ordered to join the battleship H.M.S. *Valiant* at Alexandria.

He was soon to be in the thick of battle. While the German panzers were assembling on the borders of Yugo-Slavia and Greece, Italian naval forces emerged in strength to attack our Aegean convoys. They were met off Cape Matapan by Cunningham's battleships, and in a brief night action, five Italian warships were sunk. As Philip's action station was in the *Valiant's* searchlight control position he not only had a grandstand view of the engagement but, since illumination was important, was later mentioned in despatches for 'bravery and enterprise'.

When the desperate struggle for Crete developed the *Valiant* formed part of the British naval covering forces, and at one stage she escorted to safety the destroyer which was evacuating Prince Philip's cousin, the King of Greece, from the embattled island. After Cunningham's battered ships had limped back to Alexandria Philip was anxiously waiting on the jetty to greet his Uncle Louis when the destroyer *Kipling* arrived bringing the survivors from the *Kelly* and *Kashmir*.

The time had now come for him to return to England to take his sub-lieutenant's courses for promotion, and in June 1941 he left for home in a troopship. During the lengthy voyage, which took them round the Cape, across to the South American coast and so up to Halifax to join a homeward bound convoy, the ship called in at Puerto Rica. Here her Chinese stokers, jibbing at the prospect of facing the U-boat infested Atlantic, deserted en masse, and for the rest of the voyage to Halifax the Navy men who were taking passage volunteered to replace them.

Prince Philip was one of the junior officers who wielded a shovel in the stokehold, as a result of which he received a Trimmer's certificate from the management of the C.P.R. Line who were the ship's owners!

He did unusually well during his courses at Portsmouth and Greenwich, which included higher mathematics, science, and practical navigation, obtaining four first-class passes and one second class, and thus gained nine out of a possible ten months seniority for promotion. He also achieved a distinction which fell to few naval officers while at Whale Island, when he was invited by the ship's company of that establishment to play football for them in their first eleven. On completion of the courses in January 1942, he was promoted to Sub-Lieutenant and appointed to H.M.S. *Wallace,* an old 'V' and 'W' class destroyer, employed on east coast convoy work.

This was one of the most arduous of the Navy's wartime tasks, for as deep sea ships could not be risked in inshore waters, coastal convoys formed an indispensable link in the chain of the country's transport system. Every alternate day a south-bound convoy sailed from Methil, and in due course a north-bound convoy left Southend for the return trip, each convoy comprising some 30 to 40 ships. Wrecks and sandbanks strewed the channel they had to follow, and the enemy assiduously sowed it with mines of all types, magnetic, acoustic and contact. By day the ships and their hard-worked escorts were subjected to continuous air attacks, and by night to assaults by E-boats.

During the 18 months that the *Wallace* was employed on these duties, Prince Philip, who was promoted to lieutenant in July 1942, moved up to second lieutenant, and, four months later, took over as First Lieutenant. At the age of 21 he was thus one of

O

the youngest officers to have risen to become second in command of a large destroyer.

By the spring of 1943 the tide of war had at last begun to turn in favour of the allies. The enemy had surrendered in North Africa, and with Malta relieved the sea route to the eastern Mediterranean lay open. A second front against Germany was to be launched as soon as possible. Meanwhile it was decided to attack what Churchill had described as 'the soft under belly of the Axis'. Accordingly, early in July 1943, the allies staged a seaborne invasion of Sicily. Among the vast armada of naval vessels which took part in the operation the destroyer *Wallace* helped to cover the troop landings, and was frequently near-missed in enemy bombing attacks.

She arrived back in home waters in November when Philip left her to undergo further technical courses at Greenwich. When these were completed he was appointed to be First Lieutenant of the new destroyer *Whelp,* then completing at the Hebburn yard of Messrs Hawthorn Leslie. One of eight *Wager* class destroyers, the *Whelp* displaced nearly 2,000-tons, was armed with four 4.7-inch guns and ten 21-inch torpedo tubes, and had a top speed of 36 knots. She commissioned in June 1944, and as a unit of the Home Fleet covered carrier strikes against enemy ships in the Norwegian fjords.

But after the landings in Normandy the focus of the naval war was now shifting to the Far East, and in August the *Whelp* and her sister ships, now formed into the 27th Destroyer Flotilla, left home waters to join Britain's Eastern Fleet. Under Mountbatten's command they took part in operations against the Japanese in Burma, Sumatra, and the Andaman Islands. When the British Pacific Fleet was formed under Admiral Sir Bruce Fraser to join with the American Navy in closing the ring around the Japanese home islands, the 27th Flotilla was attached to his command. Thus when on September 2nd, 1945, the final surrender of the last enemy took place in Tokyo Bay the royal sailor was privileged to be present at this historic occasion.

After the return home of the *Whelp* early in 1946 Prince Philip took over command of the ship for the last two months of her service while she was being de-stored and made ready for placing in reserve. When she finally paid off in June he joined the staff of a naval training establishment in North Wales, and two months later was transferred to H.M.S. *Royal Arthur* at Corsham, in Wiltshire, a newly created establishment to provide leadership courses for petty officers, where he became one of the two officers responsible for training. Since the courses were run on lines not greatly dissimilar to the curriculum at his old school at Gordonstoun, the prince was back on familiar ground. It was now that he became engaged to Princess Elizabeth. But before this could be made official there were certain difficulties to be ironed out.

In February 1947, therefore, he renounced his Greek claims and became a British subject, taking the name of Mountbatten and having no other title save his naval rank. In July his official engagement to the princess was announced, and four months later they were married. On the day before the wedding he was created Duke of .Edinburgh, Baron Greenwich and Earl of Merioneth, the king also bestowing on him the Order of the Garter and the dignity of Royal Highness.

For the next three months he was attached to the Operations Division of the Admiralty, and in March, 1948, he began a long staff course. When this was completed he went on half pay in order to be able to carry out various official functions which now began to fall to his lot as husband of the Heir to the Throne. But he was still anxious to continue his career in the Navy, and in October 1949 he was given the appointment of First Lieutenant of the destroyer *Chequers*. A unit of the Mediterranean Fleet, she was one of 32 destroyers of the 'C' class which had been built between 1943 and 1945.

Displacing 1,710 tons, they were of all-welded construction, armed with a new type of 4.5-inch gun, and boasted a speed in excess of 36 knots. After nine months service in the dual and difficult capacity of 'Number One' on board and 'Royal Highness' ashore, Philip was promoted to Lieutenant-Commander and informed that he had been selected to take command of the frigate H.M.S. *Magpie*.

When he left her in July 1951, his active naval service, which totalled a trifle over twelve years in war and peace, came to an end. In June 1953, he was advanced to the top of the professional tree when a supplement to the London Gazette announced that:

Her Majesty the Queen has been graciously pleased to approve the following promotion: Commander His Royal Highness the Duke of Edinburgh, K.G., K.T., Royal Navy, to be Admiral of the Fleet.

At the same time he also received the revived and historic appointment of Captain-General of the Royal Marines.

There was no doubt, however, that he, too, had thoroughly earned the right to be regarded as a very professional royal sailor.

BIBLIOGRAPHY

Allen, W.G.	*King William IV*, Cresset Press. 1960.
Arthur, Sir Geo.	*King George V*, Jonathan Cape, 1929.
Bolitho, H.	*A Century of British Monarchy*, Longmans Green, 1951.
Bolitho, H.	*George VI*, Eyre & Spottiswood, 1937.
Bryant, Sir A.	*George V*, Peter Davies Ltd., 1936.
Charnock	*Naval Biography*
Churchill, Sir W.	*The World Crisis 1911-1918*, Macmillan, 1941.
Clowes, W. Laird	*The Royal Navy*, Sampson Low & Marston, 1898.
Cookridge, E.H.	*From Battenberg to Mountbatten*, Arthur Barker, 1966.
Dalton, Canon J.N. (Ed)	*The Cruise of H.M.S. Bacchante 1879-1882*.
Darbyshire, T.	*The Duke of York*, Hutchinson, 1929.
Everitt, D.	*The 'K' Boats*, Harrap, 1963.
'Etienne'	*A Naval Lieutenant 1914-1918*, Methuen, 1919.
Fisher, H.A.L.	*A History of Europe*, Eyre & Spottiswood, 1952.
Fulford, R. (Ed)	*'Dearest Child'*, Evans Bros, 1954.
Gore, J.	*King George V – A Personal Memoir*, John Murray, 1941.
Hatch, A.	*The Mountbattens*, W.H. Allen, 1966.
Hollis, Gen. Sir L.	*The Captain General*, Herbert Jenkins, 1961.
Holmes, Sir R.	*Edward VII – Life & Times*, Amalgamated Press.
Hood, D.	*The Admirals Hood*, Hutchinson, 1941.
Hughes, E.A.	*Royal Naval College, Dartmouth*, Winchester Pubns. 1950.
Keppel, Adml. Sir H.	*A Sailor's Life Under Three Sovereigns*, Macmillan, 1899.
Kerr, Adml. M.	*Prince Louis of Battenberg*, Longmans Green, 1934.
Lewis, M.	*The Navy of Britain*, Allen & Unwin, 1948.
Magnus, P.	*Edward VII*, John Murray, 1964.
Major, E.	*George V – King & Emperor*, James Nisbet, 1911.

Marder, A.   *From the Dreadnought to Scapa Flow*, O.U.P. 1961.

Marshall   *Naval Biography*
Martin, Adml. of the
  Fleet Sir T.B.   *Letters*, Navy Records Society, 1902.
Martin, Sir Theo.   *Life of the Prince Consort*, 1880.
Mathew, D.   *The Naval Heritage*, Collins, 1945.
Milner, Rev J. &
  O. Birley   *The Cruise of the Galatea*, W.H. Allen, 1869.
Moffatt, J.   *King George was My Shipmate*, Stanley Paul, 1940.

Molloy, F.   *Sailor King*, Hutchinson, 1903.
Morrah, D.   *To Be a King*, Hutchinson, 1968.
Nicolson, Sir H.   *King George V*, Constable, 1952.
Oman, Carola   *Nelson*, Hodder & Stoughton, 1947.
Oman, Sir C.   *History of England*, Arnold.
Penn, G.   *'Snotty'*, Hollis & Carter, 1957.
Ponsonby, Sir H.   *Recollections of Three Reigns*, Eyre & Spottiswood, 1951.

Protheroe, E.   *The British Navy*, Routledge, 1915.
Roskill, S.W.   *The War at Sea*, H.M.S.O. (4 vols).
Sanders, G.   *Edward, Prince of Wales*, Nisbet & Co. 1921.
Smith, A.A.   *Sailor King*, John Shaw, 1910.
Statham, E.P.   *`Story of the Britannia*, Cassell, 1904.
Stephenson, Adml. Sir H.   *A Royal Correspondence*, Macmillan, 1938.
Thompson, G.E.   *Patriot King*, Hutchinson, 1932.
Townsend, W. & L.   *Edward VIII*, Marriott, 1929.
Trevelyan, Prof. G.   *English Social History*, Longmans, 1945.
Verney, F.E.   *'H.R.H'*, Hodder & Stoughton, 1927.
Walker, D.F.   *Young Gentlemen*, Longmans Green, 1938.
Wheeler-Bennett, Sir J.   *George VI*, Macmillan, 1958.
Windsor, H.R.H.
  The Duke of   *A King's Story*, Cassell, 1951.
Young Cdr. R.T.   *The House that Jack Built*, Gale & Polden, 1955.

Miscellaneous
Army & Navy Gazette
Britannia Magazine
Daily Express
Daily News
Dictionary of National Biography
Illustrated London News
Jane's Fighting Ships
London Gazette
Naval & Military Record
Navy Lists
Osborne Magazine
Times
United Services Gazette

INDEX